INDIA TODAY

By FRANK MORAES

Report on Mao's China
Jawaharlal Nehru: A Biography
Yonder One World: A Study of Asia and the West
The Revolt in Tibet
India Today

Frank Moraes

INDIA TODAY

THE MACMILLAN COMPANY
New York 1960

First Printing

The Macmillan Company, New York
Brett-Macmillan Ltd., Galt, Ontario

Printed in the United States of America

Library of Congress catalog card number: 60-7086

FOR D.S.

WHO WILL NOT
AGREE WITH ALL
THAT I WRITE

Introduction

THIS book deals primarily with independent India over the past twelve years. As one who has lived through the last forty years of British rule, the Gandhian era, and the early crucial years of independence, my observations, based mainly on my experience as a newspaperman who has been privileged to know many of the chief actors in this historic drama and to have watched developments closely over the past twenty-five years, may perhaps be of some interest. The views I express are my own, and I realize that a great many of them are controversial. Several friends have been kind enough to read various chapters, and I am grateful to them for their criticism and suggestions. My thanks are also due to Mr. T. R. Gopalakrishnan, who very patiently typed my many drafts and also helped me in other ways.

FRANK MORAES

Contents

I The Dance of Shiva 1
II Three Thousand Years 24
III Britain in India 45
IV The Gandhian Era 66
V The New Class 89
VI Red Harvest 112
VII Toward Unity 140
VIII Planning for Progress 166
IX Foreign Policy 190
X Men and Politics 215
Index 243

I
The Dance of Shiva

TWELVE years constitute a small span in the life of a country five thousand years old. How far has India changed or progressed since independence was proclaimed on August 15, 1947? Countries are very much like individuals, subject to not dissimilar pressures, internal and external, influenced by environment, events, traditions, and training. The past twelve years in India can no more be isolated from the context of five millenniums than an individual's life and character can be divorced from the lives of his forebears, his own background and upbringing.

The history of India is predominantly and inevitably the history of Hinduism, for out of a total population of over 390 million well over 80 per cent are Hindus. Although Hinduism as we know it today emerged in the wake of the Aryan invasion about 1500 B.C., there is some evidence to establish its origin in the Indus Valley civilization of Mohenjo-daro, which goes back to around 3000 B.C. According to Sir John Marshall who supervised excavations in the valley, enough evidence appears in the fragments recovered "to demonstrate that . . . this religion of the Indus people was the lineal progenitor of Hinduism." This would make Hinduism almost coincidental with the beginnings of Indian civilization.

The Indian Constitution of 1950 ordains that the state shall be secular; but however enlightened and well intentioned this proviso is, it cannot in itself erase the imprint of history. For better or worse, Hinduism has set its stamp on India and pervaded every sphere of life from the social and economic to the cultural and political. Unlike other religions, it is confined largely to the territorial limits of India, and gives that country its distinctive character and outlook.

Hinduism represents more a way of life than a religion, because it is inspired more by conduct than by faith. As Gandhi observed, a man may not believe in God and still call himself a Hindu. To the Mahatma Truth was God, and in saying so Gandhi echoed the Hindu concept of a pantheon of deities, each representing an attribute or quality and each invested with a form and sentiment. These deities mirror the many-sidedness of the Supreme Being known as Brahma, who can be conceived only in the abstract and who is himself devoid of attributes.

According to Hindu belief, the Godhead is mighty and divine, but a deity can share the weakness of a mortal. Some devas, like Indra and Varuna, occupy a position midway between mortals and deities. There are gods who embody compassion and love, while others may signify pride and lust. One god may be a sage and another a simpleton. A deity can topple from his high niche and even disappear. The Hindu pantheon has never remained constant.

This blend of extreme conservatism and extreme resilience, of intolerance on the one hand and passivity on the other, of meekness and truculence, of a certain confusion and distortion between vice and virtue combined with the habit of censuring inhumanity while acquiescing in untouchability is identified with the Indian character and is intrinsically a Hindu heritage. The bland combination of these contradictory qualities leads many foreigners to label Indians as smug, arrogant, and hypocritical.

The Indian is more metaphysical than spiritual. Yet many Indians are at pains to stress the high spiritual content of their civilization, which again incites foreigners to accuse them of moral pretentiousness and of a passion for verbal and intellectual hairsplitting which derives not from the spiritual but from the metaphysical. So also the average Indian's proneness to "turn away," to ignore things which he would rather simply not see, to go around or away from the difficult or unpleasant instead of confronting it. In the outsider's view this is akin to moral inertia or moral cowardice.

To understand the complexities of India one must understand the convolutions of the Hindu mind. It is a mind identified with some of the noblest thinking of man, capable of a supreme serenity in outlook and action, rich in cultural expression, often ascetic, even astringent to the point of turning away from the world of the flesh and seeking in intellectual contemplation a communion with the divine. And yet it is also a mind often earthy, self-centered, indifferent to the sensibilities or needs of others, capable of sublimating pain and cruelty, at once sadistic and masochistic. In so far as India represents a palimpsest, with layers of disparate cultures ranging from the primitive to the modern, it reflects the myriad reaches of the Hindu mind which embraces the aboriginal in the jungle and the urban sophisticate who is often an impressive synthesis of East and West.

Of the gods of the Hindu Triad Brahma, Vishnu, and Shiva, lords respectively of creation, preservation, and destruction, Shiva in the variety of his physical and moral attributes and in the paradox and contradictions of his personality is in many ways the deity most symbolic of the Hindu spirit. Like Vishnu, he has a thousand names. He is described as "three-eyed," "blue-necked and red-colored—bearing a thousand quivers." Destruction in Hindu belief implies reproduction, and Shiva, lord of destruction, also signifies reproductive power perpetually restoring that which has been dissolved. Shiva in fact embodies the triple powers of the deities of the Hindu Triad. Though he is the Maha-yogi, the great ascetic, concentrating within himself the highest perfection of austere penance and abstract meditation, he is given to revelry, drink, and dance. Shiva's popular image depicts him dancing as Nataraja, Lord of the Dance. In Hindu mysticism his dance represents the perpetual motion of the universe projecting Shiva as the embodiment of cosmic energy, a succession of cycles in which change follows change, and the rhythm of his dance is expressive of both joy and sorrow. Legend relates that he danced seven times round the world with the corpse of his dead wife, Sati, who was later reborn as Uma, daughter of the Himalayas, and christened Parvati.

In its mixture of the macabre, the mystic, the ascetic, and the near-obscene, the story of Shiva is symbolic of the emotional and contemplative mosaic which enmeshes Hindu thought and character. All is grist to the mill, and the polarization of a hundred contending and conflicting qualities within the amplitude of an amorphous creed is puzzling and sometimes repellant to the Western observer. Yet, in essence, does it not reflect the manifold attributes and spirit of man?

The West's antipathy to Hinduism, which it is impossible to ignore, derives from a fundamental difference in the conception of man's nature. The orthodox Hindu identifies a life of action with a life of the spirit and sees a kinship to the point of identification between the human and the divine. According to the Hindu, the divine element or spark is immanent from the first in man, and human growth signifies the development of this element. God is identified with Nature but God is more real than the world. On the other hand, the Western mind sees the divine as largely external to man. The world is more real than God. Did not Voltaire say that if God did not exist it would be necessary to invent him so that the world could come into being? As a result, while the conservative Hindu is primarily concerned with improving his being, or inner self, the average European seeks to master and transform his environment.

The antithesis can be pushed too far to the point of blurring and destroying the core of the argument, for its validity rests on premises which are being rapidly undermined. This is the line of distinction which divides Nehru's India from the India of Narada and Manu.* While some Indians today may look askance at the cultural and spiritual values of the West, the vast majority of them none the less envy Europe its material achievements, which they would like to emulate. Similarly, to a large extent they have adopted from the West those economic and political concepts rooted in the ancient Greek philosophy which laid greater stress on doing than on being. The facile dichotomy which identifies the West with scientific materialism and Western man as "moving into a machine age" that threatens the spiritual and contemplative values of the East is out of date.

Nehru acknowledged this when, to the dismay of some mildewed medievalists, he proclaimed India's power projects, her industrial factories, and river-valley schemes as the "new temples" of the country. Science, he realizes, influences and infects not only doing but thinking, since it encourages the habit of precise thought. "The Indian mind," he once observed, "was uncritical where fact was concerned perhaps because it did not attach much importance to fact as such." Far from being a divisive factor, science, by placing the stress on cooperation rather than on competition, can prove the primary binding force between East and West, drawing the two closer together and in the process establishing an effective medium for communication and thought. The language of science is and should be universal.

* According to H. G. Rawlinson, in *India* (London, Cresset Press), these two eminent lawgivers lived in the fourth century after Christ and founded their rules of law on the Brahmanic rules of caste. Others ascribe to them an earlier and semidivine origin.

But science by itself, as Nehru again realizes with his gaze focused on India's many social and welfare problems, is not enough. If the curse of untouchability is to be abolished and the divisive devil of caste exorcised, and if other social and legal anomalies and anachronisms are to be removed, a new attitude of mind needs to be developed. India, for all her loud-voiced sympathy for the underdog, herself needs the softening touch of humanism at home. On the long-term educational front Nehru, despite his insistence on wider and speedier scientific and technical training, is sensitive to the urgent need of kindling a new humanistic glow by the spread of humanistic studies; and these, he acknowledges, must be regarded not as an alternative course of study to science, but as complementary to it. For if the integrated individual which India and the world so sorely need is to come into being, there can be no cleavage between humanism and science. They are two facets of an integrated whole.

Similarly, an integrated individual can function effectively only in an integrated society. Here Nehru faces some formidable hurdles; for untouchability, with its concomitant of caste, is embedded deep in the fabric of orthodox Hindu society, and orthodox Hindu society comprises some 60 per cent of the Hindu population. These orthodox citadels are entrenched in archaic customs and prejudices which cannot be uprooted overnight. Aside from the linguistic agitation which demands separate states or provinces on a linguistic basis, caste poses the most potent divisive threat to India. Its ramifications permeate Hindu society. They are wide and deep, constituting a crisscross, horizontal-vertical pattern based on a complicated system of exclusiveness, segregation, taboo, and inequality. This pattern comprises the four main castes, with a legion of subcastes trailing behind each of them. The four main castes in order of priority are the Brahmans (priests or learned men), the Kshatriyas (warriors and rulers), the Vaisyas (traders and merchants), and the Sudras (serfs). Legend holds that the Brahmans grew from the mouth of the Creator, the Kshatriyas from His arms, the Vaisyas from His belly, and the Sudras from His feet. But each of these castes has its subcastes, the Brahmans alone exulting in over a thousand subcastes, each in turn governed by strict rules of intermarriage and interdining. Beyond the pale of the fourfold caste frame are some 60 million so-called Untouchables, whom Gandhi christened Harijans, or Children of God. Their status is even below that of the lowly Sudras. The prospects of this rigid structure dissolving to emerge into an integrated society are dim unless the battle for a modern, rational, forward-looking India is vigorously pursued.

Nehru can no more escape the past than can India. Five millenniums of history look down upon him. His task is to carry forward a people who range sociologically from the primitive to the most sophisticated in a country where the rate of literacy averages a little over 20 per cent of the population, with a national income of around $24,000,000,000 and a per capita income of about $60 a year. By any standards this constitutes a tremendous challenge. Add to these depressing factors a socio-religious pattern with strong divisive urges, and the gigantic proportions of the job which faces India's Government and people can be better understood.

During the past twelve years some progress has been made in curbing these anomalies and injustices, but the battle for a modern, progressive India has by no means been decisively won. On certain fronts it has still to be joined. It is a battle not only against the entrenched orthodox reactionary elements who believe that the adoption of modern ideas and institutions will undermine a society which has withstood new attacks and pressures over the centuries and has thereby helped to preserve India and Hinduism for nearly five thousand years, but also against a general habit of mind instinctively hostile to changes whose benefits are not tangible or are difficult to comprehend. The Indian, insulated in his way of life, is innately conservative.

Consider the Hindu reverence for the cow. A state such as Uttar Pradesh, which has a fair-sized Moslem minority, and which is also Nehru's home state, is foremost in urging a ban on cow slaughter. This embargo obtains there as well as in Bihar, Kashmir, Madhya Pradesh, the Punjab, and Mysore. In the Second Five-Year Plan the Planning Commission expresses concern with the disquieting increase in surplus cattle who number at least one-third of the total cattle population of roughly 200 million head, which is half of India's total human population. With further bans on cow slaughter and improvement in the control of famines and in the treatment of cattle diseases such as rinderpest, the number of surplus cattle is bound to grow, to the detriment of crops which are being destroyed increasingly by stray, unserviceable, and unproductive cattle.

Yet resistance to cow slaughter shows signs of increasing rather than of diminishing. Though it was not always so, the cow is held to be a sacred animal by the Hindus and is even venerated as a goddess. According to current orthodox beliefs *Gohatya* (killing a cow) is as great a sin as *Brahmahatya* (killing a Brahman), and in the older orthodox states such as Saurashtra, which is now merged with Bombay State, it was until very recently mandatory on a magistrate to impose a sentence of eleven years rigorous imprisonment on anyone found guilty of killing a cow. In the circumstances, the economic argument that these surplus cattle are wasteful and constitute a drain on fodder and field crops is unlikely to make any great impression.

Gandhi once described the cow as "a poem of pity." Though a rebel and revolutionary, he was deeply conservative in so far as the roots of his philosophical thinking were embedded in the ancient soil of Hindu India. His genius lay in idealizing concepts which he could not convincingly fit into the framework of his own forward thinking. Thus while condemning untouchability he connived at caste and sought to justify the system on the ground that the divisions of caste "define duties, they confer no privileges. All are born to serve God's creation." But this idealization, though typical of the Hindu approach to unpleasant problems, does not altogether accord with the facts or with common practice.

Unlike Gandhi, Nehru tends to rationalize those ideas which he cannot accept but is compelled temporarily to adopt. This might be described as a typical Western approach. Thus, though intellectually he could not give an absolute allegiance to the doctrine of nonviolence in Gandhi's lifetime, he characteristically accepted it as the right method for Indian conditions. Where he cannot immediately accept the ideas of others or implement his own, he procrastinates, keeping these ideas in the background until the time is ripe to demolish or implement them. He outlined his policy of nationalization, or socialistic planning, as far back as 1927, implementing it only over twenty-five years later as prime minister of an independent India.

Time and again during the three decades when the Mahatma and Jawaharlal worked together for independence, Gandhi chided the younger man for his "impatience" and pleaded with him to "move slowly." Had Gandhi outlived independence for a longer period than he did—he was assassinated within five months of freedom, on January 30, 1948—it is possible that he would have continued to counsel Nehru on the same lines. "I love you too well," he once wrote to Nehru, "to restrain my pen. You are going too fast." Nor was he oblivious of the younger man's intolerance and impatience. "If they [Nehru's colleagues] are guilty of intolerance, you have more than your share of it," he rebuked him. And again when Nehru, Achilles-like, sulked in his tent: "Resume your humor at the committee meetings. That is your most usual role and not that of a careworn irritable man ready to burst on the slightest occasion."

The difference between the two men extended beyond ideas to approach. Gandhi's approach to a problem, whether personal, social, economic, or political, was essentially pragmatic. He liked to deal with each issue as it arose, and was unwilling to peer into the future. "Why," he once asked Nehru plaintively, "are you bothered about stressing a precise political goal?" The query was provoked by Nehru's insistence at the time on keeping complete independence as the political goal. Ironically enough, it was Nehru who was later to influence India's decision to remain within the Commonwealth. Nehru has always believed in defining the long-time objectives, political and economic, and in giving them a clear character and content.

From this difference in outlook and approach arose another basic difference between the two men who, however, were both prepared to compromise and temporize with each other for the greater and ultimate good of the country. The rebel in Gandhi drew Nehru to the Mahatma—that, and the older man's insistence on action. But Gandhi, viewing the past, present, and future, saw the three phases blended in a flowing, continuous pattern, one leading to another in an unbroken, harmonious sequence. The timeless quality of the Hindu mind is reflected in that approach. If, said Gandhi, they opened a quarrel between the present and the past they would find that they had lost the future. Nehru demurred. Speaking at the first Asian conference at New Delhi in November, 1946, he suggested that unless they drew a line between the present and the past, while remembering the historic continuity which linked the two, the future would be merely a projection of past and present evils, and mortgaged to both. In other words, Nehru in some respects would like a sharper break with the past. The iconoclastic streak is stronger in him than it was in the Mahatma.

Because his thinking was impregnated with reverence for the traditional past while anchored also in a deep resolve to remedy present ills, Gandhi was able to carry a part even of conservative India with him. In his mind's eye India represented not only the educated few but the illiterate millions, Brahman and Untouchable, prince and peasant, capitalist and worker, the millionaire in his lordly dwelling and the aboriginal in the jungle. They were all part of India for they were India. And Gandhi's free India would have had room for all of them.

Gandhi liked to describe himself as a practical idealist, and while many might question the basis of some of his philosophical thinking few will question the fact that his strength lay in his day-to-day realism. He was both pragmatic and practical. He had an unquenchable faith in human reason, capacity, and good will, and a genuine love for his fellow men. There was nothing passive or submissive about him. He preached the gospel of activism in all fields of life. To him the elementary fact of economics was that man must eat. Above all, his approach to a problem was intrinsically Indian and, in a broad sense, Hindu. He saw no reason to break with the past in order to project the present into a more roseate future, and the countermagnetism of the Mahatma's teachings drew India very largely away from the lure of Marxism, for he filled the Indian atmosphere with an Indian idea.

There is nothing intrinsically Indian in Nehru's message of work, courage, and hope for his countrymen. His own Indianness has grown perceptibly with the years, but his interest in traditional India is cultural, not religious. Gandhi held that India's economic salvation lay in the regeneration of her villages and that her political institutions should have a grass-roots base in the villages. Economically, while recognizing the urgent need of improving agricultural output and standards, Nehru is insistent that progress can be accelerated only with heavy industrialization. The first Five-Year Plan stressed agricultural development; the second lays emphasis on industrial advance. "The three fundamental requirements of India if she is to develop industrially and otherwise," Nehru emphasized long before independence, "are: a heavy engineering and machine-making industry, scientific research institutions, and electric power. These must be the foundations of all planning." Characteristically he is setting out to achieve all three. As an Indian he is concerned in ensuring that his country's economic and political development should be governed by national conditions and considerations, and should not blindly model itself on Western or Soviet forms. But unlike Gandhi he is not enamored of the villages to the extent of regarding them as the font of democratic growth; they are too often the citadels of caste, of rigid orthodoxy, of ignorance and archaic prejudices. Nehru realizes that the devolution of power in India is seriously complicated by caste, and unlike Gandhi he would eradicate caste. To him science and humanism are the only effective answers to the prejudices which encrust orthodox Hindu society and thought. His Indian-ness is secular, being concerned with the religious pattern only in so far as it impinges on social progress. The sacred cow of Hinduism interests him not at all except as a symbol of prosperity and bounty. Nor is he kindly disposed toward redundant cattle.

Had Gandhi lived for some years after independence, the pattern of India's political and economic development would probably have been different. Even before the Mahatma's death a political clash had erupted between Nehru and the late Sardar Vallabhbhai Patel, a rugged strong-minded individual whose political and economic views were far to the right of Nehru's. Patel, it is true, had been the primary force in liquidating the princes and in integrating their states within the framework of a democratic India, but he had always visualized for them an honorable and useful place, with their dignities and privileges assured them over a specified period and with opportunities for serving the country in various capacities. These hopes and assurances have by no means been fulfilled.

Patel had no patience with Nehru's socialistic theories, which only drew from him a smile of wintry scorn. As controller of the Congress party organization, he had relied on the Indian capitalists and businessmen for his political funds, and like Gandhi he was prepared to give private enterprise a prominent place in India's economy. With Gandhi he agreed that riches were a trust to be wisely dispensed by the owners but never to be forcibly appropriated by the people. Shortly after independence Patel had induced the businessmen on the one hand and the workers on the other to accept a moratorium, pledging themselves to observe industrial peace over a period of five years. He stood for a balanced economy with the scales held even between labor and capital. Nehru had accepted this compromise reluctantly.

With the coming of independence the clash between these two strong contending personalities grew more acute, and threatened a head-on collision. Had Gandhi lived longer it is not unlikely that the Congress party would have split into two groups with the right wing led by Patel and the left by Nehru. By ensuring a strong opposition to any government in power, this arrangement would have laid the foundations of a strong two-party system and helped the evolution of a healthy, virile democracy in India. As events have developed, the main alternative to the Congress party is provided by the Communists aided and abetted at times, incongruously enough, by the communalists or Hindu revivalists.

Gandhi's sudden assassination forced an uneasy truce on Nehru and Patel, both men chafing under the joint yoke. They were far apart temperamentally and politically, and the artificial association between them intensified the cleavage. In September, 1950, the clash threatened to come to a head with the election as the Congress president of Babu Purushottamdas Tandon, a political and social conservative closely aligned with the Patel school of thought. Patel, old and weary, was dying—he died in December of that year—but at the Nasik session of the Congress party which took place in the fall he made a final effort to influence the turn of the tide. He failed. Realistic as he was, Patel was forced to recognize that while the party might incline toward him, the people were with Nehru.

With Patel's death, the last conservative brake on Nehru was removed, and he was in a position to press boldly forward with his own ideas. However able some of his present-day colleagues in the government might be, they are nowhere comparable to him in political stature or public esteem. The more outstanding among them, such as President Rajendra Prasad, Govind Vallabh Pant, Morarji Desai, and S. K. Patil, are to the prime minister's right, and in the event of Nehru's withdrawal from the political scene the complexion of the new government will probably be right of center. Whether they can hold it there depends on several factors which we shall consider.

Any attempt to push the country to the extreme right will provoke a pendulum swing to the extreme left, for the bulk of voters, with adult franchise operating in India, belongs to the unorganized in-between school represented by the white-collar workers, the peasants and artisans, all of whom, having derived certain material advantages from India's socialistic pattern of society, represent a vested interest and are in no mood to relinquish what they have gained. The Socialists, seemingly incapable of delivering the goods, are at a discount, and the initiative will therefore logically pass to the Communists.

This is the major danger implicit in Nehru's demission from the political scene, though to a large extent the issue will hinge on the circumstances of his going. In the untoward event of sudden death, the likelihood is that the administration with the gravitational pull of the conservative religious and social elements who are biding their time might swing to the extreme right, but in that event the pendulum pull to the extreme left would not be long delayed. Should Nehru voluntarily retire from office or die in normal circumstances as prime minister, his successor would probably steer the government somewhere right of center and keep it there. Even if a military revolution took place in the country, which at the moment seems unlikely, and if the armed services assumed control, the pendulum would in all likelihood stay right of center.

Nehru's government stands left of center with the balance tilted in favor of the "have nots" and weighted heavily against the "haves." If the "have nots" represent the economically depressed, the majority of them also belong to the socially oppressed, and therefore constitute a considerable segment of the population who are strongly behind Nehru's forward economic and social policies. In a country enjoying adult franchise this signifies a decisive political advantage. Not unaware of this, Nehru is attempting to hustle the pace of history. Early in 1953, less than three years after Patel's death, he opened negotiations with the Socialists in an unsuccessful attempt to persuade them to enter his government. Barely two years later he got the Congress party at its session at Avadi, near Madras, to pass a resolution committing India to a socialistic pattern of society. It was not the dogmatic Socialism of the West, for the two main ingredients ostensibly inspiring it were industrial or scientific development, which represents progress largely under governmental auspices, and humanism, which stands for enlightened understanding and action. Could Patel have foreseen that India would go Socialist within less than five years of his death?

As long as Patel lived, the Congress subsisted structurally as a party, for his very presence ensured that his views, in many important ways opposed to Nehru's, would not go unheard or unheeded. Even in his last few declining years, though ill and weary, he remained resolute and purposeful. But even he, with his strong grip on the party machine, could not neutralize Nehru's magic with the masses. His death left Nehru in supreme control of the government and the party, for however deeply the prime minister's colleagues may differ with him they dare not shed him, being well aware that were he to appeal to the people over the head of the party they would find themselves isolated.

Nehru cumulatively exercises a power greater than even Gandhi wielded. The Mahatma controlled no government, while Nehru, sharing Gandhi's hold over the masses, is virtually head of the state, the country, and the party. Though enjoying supreme executive power since independence, he has never lost contact with the people; this contrasts strikingly with the majority of his colleagues. In Gandhi's lifetime there were men, including Nehru and Patel, who were strong enough to oppose the Mahatma and even at times force him into political retirement. On first principles Gandhi was uncompromising. None of Nehru's colleagues* can afford to oppose him to the point of compelling him to relinquish office, since their influence is derivative. It derives from his pervasive power, as he demonstrated when he threatened to retire temporarily in the summer of 1958. His colleagues then fell over one another to induce him to stay. On the other hand Nehru is more amenable to compromise than Gandhi.

After Gandhi's death, and during Patel's lifetime, not only the Congress party but the bureaucratic system and the country as a whole suffered from a type of political schizophrenia, with the loyalties of the politicians, the administrators, and the people

* A possible exception was a Moslem, the late Abul Kalam Azad, who was Minister for Education in the Union Government and who always spoke his mind to Nehru freely and fearlessly.

divided between Nehru and Patel. Now Nehru finds himself in unchallenged supremacy. However brave the words of difference and even defiance his colleagues may whisper in the close circle of their own confidants, they have not been known to lift their voices in challenge of India's undisputed ruler. Their contact with the masses is of the slightest. The result is that the Congress party as a whole has ceased to have deep roots in the people, who by and large regard the upper hierarchy, with very few exceptions, as no better than tuft hunters who having tasted power are reluctant to relinquish it. Even the lower echelons of the party, maintaining a precarious contact with the people, comprise men of inferior ability and small political skill who in turn are fired with dreams of also achieving office and who, basking in the glow of far-away ministers, strut the petty world of rural villages and small district towns like pinchbeck Hampdens ordering local officials about and patronizing the people. This, of course, until election time, when their tone perceptibly changes.

Before independence the structural cohesion of the Congress party was maintained not only by the leaven of Gandhi's tremendous personality and prestige but by the no less important fact that the Congress was a party in opposition dedicated to the task of dislodging British rule and authority from the country. It had thus simultaneously a focal point of attack and cohesion. The genius of Gandhi lay in his ability to attract men and women of widely disparate temperaments and views, such as Patel and Nehru, Vinoba Bhave, and Sarojini Naidu, and harness their talent and energy in the service of the country. Moreover the Mahatma not only attracted the most varied individuals to the Congress but also built them up into leaders imbued with a sense of service to the country. Nehru has conspicuously failed to do this. Nor has he the strong organizational sense which Gandhi possessed. He relies more on individuals en masse than on institutions. Gandhi relied on both, and could make each the perfect instrument of his direction and will.

Before independence, service to the Congress party was identified with service to the country. In the circumstances then prevailing, such service had to be selfless, for it involved suffering and sacrifice with no immediate hope of monetary or ministerial reward. Today the popular mind regards the average congressman as symbolizing self before service. And indeed the unseemly scramble for ministerial, diplomatic, and other lucrative appointments with the perquisites and privileges which go with them have demeaned many congressmen in the eyes of the masses. It seems to the people as if these men are no better than professional patriots who regard patriotism as an investment which with the coming of independence entitles them to dividends and returns. Not a few have cashed in heavily on freedom. For them independence has meant patriotism plus 20 per cent.

Not that the Congress party enjoys a surfeit of administrative talent and experience. The paucity of good material in its ranks is beginning to have its effect on the country, where the general standard of living has admittedly risen in the past twelve years but where other standards have declined. And yet the Congress is noticeably reluctant to utilize competent talent outside its ranks. This doctrinaire attitude to those beyond the Congress pale is no new phenomenon, being largely a hangover from the puritanical postures which some of the Mahatma's more ascetic teachings induced. But whereas in the past it expressed itself by claiming a monopoly of virtue and patriotism, it is compelled by the exigencies of today to assume a monopoly of wisdom. Thus several congressmen, who are ignorant of the elements of economic tenets and theories, and who in many cases are financially better off than they ever were or hoped to be before independence, loudly proclaim—without understanding—the virtues of socialistic living.

The dilemma which faces Nehru today is largely of his own creation. He strides in seven-league boots. He is not only ahead of his own generation but also of the younger generation which once followed his footsteps and whom he drew to the Mahatma. Young no longer, and enveloped in the cozy portliness of middle age, they look askance at his economic theories and practices and are concerned by the drift toward a Socialism which in some aspects seems to them near-Communism. While approving generally of Nehru's foreign policy, they are disturbed by his inclination to lean more heavily and more often in favor of the Sino-Soviet bloc. Nor, whatever the outer manifestations, does Nehru command within the Congress party itself the fervent allegiance which Gandhi did. In their more exuberant moments of frankness, congressmen at all levels can be heard disparaging the very ideas to which in Nehru's presence they pay lip service. At the higher echelons there are murmurings against the bias in his foreign policy and economic plans, while the socially conservative traditionalists at all rungs of the party ladder disapprove of his sledgehammer efforts to change the fabric of Hindu society and are irked by what they regard as his undue tenderness for the minorities, particularly the Moslems.

What then is the force which holds the ramshackle Congress party together? It is Nehru. Apart from his influence over the masses, he represents the Great Dispenser and Provider. As head of the government Nehru exercises a power which Gandhi never enjoyed—the power of patronage which enables him to smile or frown on a colleague or follower, to appoint and remove ministers, ambassadors, governors, and a host of other functionaries in and outside the country. The plums of office are his to bestow, and however loud their patriotic protestations the paramount urge of the vast majority of congressmen, as of politicians the world over, is to get into office and stay there. Gandhi could only offer them blood, tears, toil, and sweat. But Nehru can transport them to the gleaming desk of a minister or to the plush and cushioned ease of an embassy. The cohesive bond before independence was the urge to remove the British raj. Today it is the urge to remain in office and to enjoy its power and perquisites. This does not apply to Nehru, but it does apply to the vast majority of congressmen.

Though Nehru needs the Congress party, he needs it less than the party needs him. As long as his magic with the masses prevails, he can appeal from the party to the people, well knowing that within the Congress there is no one even among his senior colleagues who commands his close communion with the people. If anything, the link which binds the better-known Congress ministers with the people grows daily more tenuous. Power makes most men cynical, and it has not left India's politicians untouched. The loyalty which his followers protest for Nehru, and which is felt genuinely by only a microscopic few, has engendered in turn a wholly cynical public attitude, verging on the contemptuous, toward most Congress politicians.

Having lost the opportunity during Gandhi's lifetime to divide into two groups, the Congress party is now slowly disintegrating into a congeries of small groups riven by regionalism, provincialism, linguism, caste and personal rivalries. In recent years these issues have appeared on the surface in states such as the Punjab, Uttar Pradesh, Andhra, Bombay, Bihar, Orissa, West Bengal, and Rajasthan, while forces exert pressure underground in various other states. Nehru is the cement that temporarily holds them together, but with his passing from the political scene will his successors be able to keep the party united and intact? It seems unlikely.

However often and loud Indians—particularly congressmen—may invoke Gandhi's name, not many of his ideas and teachings have survived the first decade of independence. The legacies that remain and are remembered are few. Foremost among them are his battle against untouchability and his fight for the emancipation of Indian women, whose social independence and equality he did much to foster between and during his civil-disobedience movements. He taught India to shed fear and hate, and the lesson lingers. One recalls, too, his respect for poverty and simplicity, though it cannot be said to shine in the way of life of most Congress ministers; and there are also his more puritanical ideas, such as prohibition, which unhappily burdens no one but the taxpayer and which has led to more corruption and disrespect for the law than most legislative enactments. His own inspired sense of dedicated service is shared by only a few. To the younger generation the Mahatma is a memory or a misty name whose reputation is not enhanced or embellished by the behavior of the average congressman of today.

Nehru's is a battle for time and against time. He has failed signally to infuse a single colleague with his daemonic drive, his passion for social and economic justice, his political understanding, and his genius for communion with the people. Whoever succeeds him will never attain to his stature or even approximate to it. Nehru himself has explained that he is not interested in a particular successor but that he is more concerned to have certain habits of outlook and action sink deep into the minds of the people. Has he succeeded in doing so? To a certain extent he has, but this section, overwhelmingly representative of the "have-nots," while armed with the weapon of adult franchise, is neither economically, educationally, nor politically strong enough to assert itself against the vocal politicians entrenched in power and skilled enough to cajole or bludgeon any opposition into ineffectualness. In the absence of Nehru, a demoralized Congress party divided into groups torn by internal feuds and rivalries, and tainted by incompetence, nepotism, and corruption will be easy prey for the Communists. It has happened in Kerala and could happen elsewhere in India. For the only alternative to the

Congress today are the Communists or communalists—the opportunists of the extreme left or the traditionalists of the extreme right. The recently formed Swatantra party has still to assert itself.

Nehru's major task is to salvage and save India from both. Here he is handicapped by the apathy of his followers, bemused for the most part with power and eager only to enjoy the fruits of office, who regard their leader with a mixture of cynicism, bewilderment, and awe—useful as a talisman at home and abroad but embarrassing in some of his ideas and ways, particularly in his insistence on eradicating social and fissiparous evils such as caste, linguism, and regionalism, which threaten the unity of India. While Nehru inveighs against caste and linguism day in and day out, it is significant that very few of his colleagues, even at the top rungs, echo his denunciations publicly. Perhaps his impatience with the social and economic rigidity of his right-wing colleagues, of whose views he is well aware, leads Nehru occasionally into overemphasizing the socialistic aspects of his policy, making them almost indistinguishable from Communism. Thereby he confounds the masses and rejoices the Marxists. Meanwhile the right wing of the Congress party, which at certain levels is indistinguishable from the Hindu revivalist groups such as the Jan Sangh and Hindu Mahasabha, bides its time.

Gandhi's campaign, which extended over some thirty years, had succeeded in cracking the outer layer of the crust beneath which are embedded Hindu orthodoxy and prejudice. Nehru would like to break the crust before he goes. Hence the hustle. But even fifty years represent a microscopic period of time within which to throw off the encrustations of five millenniums. Nehru, though himself a politician, is slightly contemptuous of politicians. In his view what the people think, say, and do will

The tendency of many Indians to avoid facing a difficult or unpleasant situation and of treating it as if it did not exist derives from this doctrine and is the modern expression of the ancient tenet of maya. Allied with the idea of maya, but distinct from it, is moksha, or freedom, signifying release or salvation from the material world, from all desire and action. Hinduism is based on the renunciation of the immediate material world even while a devout Hindu may simultaneously accumulate worldly wealth. Christianity, far from renouncing, accepts the world and tries to make the best of it.

This habit of mind had assumed a mold by the beginning of the first century of the Christian era, and was to influence Indian history through the centuries to come. The separatist urges inherent in Hinduism are high-lighted in the Western mind by varna, or caste, but the other four concepts of dharma, karma, maya, and moksha have been no less influential in shaping action and thought. Among the five they have tended to discount initiative and to produce a static outlook seemingly indifferent to material progress.

While Hinduism has been a great unifying force, it has also made for division and a sense of separateness. Caste, as we have seen, has primarily induced this cleavage. Whatever its origin—whether induced by race, color, occupation, or the mere fact of conquest—caste has been the major divisive force throughout Indian history to the present day, and so pervasive has its influence been that it has even permeated non-Hindu groups. Among Moslem converts from Hinduism such as the Khojas and Bhoras, the separatist tendency is marked, while within Sikhism exist castes like the Ramgarhias (or carpenter caste) and the Nebs, also known as Ahluwahia, who are potters. In South India there have been Christian churches with separate pews for Brahmans and non-Brahmans. Caste, ironically enough, prevails even among the Harijans, who classify a tanner above a scavenger.

Inside Hinduism occupational frontiers have been largely

erased, but occupation to a considerable extent still serves as an index to caste. No non-Brahman, for instance, can be a priest. The taboos that characterize caste relate mainly to intermarriage and interdining but also extend to matters of touch and pollution. Until fairly recently an orthodox Brahman would deem himself defiled if the shadow of a so-called Untouchable merely fell across him while he walked down a street. In many Indian villages, Harijans are still denied access to wells, though the Constitution prohibits such embargoes.

Communications and transport have helped to eradicate caste prejudices, since a Brahman might find it difficult to avoid sitting alongside an Untouchable in a train, bus, or tram. The British system of law, by equating all before the majesty of a court, also helped this process, and Gandhi's campaign to eradicate untouchability accelerated progress. But the practice of untouchability, or caste, persists in modern India. It lingers with varied vitality.

The period of the Upanishads (circa 800–600 B.C.) was one of divine discontent, generating in time a process of religious fermentation. This discontent found expression in the birth of two new religions in the course of the sixth century B.C.—Buddhism and Jainism. Both offered a challenge to certain aspects of orthodox Hinduism, protesting particularly against the sacerdotal authority of the Brahmans. Both were to influence Hinduism to some degree, though neither was capable of displacing it. In this period men the world over were searching for the key to the manifold mysteries of life, and the Buddha's contemporaries ranged from Confucius and Lao-tse in China to Thales and Solon in Greece. Herodotus was born a few years after the Buddha's death, and about the same time Pericles set about rebuilding the Parthenon.

Siddhartha Gautama, founder of Buddhism, who is believed to have lived between 560 and 480 B.C., preached the Noble Eightfold Way based on the Four Noble Truths which embody the truth of suffering and the way in which nirvana can be achieved. Through right action and right thoughts, he declared, lay the path to salvation. Buddhism has been described as the Protestant Reformation of the Eastern world, and it says much for the stubborn strength of Hinduism that, while influenced by Buddhism, it was never at any period completely subdued by it. Brahman opposition succeeded finally in edging it out of India, though Hindu resilience by adapting and adopting certain Buddhist beliefs obliquely erased the influence of Gautama's teachings. Characteristically, Hinduism also attempted to absorb Buddhism by making the Buddha one of the avatars or incarnations of Vishnu. By the fifteenth century of the Christian era, Buddhism survived only as a dim, decaying cult in Bengal, with its main strongholds abroad, in China, Japan, Tibet, Burma, Siam, and Ceylon. But Buddhism served both external and internal purposes. Externally it served as the main vehicle for the penetration of Indian culture to the Far East and to what is known today as Southeast Asia. Internally Buddhism failed to destroy the caste system, but it succeeded in reforming Hinduism in such extreme aspects as Brahman polygamy, which was abandoned, and in other spheres of religious thought, such as the development of theism.

The founder of Jainism, Vardhamana, later known as Mahavira, lived in northern India around 599 to 527 B.C. He was thus an elder contemporary of the Buddha. Jainism's paramount doctrine is ahimsa, the doctrine of hurting no one, and it is not without significance that surviving, as Jainism does today, chiefly in Gujarat and Rajputana, where it counts about two million followers, its principle of ahimsa should have deeply impressed Gandhi, a Hindu who came from Gujarat. Asceticism is another of its principles, and this has also left its imprint on Hindu thought, as it did on Gandhi's outlook.

From thought to action, from religion to war. If India's history in these three thousand years saw the assimilation of ideas and the absorption of cultures, it also witnessed turmoil and tumult with each successive wave of invasion. The first and most famous of the many military invasions of India was that of Alexander the Great. At the time the Macedonian entered India in 326 B.C., following the course of the Kabul River through Afghanistan, Hinduism had acquired a pattern, while the political map of the country had also taken shape. India's history, in the true sense of the term, begins from this date, for all that happened before it is inference and guesswork. India was at this time carved into a number of kingdoms and tribal republics. Of the former the most important was the Nanda dynasty which, originating in Magadha or South Bihar around 500 B.C., extended its realm successively to North Bihar, Banaras, and Oudh, establishing its capital of Pataliputra, the modern Patna, on the banks of the Ganges. Later it spread to the western Gangetic plain and seeped southwest.

To enter India, Alexander had to cross the Indus into the area now known as the Punjab, the land of the five rivers. Here there existed a number of kingdoms, among them Gandhara, lying between the Indus and the Jhelum, with its capital at the celebrated university town of Taxila. East of the Jhelum and extending to the Chenab ran the realm of the Paurava monarch whom the Greeks christened Porus and whom Alexander was to defeat in battle. The Greeks crossed the Indus at Attock. Ambhi, King of Gandhara, offered no resistance to the invader, who allowed him to retain his kingdom and rule it as governor. Gandhara became a Greek satrapy. Marching eastward to the banks of the Jhelum, the Greek Hydaspes, Alexander found his way barred by the army of Porus. The forces of the Paurava king, which were drawn up in a dense mass with two hundred elephants, were no match for the nimble Greek cavalry. Plutarch gives a vivid account of this battle. Alexander was magnanimous to the vanquished Porus, whom he also appointed governor of his domain.

Had the Greek had his way he would have marched against the kingdom of Magadha, but on the banks of the Beas his weary soldiers mutinied and refused to go further. Alexander turned back to the mouth of the Indus. But before turning homeward he divided the Punjab into three satrapies, appointing governors for each of them and another for Sind, which his army had also penetrated. Some of the governors were Greeks, while others, like Ambhi and Porus, were Indians.

The rule of imperial Greece was to vanish from these provinces within twenty years, to be replaced by the Indian Empire of Chandragupta Maurya although local Greek rulers continued in the Punjab until displaced by the Sakas. Alexander's incursion left some traces of Hellenic influence on Indian sculpture and architecture. The Buddhist Gandhara, or Indo-Greek, school whose creations and relics survive in Taxila produced sculptures distinctly Greek in type, both in relief and in the round, with the Buddha endowed with a Grecian profile and wearing his robes like classical drapery. Greek rule also left behind an imperial tradition. The Maurya Empire established within four years of Alexander's invasion was the first dominion of its kind in India.

Of the Mauryan rulers, the most outstanding was the apostle-emperor Asoka, who reigned from 273 to 232 B.C. and who was converted to Buddhism. He relinquished war, espoused the creed of nonviolence, and has left the principles he cherished carved on stone in his fourteen rock edicts and seven pillar inscriptions. The charkha, or wheel, which adorns independent India's national flag, appears on the abacus of the lion capital which Asoka raised at Sarnath to mark the spot where the Buddha first initiated his disciples in the Eightfold Way. So also India's national emblem of three lions mounted on an abacus carrying a charkha flanked by a bull and galloping horse is an adaptation of the same capital. "The chief conquest is not that by force, but by righteousness," reads one of Asoka's edicts. Some two thousand years later Gandhi was to echo this teaching.

Half a century after Asoka's death the Greeks from Bactria were still active in the Punjab, and at least one Greek ruler, Menander, King of Sialkot, survives in Buddhist literature and Indian tradition as Milinda. Menander was probably an Indo-Greek and was a convert to Buddhism. He was renowned as a scholar and soldier, entering on one occasion into a famous philosophical discussion with the Buddhists which is preserved for posterity. Buddhism remained predominant in India for five centuries after Asoka, but thereafter waned.

It would be misleading to infer from this that Hellas left a strong stamp on the face of Hindustan. The impress was slight, even ephemeral, but in so far as it wove another strand into the multiwarped fabric of Indian life it is not without interest and significance. Some years after Alexander's death the Greek ruler of West Asia, Seleucus Nicator, dispatched an ambassador named Megasthenes to Chandragupta's court at Pataliputra, and Megasthenes' vivid descriptions of the contemporary Indian scene are preserved for posterity in the writings of the Roman geographer Strabo. Not for another six centuries was a foreign chronicler to write on India.

In the hundred years before the birth of Christ Hindustan comprised a mosaic of kingdoms, petty principalities, and pockets of republics, the Sungas, once subordinate to the Maurya dynasty, holding the center of the country and overlapping into the western Gangetic plain. About this time the invading Saka tribes from Central Asia, also known as Scythians, dislodged the Greeks from the Punjab, and shortly afterward came the Parthians and Kushans who from the first century B.C. to the second century after Christ dominated Afghanistan and northwest India.

It was at the court of a Saka prince, known to the Greeks as Gondopharnes, that according to legend Thomas the Apostle arrived to preach Christianity. The Kushan invasion interrupted his work, and Thomas later fled to Muziris on the Malabar coast where, around A.D. 50–60, he founded the church in Malabar. If this is true, Christianity came to India within less than three decades after the death of Christ.

Kanishka was the greatest of the Kushan rulers who looked upon Central Asia, and not India, as their homeland. Nonetheless the reign of these rulers, which formed a prelude to the Golden Age of the Guptas, inspired much cultural activity in India. The Kushan Empire began to disintegrate around A.D. 220, but before then classical Sanskrit had evolved, the new religion of Christianity came in contact with Buddhism and Hinduism, art acquired a fresh impetus and literary output new forms. In the south the same pattern of kingly domains prevailed. The Andhra rulers who were to maintain their position until A.D. 388 lorded the Deccan, while below them the peninsula was occupied by three other dynasties—the Cholas on the east, the Keralas on the southwest, and the Pandyas on the southeast. We shall have occasion to refer to these later.

This was the picture India presented when the world moved into the Christian era. Although Hinduism had proved a strong unifying bond, resisting the challenge of Buddhism even as it was to resist the Islamic onslaught in the centuries to come, India had at no time in this period constituted a single nation or state. Not even Asoka's empire covered the entire country, for while in the north it stretched from the borders of Assam to the Hindu Kush, in the south it ended at Mysore. There was a consciousness of being Hindu but no consciousness of being Indian. That consciousness was to come only with the lapse of some centuries.

In the India of the first century after Christ, the impress of caste was strong and the Brahman reigned supreme in the Hindu hierarchy. One reason why Hindu India was later to collapse under the Islamic onslaught was that the business of fighting was left to a single caste, the Kshatriyas, who were represented by the Rajputs. The vast mass of the people, though occasionally subjected to suffering, was not materially affected by the convulsions and upheavals around them. India grew up compartmentally—not only in the social sphere but economically and politically. Economically, caste militates against the concept of the dignity of labor, and lack of communications not only isolated but insulated village from town and town from city. The country's economics have always been subsistence economics with the great mass of the population enduring a marginal existence. In the India of the first century, as for centuries thereafter, industry consisted of small handicrafts for local use and of luxuries to meet the demands of the rich and princely. The former comprised such articles as coarse cotton cloth, earthen pots and jugs, brass vessels and trifles in the shape of trinkets and cheap jewelry. The rich demanded silk, calico, muslin, gold, silver, and ivory.

The fifteen hundred years before the Christian era were succeeded by another fifteen hundred years before the advent of Europe in Asia. This latter period is notable for the intrusion of a new force and factor—Islam—into Indian life which was to influence profoundly the course and character of the country's history. Islam made its first impact on India with the conquest of Sind by an Arab, Mohammed bin Kassim, in the eighth century, but Kassim's was a sporadic incursion. Only with the closing years of the tenth century did the full flood of Islamic invasions sweep the country, culminating in the establishment of the Mogul Empire by Babur in A.D. 1526, less than thirty years after Vasco da Gama cast anchor off Calicut. Along with the Moslem invasions, the high-lights of this period were the rule of two

Hindu dynasties—the Gupta era which lasted from A.D. 320 to A.D. 490, and the reign of Harsha.

One of the most lively pictures of the Gupta era comes from the pen of a Chinese scholar, Fa Hsien, who visited India during the reign of Chandragupta II when the dynasty was at the apex of its glory and prosperity. The Gupta period, which is often compared to the Age of the Antonines, was prolific in art, letters, and science, and its galaxy of writers was headed and graced by the celebrated lyric poet and dramatist Kalidasa, the Indian Shakespeare, author of the greatest of all the classical Sanskrit dramas, *Sakuntala.* Written books produced on birch bark and palmyra palms were in common use in India by the fourth century.

Fa Hsien was in India for six years, from 405. He describes the country as peaceful, prosperous, and well governed, touches on the caste system, and generally presents a highly romanticized picture of India. More reliable and informative is the account of another Chinese pilgrim, Hieun Tsang, who arrived in India in 630 during the reign of Harsha, remaining in the country for fifteen years. Harsha called himself emperor of the "Five Indies" —the Punjab, Kanauj, Bengal, Mithila or Dharbanga, and Orissa— but, though extensive, his empire stopped short of the Vindhyas, and he was checkmated when he tried to invade the Deccan. He was religiously tolerant and, so far as a ruler could be, a recluse. His reign followed a century of confused history when India was subjected to invasions by the Huna, or White Huns, who, swooping southward from their home on the banks of the Oxus, devastated the Punjab, destroying the university of Taxila. With them came the Gurjara and other nomadic tribes who made their way across the deserts of Central Asia in the fifth and sixth centuries. These incursions mark the dividing line between ancient and medieval India.

We pass from Harsha over two centuries, dim and confused, to discover a new order of society centering upon the Rajputs, a martial race comprising numerous clans who modeled their principles of conduct upon the heroes of the ancient Hindu epics. The Rajputs appear on the stage of Indian history around the ninth century, though there are traces of them even before the fifth century. Organized loosely as clans or tribes, they built up various kingdoms under their chieftains in the area now known as Rajasthan, and with their martial spirit, bardic poetry, and distinctive architecture made it the cradle of Hindu chivalry and culture. It was the Rajputs who offered the main Hindu resistance to the early Moslem invaders.

On the eve of the Moslem invasions the Hindu social structure had acquired a settled form and so had the Hindu religion, influenced, as we saw, to some extent, though never materially affected, by Buddhism and Jainism. Other religious movements, such as the ritualistic Mimamsa doctrine preached by Prabhakara and Kumarila in the sixth and seventh centuries and the teaching of Sankara Acharya, the greatest of the Advaita Vedanta philosophers, a Hindu Thomas Aquinas who systematized Hindu philosophy and was prominent in the revival of orthodox Brahmanism against Buddhism, left more enduring traces. Later came Ramanuja who reinvigorated the doctrine of bhakti, the religion of love which is also a monotheistic cult preaching devotion to a personal deity. Its inspiration is to be found in the Bhagavad-Gita. Much later, in the nineteenth century, Ramanuja's disciple Ramakrishna and the latter's disciple Vivekananda carried this revivalist creed abroad.

Buddhism retreated before these inroads. By the ninth century it had ceased to be a vital religion in India, though it lingered on, and by the end of the tenth century Hinduism was paramount. As throughout the greater part of its previous history, India was then a congeries of kingdoms and domains, economically a society ranging from affluence to bitter poverty, and politically divided and weak. Fratricidal quarrels, inflamed by the clan spirit of the

Rajputs, who knew no imperial tradition or loyalty, left northern India an easy prey to the invader. Not even when faced with the Moslem onslaught was Hindu India able to unite in resistance and defense.

Islam's initial impact on the world was terrific, perhaps unparalleled, for within a period of about fifty years, between A.D. 670 and A.D. 711, the Arabs straddled half of the known world from the borders of China to the fringes of the Atlantic Ocean. In the eleventh century Mahmud of Ghazni, son of Sakubtagin, a Turki soldier of fortune who had earlier taken Peshawar from its Rajput defenders, descended on India, plundering the countryside and putting thousands of Hindus to death. His visitation is notorious for the sack of the holy city of Mathura and the destruction of the temple of Somnath, dedicated to Shiva. Amidst trumpeting elephants and the shrieks of terrified dancing girls, Mahmud entered the temple, walking into the holy of holies where the great idol stood. With his whirling mace he smashed it to smithereens, and "out gushed a store of rubies like splinters of ice, and emeralds like sprays of myrtle, and pearls as big as pigeon's eggs." In his reign of thirty-three years Mahmud plundered India sixteen times. The next Moslem invader, a Turki chief named Mohammed Ghori, after defeating the Rajput leader Prithvi Raj, captured Delhi in 1191. From then on until 1858 a Moslem king was to rule in Delhi. From Delhi the Moslem invaders moved east. Banaras, a sacred center of Hinduism, was taken by Mohammed Ghori's general, Kutbud-din Ibak, and the conquerors, penetrating farther east into Bihar, destroyed the great university of Nalanda and swept into Bengal. A little after A.D. 1200 the whole of northern India, with the exception of Rajputana, Malwa, and part of Gujarat, was in Moslem hands.

Following Mohammed Ghori's assassination the dynasties known as the Delhi Sultanates were set up. The wave of invasions continued. During the reign of Altamish, most prominent of the so-called Slave Kings, the Mongol hordes of Ghengiz Khan moved from the desert wastes of Karakorum into India, penetrating to Peshawar, and plundering and killing as they turned back from Peshawar into western Asia. They did not get beyond the Indus. Like their predecessors, the Huns, the Mongols were regarded as no better than savages by the Turkis who now ruled North India. "Their eyes," writes the poet Amir Khusru, "were so narrow and piercing that they might have bored a hole in a brazen vessel. Their stink was more horrible than their color." In the closing years of the fourteenth century the dreaded Timur the lame, the Tamerlane of English literature, descended on Delhi from the Gobi Desert and reduced that city to ruins. On his way through northern India he defiled the temple at Hardwar, an ancient place of Hindu pilgrimage, and left terror and rapine in his wake. "For two whole months not a bird moved a wing in the city," observes a chronicler commenting on Timur's sack of Delhi.

From the fourteenth century to the sixteenth, the Sultanate at Delhi was subjected to attacks by the Mongols from the north and by the Hindus from their lairs in Rajputana and Malwa. Around 1310, Malik Kafur, a general commanding the armies of the Delhi Sultan Ala-ud-din, entered South India and, marching through the hitherto inviolate Tamil kingdoms, ravaged the countryside. Hindu rule in the south was virtually extinguished, to rise again only with the foundation of the empire of Vijayanagar which at the height of its power stretched from sea to sea south of the Kistna. This Hindu empire perished in 1565 before the combined onslaught of the five Moslem states of Bijapur, Berar, Ahmadnagar, Golconda, and Bidar, relics of the Moslem Bahmini kingdom which had lasted until almost the close of the fifteenth century.

The impact of the Islamic invaders on India was altogether different from that produced by the previous intruders. Hinduism was able to absorb and assimilate in its social fabric Greek and Saka, Kushan and Huna. But the Moslems it could not absorb. Nor was Islam able to uproot Hinduism and destroy its ideas and institutions. Hitherto Hindu society was divided horizontally; but with the intrusion of Islam into India, society was split vertically, living in two parallel but separate worlds, divided one from the other by differences in outlook, ideas, religious and social philosophy, dress, manners, and customs.

Against the amorphousness of Hinduism Islam posed a positive, definite challenge. Religiously Islam rejects idolatry, believes in one God, possesses a creed and a book (the Koran), upholds the equality of all Moslems and, cherishing the transcendence of God, denies the idea of incarnation. Idolatry and polytheism are particularly repugnant to the Moslem. The 112th sura, or chapter, of the Koran, which Mohammed the Prophet declared was equal in value to a third part of the Koran, runs: "God is one God, the eternal God: He begetteth not neither is He begotten: and there is not any like unto Him."

In outlook and ideas Islam is near to Christianity and Judaism. Like the Christians, the Moslems hold the world to be important and seek to make the best of it. Like the Jews, the followers of Mohammed celebrate their Sabbath on a day of congregational prayer, and the Jewish idea of fasting finds expression in Ramadan, the annual month of fasting which orthodox Moslems observe. The Greeks also influenced Islamic thought and practice in science and the law. *Yunani*, the term for the Moslem system of medicine, is Greek in origin. Islam ordains four primary or practical duties: (1) prayer, (2) fasting, (3) almsgiving, and (4) the Haj, or pilgrimage to Mecca. A man who confesses the unity of God and performs the four practical duties is called a *mumin*, or believer. He who rejects these is a *kaffir*, or infidel.

Thus Islam in its beliefs and practices is sharply antithetical to many aspects of the Hindu faith. There is, however, another side to the picture. Though surviving separate and distinct, Hinduism and Islam when brought in proximity with each other over a long period of time have exercised their influence, the one on the other. Caste, as we have seen, infected certain Moslem groups. Conversely, Hindu society was affected by the social customs of its new rulers, the higher classes adopting the Moslem practice of secluding women. Moslem court dress and ceremonial also became fashionable, and though Persian was the court language a lingua franca known as Urdu, or camp language, a form of western Hindi with a large admixture of Persian and Arabic words, came into being at the end of the thirteenth century. Nor was religion uninfluenced. On the Moslem side the Persian Sufis, a school of mystics who numbered some famous poets, were attracted by the Hindu tendency to identify God and Nature, and evolved a philosophy which approximated to Hindu pantheism. The unity and moral character of God, which is a prominent feature of Islam, led to liberalizing movements within Hinduism, giving birth to Sikhism, which came into being in the fifteenth century in one of the periodic attempts to find a common bond between Hinduism and Islam.

The founder of Sikhism, Guru Nanak, was influenced greatly by the teachings of Kabir, a Moslem weaver who also advocated a religious synthesis of Hinduism and Islam, and attracted both Hindu and Moslem disciples. "God is one," preached Kabir, "whether we worship him as Allah or as Rama. The Hindu worships him on the eleventh day, the Moslem fasts at Ramadan; but God made all the days and all the months. The Hindu God lives at Banaras. The Moslem God at Mecca. But he who made the world lives not in a city made by hands. There is one father of Hindu and Moslem, one God in all matter. He is the Lord of all the earth, my guardian and my priest." With the Hindus the Sikhs believe in karma and in transmigration but they reject the Vedas, idolatry, and the overlordship of the Brahmans. Nanak frowned on the caste system, though it was too strongly entrenched for him to uproot it even among his followers. Like the Moslems, the Sikhs are monotheistic, believe in a common brotherhood and in a holy book, the *Granth Sahib*, and are organized in the khalsa, a militant fraternity of "the pure and faithful."

The early Islamic invaders in pre-Mogul India also influenced Hindu architecture. The Turki conquerors brought with them the new concepts of the arch, the dome, and the minaret. Just as Alexander's invasion left its cultural traces in the Buddhist Gandhara or Indo-Greek school of architecture, so too the early Moslem rulers helped to evolve a new Indo-Moslem architecture, a fusion of Central Asian and Hindu motifs, of which the Kutb Minar, Ala-ud-din's Alai Darwaza (a gateway of red sandstone and white marble) and Kutb-ud-din's mosque named Kuwat-ul-Islam, all of them situated in Delhi, are examples. In the building of these structures Hindu craftsmen and artisans cooperated with Moslem architects. The mosques, palaces, and gateways which adorn Ahmedabad and Mandu belong to this period. Administratively also the Islamic period saw close cooperation between Hindus and Moslems, the lower rungs of the official ladder being manned largely by Hindus during the rule of the early sultans; but in the later Mogul era, particularly in Akbar's day, Hindu dignitaries such as Raja Todar Mal served the emperor in the upper hierarchy, Todar Mal devising the revenue system which was to survive into the British period. Out of 415 major officials of Akbar's empire, fifty-one were Hindus. Birbal, the court jester and one of Akbar's closest friends, was a Brahman whom Akbar elevated to the rank of raja and general.

The Mogul Empire functioned effectively for seven generations, from its foundation in 1526 to Aurangzeb's death in 1707, although it continued as a phantom dynasty until 1858. Long before the British entered the political field the twilight had descended on this dynasty, whose death knell was sounded by the

Persian warrior Nadir Shah, who in 1739 sacked Delhi, carrying away with him the famous Peacock Throne to Persia. Not since Timur's days had Delhi seen so dread a holocaust. "The streets were strewn with corpses like a garden with dead leaves. The city was reduced to ashes and looked like a burnt plain."

Akbar's reign (1556–1605) marked the apogee of Mogul rule, and his attempt to unite the peoples of India, particularly the Hindu Rajputs and Moslem aristocracy, although it failed and found little sympathy with his successors, was to leave its impress in several fields. In the domain of painting, the fusion of Hindu and Persian styles developed further to produce a distinctive school of art. Akbar abolished the hated "head tax" hitherto levied on "infidels." He was religiously tolerant, and attempted, again without success, to found an eclectic creed called Din Ilahi, or the Divine Faith. He tried to promote tolerance by himself marrying a Hindu princess from Jaipur whose son, Jehangir, succeeded his father. He also got Jehangir married to a Rajput princess from Jodhpur and entrusted the education of another son, Murad, to a Jesuit. The Taj Mahal at Agra, built by Jehangir's son Shahjehan, is thus the creation of a Moslem emperor whose mother and grandmother were Hindus. Akbar, though he could not read and only with difficulty signed his name, loved to listen to the philosophical and religious debates among the Moslem maulvis and the Jesuits at his court. He also for a time studied the Vedanta with the Brahmans. On the Gate of Victory which he set up at Fatehpur Sikri, not far from Delhi, Akbar ordered the following words to be inscribed, "Said Jesus on Whom be peace: 'This world is a bridge, pass over it, but build no house there.' " He lived in an age of great contemporaries who included Elizabeth of England, Henry IV of France, and Shah Abbas of Persia. Some historians reckon him greater than these three. At his death his empire extended over the whole of North India from the

Indus to the mouth of the Ganges, and from the Himalayas to the Vindhya Range.

Akbar's great-grandson, Aurangzeb, further extended the Mogul domain which with his conquest of the Deccan covered the greater part of the country, reaching out from Kabul almost to Cape Comorin. But Aurangzeb's religious intolerance and his persecution of the Hindus and Sikhs induced a non-Moslem renascence which saw the rise of two militant races, the Marathas in the Deccan and the Sikhs, who under the great Ranjit Singh were later to consolidate themselves into a powerful military state, west of the Sutlej. Between 1675 and 1708 the Sikhs under their tenth guru, Gobind Singh, developed into a military clan not unlike the Knights Templars of medieval Europe. The Marathas and Sikhs were the last two Indian races to go down before British arms.

So the story of India for three thousand years from 1500 B.C. falls into two broadly even divisions—the first period from the coming of the Aryans to the dawn of the Christian era, the second fifteen hundred years ending with the entry of Europe into Asia. During the first period Hinduism crystallized in form and character, imparting a sense of unity to the people of the country but never able to unify them either politically or sociologically. Imbued with stubborn strength but also with resilience, Hinduism was able within this period to withstand the religious challenge of Buddhism and to absorb and assimilate invaders ranging from the Greeks to the Kushans. To this era also belongs the rule of the Mauryan Empire, which reached its zenith in the reign of Asoka.

The second period of fifteen hundred years, notable for the Gupta era and the reign of Harsha, is also notable for the Islamic invasions which were to alter the face of India, politically, culturally, and socially. The memories of seven centuries cannot easily be effaced, and in this long period Islam set its impress, leaving behind not only the marks of terror, tumult, destruction, and upheaval but also a new tradition and way of life basically distinct from that of Hinduism but blending with it in many constructive, creative forms. For the greater part of this time the land was in turmoil. Not until Akbar came to the Mogul throne did India know a period of prosperity as great as that of the Guptas.

The battle of Plassey which gave the East India Company dominion over Bengal and laid the foundations of British power in India was still fifty years away when Aurangzeb died. With the disintegration of the Mogul Empire Hinduism faced Islam, neither of them a cohesive, compact political force and each acutely aware that a third factor was preparing to step into the struggle for power.

Europe had entered Asia.

III
Britain in India

DEMOCRACY, like nationalism, is a concept new to Asia. So is industrialization, which with science and technology stirred Europe in the second half of the eighteenth century to a new ferment of intellectual activity and thought. No such feeling as nationalism in its modern sense was known in the East, where loyalties were primarily local and where the vast mass of the people were untouched by the dynastic clashes around them. In India the caste system, which enabled the peasant in the field and the artisan in the town to carry on their traditional pursuits largely immune from and impervious to the tumult and conflict around them, accentuated this tendency.

Europe decries today the aggressive nationalism of Asia, but it was in Europe that nationalism first ran amok, producing in our own day two global wars within one generation. The latter half of the fifteenth century, which saw the culmination of the Renaissance in Europe, by stimulating the old Greek passion for knowledge and exactitude led to a scientific revolution which in turn ushered in the Industrial Revolution three centuries later. The decisive half-century ending in A.D. 1500 witnessed the discovery of America, the retreat of Islam from Europe which followed the expulsion of the Moors from Spain, and the exploration of the Indian seas when the Portuguese opened the sea route to India around the Cape.

In the five or six hundred years before Bartolomeu Dias discovered the Cape route and Vasco da Gama anchored off the port of Calicut on the southwest coast of India, the contacts between Europe and Asia were negligible, almost nonexistent. But the impact of Europe when it erupted on Asia in the course of the sixteenth century was explosive. Its influence on the thought, politics, government, and economy of the East was in time to be revolutionary.

Politically, economically, and intellectually Europe altered greatly as the Renaissance was followed by the Reformation in the first half of the sixteenth century. Not only was Western Christendom disrupted into two camps, but the Reformation, by destroying any hope of a single theocratic civilization, generated nationalist ideas and led to the creation of a congeries of competing nation states. The first faint glimmerings of democracy became apparent in countries such as Holland and Britian, where opposition to tyranny led to closer association of the people with the government. Trade also stimulated equality. Intellectually this trend expressed itself in a belief in individual freedom—a heritage from the Greeks—and in a differentiation between religious and secular power. Europe moved away from the otherworldliness of the East, seeing in history a purposefulness to which growing commerce gave an intensified material edge. The seeming paradox of the Quakers combining religious pietism with keenly developed business acumen is explained by the Puritan tradition which associated a sense of religion with an urge for hard work not only in field and factory but also in the counting-house.

In May, 1498, eleven years after Bartolomeu Dias rounded the Cape of Good Hope, Vasco da Gama with a Portuguese fleet of three small vessels and about 160 men cast anchor in the harbor of

Calicut. At that time, as we saw, the waning Sultanate of Delhi exercised a shadowy authority in the north, while south of the Kistna River ruled the empire of Vijayanagar which was Hinduism's answer to the challenge of the earlier Moslem invasion of South India. Prior to the establishment of this empire, three Tamil dynasties—the Cholas, Pandyas, and Keralas—had held sway in this region. The Cholas, who in their heyday were a considerable force in the country, vanished from history by about the end of the thirteenth century. But the Pandyas and Keralas survived as subordinates of the rulers of Vijayanagar and their successors—the Pandyas until the seventeenth century and the Keralas into British days as rulers of the two States of Travancore and Cochin. These two states are merged today in a single state known as Kerala, which for twenty-eight months, until July 31, 1959, had a Communist government, the only one in India.

Until about the seventeenth century India's economic condition was not vastly different from that existing in many countries of Europe. Akbar, as we noted, was a contemporary of Elizabeth of England, and in the India of his day the per capita income probably approximated that of England, while the quantum of surplus wealth at the disposal of the Mogul dynasty was in fact larger. One reason for this was that the greater part of the country's wealth from foreign trade, agriculture, handicrafts, and small industries found its way to the royal exchequer. Akbar's total annual revenue has been estimated at 60 million dollars.

During Akbar's reign three Englishmen named John Newberry, William Leedes, and Ralph Fitch visited India, and Fitch has left an interesting acount of their travels. He describes the city of Agra as "much greater than London and very populous," and notes that in the bazaars were "a great resort of merchandise from Persia and out of India, and very much merchandise of silk and cloth and precious stones, both rubies, diamonds and pearls." Sir Thomas Roe who came to the court of Jehangir as James I's ambassador was not overly impressed by the emperor but was struck by the ostensible signs of prosperity as evidenced by the display of bullion, silver, jewelry and precious stones. "Europe bleedeth to enrich Asia," he lamented. At the time India's chief exports were printed cotton goods, silk, indigo, spices, sugar, opium, and saltpeter, while the East India Company ships brought in bullion, quicksilver, copper, zinc, lead, jewelry, velvets and brocades, clocks and mechanical toys.

India may have seemed rich to the casual visitor who only roamed its cities and palaces, but not to the discerning onlooker. A more perceptive observer than these Englishmen was the Frenchman François Bernier, who was in the country during Aurangzeb's reign. Bernier writes enthusiastically of the Moslem palaces and courts in the north, but he also took time to peer below the surface. "The inhabitants," he notes, "have less the appearance of moneyed men than those of many other parts of the globe." As in the India of very much later days, the disparity between ostentatious wealth and extreme poverty was perhaps even then too obstrusive to be missed. But by and large these contrasting extremes also existed in Elizabethan England.

The interesting and significant point is that while India and Asia generally have always been poor in relation to the West, the economic gulf between the Occident and the Orient has continued to widen since the middle of the seventeenth century. From then on, Asian countries have been relatively much poorer. The development of the Industrial Revolution in England noticeably affected the economic fortunes of India, which declined steeply during the eighteenth and nineteenth centuries. In the seventeenth century textiles formed the base of the country's export trade, and these were hopelessly disorganized and crippled by the inflow of Western machine-made goods, particularly cheap but durable textiles, which were flooding the Indian market by 1800. This influx dislocated local trades and handicrafts, drove the weaver back to the land, thereby disorganizing rural economy; limited the textile trades to the production of coarse cloth supplemented by a few handwoven luxury lines for the wealthy, and cumulatively depressed India to the status of a colonial economy producing raw materials for manufacturers abroad.

By 1818, with the defeat of the Marathas, the British, controlling the whole country east of the Sutlej, were the paramount power in India. By that time Britain was well on the way to becoming the workshop of the world. Through an unfortunate juxtaposition the early years of the Industrial Revolution coincided with the laissez-faire ideas of Adam Smith and the utilitarian theories of Jeremy Bentham and of James and John Stuart Mill which impelled the dawn of free trade and free enterprise with their concomitants of no tariff barriers and no commercial restrictions. Internally the removal of trade barriers helped Indian commerce. But externally free trade struck a disabling blow to the country's crafts and industries.

India's peasant economy suffered grievously from the impact of the free influx of foreign machine-made goods. In the nineteenth century there were widespread economic confusion and disintegration in the country. The lingering suspicion that India was being exploited for the benefit of Britain, initially aroused by the theories of free trade and free enterprise, was intensified by measures such as the imposition of the cotton excise in 1894 which was manifestly more for the good of Lancashire than of Bombay. In the name of economic freedom India's infant industries were denied the safeguard of tariffs at a time when the youthful, independent United States was raising these protective barriers. Indeed, only after the First World War was the country's growing textile industry allowed the benefit of sizable tariffs.

Politically and economically the effect of these ideas and measures on the thinking of educated Indians was far-reaching and in some respects disastrous. Politically it led the vast majority to equate colonialism with capitalism, seeing the former as the natural corollary of the latter, since the new capitalism born of the Industrial Revolution relied for its cheap labor, raw materials, and untapped markets on the exploitation of the politically weak, economically underdeveloped countries of Asia and Africa. With capitalism were also identified free trade and free enterprise, a conjunction which conspired to denigrate all three in the eyes of Asia. These initial antipathies were to color much of India's later economic thinking even if, with the country's lack of financial resources, its comparatively small entrepreneur and managerial class, and its huge reservoir of idle manpower, a welfare state on a socialistic pattern was almost inevitable when India became independent.

In the years to come, certain other factors were also to impinge on Indian thinking. First the Soviet experiment, whose Five-Year plans attracted the attention and interest of many thoughtful Indians, including Nehru, and influenced not a few. A number of these were students in American and British universities in the late 1920's and early 1930's when Socialism was fashionable, and not all of them appreciated the fact that there were industries in Russia before the Bolsheviks took over or that the Soviet experiment in its early stages owed much of its industrial success to Western technical aid. Similarly today many Indians, more particularly of the growing generation, gaze starry-eyed at Communist China's economic advances and see in them a manifestation of the wonders of state control. They forget that in the world as it exists today there is no such thing as an economy run entirely by private enterprise—not even in the United States. Nor for that matter can a Socialist economy be run completely by the state, as India itself proves.

The benefits which British rule brought the country were considerable and cannot fairly be ignored. It is ironical but true that not until the British era did the consciousness of India and of being Indian grow. In that sense, the concept of India is really a British creation. Hieun Tsang, the Chinese pilgrim, referring to India as Intu, remarks that the people of that land "call their country by different names according to the district." Until the establishment of British rule, loyalty was very largely a local affair. To the Marathas and the Sikhs the Moguls were as much intruders as the British. In the Great Rebellion of 1857 Hindus and Moslems fought the British, though they were actuated by different and varied motives; but the Sikhs, with lingering memories of Mogul persecution, actively assisted the new conquerors.

India passed under British dominion largely because of its own intrinsic weakness. As Mogul power waned, Maratha aggressiveness grew. But even the Marathas were divided by internal dissensions and they could never offer a united front against the British. The Portuguese had faded out of the picture by 1615, but Britain and France were to contend for commercial power until 1761, when the loss of Pondicherry and lack of sea power forced France out of India. In the period of Anglo-French rivalry the British and the French had in turn backed rival kingdoms, playing one dynasty against another until with the withdrawal of the French the British were left as the chief contending power for the dominion of the country. Britain conquered India with the help largely of Indian mercenaries.

Distance combined with lack of communications to compartmentalize Indian life and to create widely spaced pockets of population with distinct social and ethnic modes of living. The development of transport and the opening of communications under British rule brought the self-contained village communities, the immemorial core of Indian economy and life, into closer contact with the towns and cities; and as urban industrialization grew, the drift of population from villages to towns and towns to villages mixed the people appreciably. The curse of political instability ceased with the consolidation of British rule, and the

Pax Britannica enabled the country to settle down to a more ordered and orderly pattern of social and economic life. Peace in the village meant peace for the community, which in turn meant security for the country as a whole. And security, if it intensified the dead weight of foreign rule, also stimulated progress in various directions.

The British gave India roads and railways, sanitation and irrigation projects. Better sanitation and health led to an increase of population, which rose perceptibly from around 1880. Simultaneously, improved communications stimulated internal trade and industry and by facilitating the transport of foodstuffs from one area to another minimized the ravages of famine. Not that these pestilences ceased to afflict India. The great famine of 1877, which affected an area of 200,000 square miles and a population of some 36 millions, proved that though the railways could transport food grains and foodstuffs, a more effective system of distribution remained to be devised. But as long as a sufficiency of food was available in the country, or could be freely imported, the more devastating consequences of a famine could normally be controlled. More roads and railways also meant the development of productive industries and trades, such as coal, iron, wheat, and cotton, in the interior. Externally the opening of the Suez Canal in 1869 linked India's economy closer with that of the world.

In time, the advent of British rule, symbolizing the exercise of political power based on superior scientific, technological, and industrial techniques, generated a train of thought in the minds of many Indians. If their own country was to advance and be politically independent, they had to emulate the West in some decisive directions, grafting and adopting certain Western ideas and methods to Indian conditions and needs, evolving ultimately a synthesis neither wholly Western nor Indian but a combination of the best of both. Some such ideas inspired the early pioneers and reformers, notably a Hindu, Ram Mohun Roy and, much later a Moslem, Syed Ahmed Khan.

From these urges evolved a new phenomenon, the Indian middle class, which again is primarily a British creation. This class, initially visualized by Bentinck and Macaulay* as the mainstay of British rule in India, was ultimately to prove its undoing. As a class it was influenced strongly by British ideas and institutions in which it saw first the chief instruments for ensuring progress and later for securing political freedom. The seeds for its germination came in 1835 from Macaulay's celebrated Minute on Education, which decreed English as the medium of instruction while simultaneously English displaced Persian as the language of government and the higher law courts. Even before this time a few educated Hindus could converse in English, among them being Ram Mohun Roy, who learned English in 1792 at the age of twenty. Roy's was an exceptional case, but by 1818 a fair number of cultivated Hindus could read and write English.

Unlike Warren Hastings, Macaulay had a contempt for Hindu learning and knowledge. While governor and later governor general in Bengal from the years 1772 to 1785, Hastings, assisted and encouraged by a remarkable Orientalist, Sir William Jones, had founded Sanskrit and Arabic colleges, published a Persian grammar and was interested in both the Hindu and the Moslem cultures. In recommending English as the medium of education, Macaulay, as he writes in his Minute, planned "to form a class who may be interpreters between us and the millions whom we govern; a class of persons, Indian in blood and color, but English in taste, in opinions, in morals and in intellect. To that class we may leave it to refine the vernacular dialects of the country, to enrich those dialects with terms of science borrowed from the

* Lord William Bentinck was governor general of India from 1828 to 1835. Lord Macaulay, scholar, poet, and historian, was Legal Member of the governor-general's council under Bentinck.

Western nomenclature, and to render them by degrees fit vehicles for conveying knowledge to the great mass of the population."

Thus Macaulay's Minute led to the emergence of a new educated class of English-speaking Indians designed initially to provide a link between rulers and ruled and to interpret Western, more particularly British, ideas and institutions to their countrymen. Prior to this, in the eighteenth century indigenous instruction was confined among the Hindus to a small and privileged group, higher learning being a Brahman preserve. In many localities throughout the country there were Hindu and Moslem schools, usually attached to a temple or mosque with Hindu pandits or Moslem maulvis as teachers. Much of the instruction was obscurantist and ineffectual, and since it was imparted largely in religious institutions the lower castes and primitive tribes were excluded. The troubled state of the country in the eighteenth century also put learning out of joint.

The substitution of English for Persian had some important results and revolutionized the relations between Hindus and Moslems. In the eyes of the British raj, the active participation by the Moslems in the Great Rebellion when a titular Mogul emperor still reigned in Delhi made the Moslems politically suspect. To the Moslems in the early stages the establishment of British rule was more repugnant than to the Hindus, for memories of the long Mogul dominion survived with them. British rule meant the separation of church and state, which was contrary to Islam's theocratic conception of government. Less adaptable than the Hindus, the Moslems for many years eschewed English education, their orthodox religious leaders encouraging a boycott of secular schools. Only in 1875, when Syed Ahmed Khan founded the Moslem Anglo-Oriental college at Aligarh, now the well-known Aligarh university, did his coreligionists shed their prejudice against English learning. Moreover the bulk of Indian Moslems residing largely in the Punjab and Northwest Frontier came under British influence at least a generation later than the Hindus. As a result the Hindus began with an initial advantage, and their priority in education affected them in various spheres. Socially, it led to a divergence in education between the two communities which weakened the cultural links between them. Economically, because of their boycott of English, Moslems were slowly ousted from government posts and their places taken by Hindus. As India advanced, this economic rivalry was projected into the political field and had its logical outcome in the establishment of Pakistan. Despite these disruptive consequences the introduction of English impelled a wide release of mental energy. It brought some far-reaching social changes and opened new horizons of political, economic, and scientific thought from which all communities, Hindus, Moslems, and others, were to benefit in varying degrees.

Almost as revolutionary as the introduction of English was the establishment of the rule of law. This ensured the equality of all men, whether Brahman, Sudra, or Untouchable, before the courts, and affirmed the individual's rights as an individual. Hitherto Hinduism had differentiated between Brahman and non-Brahman, while Islam observed one law for Moslems and another for "infidels." Both the Hindu law of inheritance and the custom penalizing the marriage of Hindu widows were modified.

In the hundred-odd years between Aurangzeb's death and the effective establishment of British rule, there had existed a vacuum not only political and administrative but also ideological. Into this vacuum the British injected new ideas and institutions. As the country settled down and was administratively unified, the governmental system gained in stability and strength, and the emergence of an educated middle class saw successive rungs of the administrative ladder slowly manned by Indians. With political stability and improved communication came an expansion of trade and industry which again demanded, at first in the lower echelons, the services of qualified Indians. From the end of the First World War the industrialization of the country got under way with the gradual development of heavy industries, particularly coal, iron, and steel. Tariffs offered protection to national industries, the opportunities for indigenous participation expanded, and these were accelerated by the Second World War.

Much more vital and far-reaching was the impact of ideas in an atmosphere receptive to positive influences and new trends. Through English the educated Indian was enabled to read not only the thought of the West but to rediscover his own culture and civilization. Until the research of the early European scholars little or nothing was known of the pre-Islamic period in India. British scholars rediscovered and rejuvenated Asoka. Prinsep's discovery of the clue to the Brahmi and Kharoshti alphabets in 1834 enabled the ancient Hindu scriptures to be deciphered and unraveled. In 1785 Charles Wilkins published a translation of the Bhagavad-Gita, and five years later Sir William Jones translated Kalidasa's *Shakuntala*, which Goethe hailed with enthusiasm and delight. The German Max Müller and the Frenchman Emile Burnouf unearthed the treasures of Sanskrit and Pali learning. Through English the educated Indian was also able to discover the liberal thought enshrined not only in the writings of Burke and Mill but in political documents like Magna Carta and the story of the Long Parliament and to know something of the economic theories of Adam Smith and the utilitarian teachings of Jeremy Bentham. He came to hear of the humanitarianism of Wilberforce and Shaftesbury. He read avidly the works of Shakespeare, Milton, and John Bunyan. The marvels of Western science and technology unfolded before him, and concepts like democracy, the rule of law and parliamentary government, Marxism and dictatorship came within his ken. These cumulative developments produced mental stirrings at first vague but gradually more defined. The educated Indian saw and recognized that

British power was based on some positive qualities—on stability and strength, on unity, industrial initiative, economic enterprise, a live social conscience and discipline. Behind it were long years of knowledge and experience.

These mental stirrings in turn produced a dual reaction—a desire for modern reform on the one hand and an urge for the preservation of old ideas and institutions on the other. Under the evangelical influence of Wilberforce and Charles Grant, Bentinck in 1828 had suppressed suttee (the practice of immolating widows), forbidden infanticide and child sacrifice, and crushed out of existence the combined ritual of murder and robbery known as thuggee. Slavery was abolished some years later. Orthodox Hinduism hardened in self-defense, as it had done long before against the inroads of Islam, but reformist schools of thought also began to assert themselves. The most prominent of the early Indian reformers, as we noted, were Ram Mohun Roy on the Hindu side and Syed Ahmed Khan on the Moslem.

Of these two remarkable men the older was Ram Mohun Roy, who was born in 1779, nearly fifty years before the birth of Syed Ahmed Khan. Roy, a Brahman, of orthodox Hindu parentage, had an encyclopedic mind—he was fluent in eight languages—and a strong social conscience which was moved to moral indignation when as a young man he witnessed the immolation of his sister-in-law on her husband's funeral pyre. He had earlier denounced such practices as suttee and idolatry while upholding the teachings of the Vedas and Upanishads. These, according to him, represented the pure font of Hinduism which was sullied by later-day superstitions and accretions. Roy thus strove to reform Hinduism by rationalizing it on the basis not of Western religious beliefs but of the old Hindu scriptures. The Bible also attracted him, and in order to comprehend it better he acquired a knowledge of Hebrew and Greek. Like Gandhi, he was drawn to the Sermon on the Mount, which he felt reflected and projected the every-day ethics preached in the Gita. The Brahmo Samaj which he founded around 1829 was designed to propagate this reformist creed. It had its roots in the Hindu scriptures and thought but its outlook was modern. Although the Samaj attracted many of Bengal's leading writers and thinkers, notably some members of the Tagore family, it fell, perhaps inevitably, between two stools, with certain members drawn more toward Christianity than to Hinduism, while others were content to be philosophically quiescent.

Like Ram Mohun Roy, Syed Ahmed Khan also attempted to achieve a synthesis between Eastern and Western thought, and like the Hindu the Moslem sought to graft a rational outlook on a traditional culture. Islam was encrusted with medieval scholasticism, and Syed Ahmed Khan, in trying to break this crust, invoked both reason and authority. He strove, like Roy, to reconcile traditional beliefs with modern needs. Realizing that the root cause of Moslem backwardness was the reluctance of Moslems to take to English learning, he worked for many years to break down this prejudice. The establishment of the Moslem Anglo-Oriental college at Aligarh in 1875, to which we have referred, is a monument to the progressive outlook and constructive genius of this farsighted man. Like Roy again, Syed Ahmed Khan visited Europe at a time when very few Indians traveled west. Roy had gone to England in 1830 to voice some grievances of the Mogul emperor before the directors of the East India Company and while there was presented to William IV. Nearly forty years later Syed Ahmed Khan went to England, where among other personalities he met Thomas Carlyle.

There were other reformist movements on both sides. One reaction to Ram Mohun Roy's Brahmo Samaj was Swami Dayananda's Arya Samaj founded in 1875. Dayananda regarded the Brahmo Samaj as too rationalistic in its outlook and felt that the only way to purify Hinduism was to go back to its primeval source in the Vedas. In the early Vedic days Hinduism was not riven by caste nor was it cluttered up with customs such as child marriage, the seclusion of women, and suttee. Dayananda denounced idolatry and caste, calling on Hindus to rejuvenate and purify themselves by a return to the old religion of their forefathers in its pristine form. He might be described as a Hindu Luther. The Arya Samaj had a militant aspect, being actively hostile to Christianity and Islam, and its militancy expressed itself in the *shuddhi*, or reconversion, movement. On the other hand, its sense of enlightened reform helped to raise the marriage age, improve the status of the widow, and encourage feminine education. Today it counts around half a million followers, mostly in the Punjab. Its appeal to Hindus, being clear-cut and decisive, was stronger than that of the Brahmo Samaj.

On the Moslem side were parallel reform movements, notably the Ahmaidya movement, also located largely in the Punjab. It was inaugurated in 1889 by Mirza Ghulam Ahmad who came from the town of Qadian and who, like John the Baptist in the power and spirit of Elijah, claimed he was the recipient of divine revelation and had been sent into the world "in the power and spirit of Jesus." According to him, Jesus did not die on the cross but was taken down unconscious, survived, and eventually died at the age of 120 in Kashmir, at Srinagar. Orthodox Islam brands the followers of this movement as heretics, and it has made small headway, though it has successfully attracted the attention of many Europeans to Islam.

Much later Sir Mohammed Iqbal, the well-known poet and philosopher, who was influenced greatly by the Sufis, attempted to reinterpret Islamic doctrine on modern lines. In his poems he combines the ideas of the Sufi mystics with the beliefs of Nietzsche and Bergson. Not surprisingly, this subtle exercise had a limited appeal, being confined largely to intellectuals who were interested more in academic theories than in practical pursuits.

A Moslem counterpart to the Hindu Arya Samaj was the Wahabi movement, which also preached a return to primitive Islam. The Wahabis are the Puritans of Islam who interpret the Koran literally, frown on extreme veneration of the Prophet, and avoid tobacco, spirituous liquor, card playing, and usury. They count some followers in India, but their influence is not considerable.

The struggle between those who wanted India to develop on modern lines and those who set greater store by ancient ways and teachings was thus fought out on various fronts. So it continues today. The new middle class who propagated these ideas were in time to direct the country in many fields, manning the administrative machinery, the armed services, the professions, industry, and commerce, the managerial cadres and a large proportion of ministerial and public offices. From being governed they were to govern.

What of the princes? The India of the early British administrators was a peasants' and princes' India. When the British established their political primacy, not all the country was directly ruled by them. A considerable territory was in the hands of the Indian princes and chiefs who had accepted the suzerainty of the British in return for their own continuance as rulers. At the time of independence in August, 1947, they numbered 562, ranging in size and importance from states such as Hyderabad and Kashmir, nearly as large as Great Britain, to a titular estate like Bilbari in Gujarat with an area of under two square miles and a population of less than thirty.

These princes were subject to few internal checks, and as a result their states, with a few honorable exceptions, were notorious for misgovernment. This was a natural consequence of divorcing power from responsibility and of converting the princes into subsidiary allies of the British. Lord Dalhousie who came to India as governor general in 1848 attempted to check princely misrule by initiating a policy to absorb their states gradually into British India. This policy, known as the Doctrine of Lapse whereby a state on the death of its ruler without a male heir lapsed to the British, resulted in the Maratha States of Satara, Nagpur, and Jhansi being taken over by the East India Company, and in the annexation of Oudh. Princely resentment over this policy was one reason for the Great Rebellion. The Rani of Jhansi, widow of the ruler whose state had lapsed, was significantly one of the principal rebel leaders.

After the rebellion the British returned to their old policy of subsidiary alliance which entitled the princes to military support and freedom from foreign invasion and undertook to respect their "rights, dignity and honor." At the same time India passed from the rule of the East India Company to the Crown. But the British could never quite escape from the dilemma created by the invidious position of the princes. Their attempts to modernize them failed except in a few cases like Baroda and Mysore, and what Dalhousie had initiated an independent Indian Government was to complete. When Britain relinquished its dominion over the country the peasants and princes were still there—the latter occupying over two-fifths of the territorial area and ruling over less than a quarter of the country's inhabitants. With the departure of the British this feudal order lost its pomp and power. Princely India was absorbed within a democratic framework.

If the road to independence was long and hard, the urge for political freedom was again a reaction to the British impact. The spread of education and the growth of new and wider opportunities in many fields inevitably led to a demand for self-government, though in its early manifestations this merely took the form of a request for equal and more extensive Indian association with the British in the government of the country and for the gradual infiltration of indigenous personnel into the higher ranks of the Civil Service. Since 1858 Indians had been permitted to compete for places in the Covenanted Civil Service, but very few had done so. Lord Lytton, who was viceroy from 1876 to 1880, had toyed with the idea of enlisting the services of the big landholders as magistrates and local administrators and of encouraging their sons to enter the Civil Service. In this he was opposed, as his successors were to be, by the vested interests represented by the British administrators. A viceroy, however able, was not capable of achieving much in his five-year term of office, the real rulers of India being the British officials.

The viceroyality of Lytton's successor, Lord Ripon, was notable for a more positive liberalism than that practiced by any of his predecessors. In India he is remembered for the storm which his attempt to remove racial discrimination in the legal field generated. At that time no European could be tried by anyone except another European. Since a few Indians had by then achieved the rank of district magistrates, the issue raised was by no means academic. Ripon decided to abolish this racial discrimination, and with that object in view introduced the Ilbert bill, named after the then Law Member, which provoked a tremendous uproar in the European community. He was compelled to amend the bill and to allow a European brought for trial before a district magistrate to be tried by a jury of which half were Europeans. The controversy had some important repercussions. If European agitation could compel the government to retreat, so could a well-organized Indian agitation. The Indian National Congress was founded in 1885, within two years of the Ilbert bill, though initially it was designed more as a safety-valve for Indian political feeling than as a platform for political agitation.

The movement for self-government thus goes back many years before Gandhi's day. It may be said to have surfaced when the Indian National Congress held its first session in Bombay with a Scotsman, Alan Octavian Hume, a former member of the Indian Civil Service, as its prime founder. When Hume called for "three times three cheers for Her Majesty the Queen Empress," the delegates responded enthusiastically. The Congress in its early days was essentially an institution of moderates, and remained so for thirty years until after the death in February, 1915, of Gopal Krishna Gokhale, perhaps the most eminent of the early liberals, when the extremists led by Bal Gangadhar Tilak captured the organization. Tilak's death in July, 1920, brought Gandhi to the helm of Congress, although even earlier, around 1917, when he launched his first indigenous experiment in nonviolent non-cooperation on behalf of the indigo plantation laborers at Chambaran in North Bihar, the Mahatma had begun to attract the country's attention. With Tilak's death there was no one to challenge Gandhi's political primacy.

While inside the Congress the moderates and extremists contended against each other, the rivalry between Hindus and Moslems also developed on the broader national plane. Although the first four presidents of the Congress were respectively a Christian, Parsi, Moslem, and Briton,* and the Congress was Indian and not communal in character, it was inevitably dominated by the Hindus. Sir Syed Ahmed Khan, even while describing Hindus and Moslems as "the two eyes of India," urged the Moslems to keep away from the Congress. The second half of the nineteenth century saw a great upsurge of Hindu revivalism, which was accelerated and intensified by the partition of Bengal in July, 1905. This pleased the Moslems, since the majority of them resided in East Bengal, but irked the Hindus, for the creation of a separate province in eastern Bengal was regarded by the latter as a counterpoise to the politically dominant Hindus. In turn, Hindu agitation against partition alienated many Moslems, and their reaction was reflected in a drop in Moslem membership of the Congress. Whereas in 1890 out of 1,702 delegates to the sixth

* W. C. Bonnerjee (1885); Dadabhai Naoroji (1886); Badruddin Tyabji (1887); George Yule (1888).

session 153 were Moslems, in 1905, at the twenty-first session, out of 756 delegates only 17 were Moslems.

Slowly a separate Moslem national consciousness came into being, expressing itself around 1906, some eight years after the death of Sir Syed Ahmed Khan, in the formation of the Moslem League which demanded separate electorates for the Moslems. This was conceded by the Indian Councils Act of 1909, more popularly known as the Morley-Minto* reforms. Thereafter political agitation, which was concerned in the early stages mainly with a division of the loaves and fishes of office, was channeled into two distinct streams. The system of separate electorates was confirmed by the Government of India Acts of 1919 and 1935 which took the country further on the way to self-government. As the communal virus bit into the Indian body politic, separatist influences grew. Separate representation created a balance of interests, classes, and communities whose chief concern it soon became to perpetuate these divisions. The logical culmination was Pakistan.

Within the Congress the division between the moderates and the extremists also displayed an interesting cleavage in religious outlook. Moderates like Gokhale and Phirozeshah Mehta, a Parsi from Bombay; Dadabhai Naoroji, the first Indian to sit in the British House of Commons; Narayan Chandavarkar, a well-known social reformer; Bhupendranath Basu of Bengal and Subramania Iyer of Madras, were advanced in their outlook, politically concerned only in hastening the country's progress to self-government. On the other hand Tilak, the extremist leader, was a curious blend of religious obscurantism and revolutionary ardor. He appealed to Hindu revivalism, urging his coreligionists to save the country from being absorbed into an alien civilization and to prevent Hinduism from disintegrating and thereby allow-

* After Lord Morley, secretary of state for India at the time, and Lord Minto, the viceroy.

ing a foreign order to take its place. Tilak, though a political revolutionary, was a religious conservative, and bitterly opposed the Age of Consent bill which was designed to mitigate the evils of child marriage.

"Swaraj is my birthright and I will have it" was his slogan, and it attracted not only orthodox Hindus but militant young men who regarded the moderates as being cautious to the point of timidity. Tilak's teachings, first localized in western India in Maharashtra, soon spread their influence to other parts of the country, notably to the Punjab and Bengal. Unlike Gandhi, Tilak preached no political ethics. He supported violence and even condoned assassination. The cult of the pistol and the bomb extended from Maharashtra elsewhere and resulted in the murder of some Europeans. In 1908 Tilak was prosecuted for sedition and sentenced to transportation* for six years. About the same time Lala Lajpat Rai was deported from the Punjab and lived for many years as a political refugee in the United States. Not long after Gokhale's death, Tilak returned to the Congress fold, captured the organization, and was among its most outstanding figures until Gandhi appeared on the scene.

Gandhi's entry on the political stage changed the course of Indian history. When noncooperation threatened to become the official policy of the Congress, the moderates withdrew to form in time their own group, known as the Liberal party. Inside the Congress Gandhi was dominant. He was soon to dominate the country. The Gandhian era had begun.

* Imprisonment outside India. Tilak was in prison in Burma.

IV
The Gandhian Era

GANDHI appeared on the Indian scene in 1915, thirty years after the founding of the Congress and thirty-two years before the achievment of independence. He had been away in South Africa almost continuously since 1893, returning to India only twice—for about a year's stay in 1901–1902, and earlier for a brief visit in 1896. On the advice of Gokhale, the liberal, he desisted from active politics for twelve months, and in this period traveled around the country, acutely observant. The first Congress session which the Mahatma had attended was in 1901 at Calcutta. Fifteen years later he attended the Congress session at Lucknow where for the first time he met Jawaharlal Nehru, then twenty-seven. Gandhi was twenty years his senior. Neither seems to have made any great initial impression on the other.

The Mahatma was not to be an active force in Indian politics until 1918, when the moderates withdrew from the Congress. Two years later Tilak died, and this, as we saw, left Gandhi the dominant figure in the Congress. Many in and outside India associate the terms *swadeshi* (Indian-made goods) and *swaraj* (freedom) with him, but these phrases were current long before the Mahatma. The ideal of swaraj was first proclaimed from a Congress platform by Dadabhai Naoroji at the Calcutta session of 1906. The swadeshi movement for the boycott of foreign goods was launched in August, 1905, again in Calcutta, at a meeting called to protest against the proposed partition of Bengal.

What then were the new elements which the Mahatma injected into India's political life? His first and most important contribution was that he took politics to the people. He identified the struggle for freedom not with the middle classes but with the masses. Others, like Tilak, had taken it beyond armchair agitation to aggressive action; but neither Tilak through the columns of his popular newspaper *Kesari* (Lion) or by his revival of the Shivaji* cult and the Ganapati† festival nor Aurobindo Ghose, later to retire as a famous recluse to his ashram at Pondicherry, was able to influence many beyond the fringe of the restive, educated middle class. Gandhi spoke in a language which the masses understood. He imported a new idiom and a new common denominator—the ordinary peasant and worker for whose benefit and progress, he claimed, independence was vitally necessary.

So far most Congress politicians had been content merely to register their protest against the British Government's sins of commission and omission. Gandhi went further. He insisted that a wrong should provoke not only protest but resistance and that resistance must be nonviolent. Tilak had preached passive resistance before him, while writing and speaking in terms which could be construed as an incitement to violence. Gandhi stressed the active quality of his resistance, which he christened *satyagraha*, meaning literally "force of truth" but signifying broadly nonviolent noncooperation. It was a weapon, he declared, of the strong, not the weak.

With the advent of the Mahatma the Congress widened its political appeal to include the masses and the classes and in time

* Shivaji (1627-1680), famous Maratha warrior and leader of the Maratha resurgence.

† Ganapati is the God of Wisdom and remover of obstacles.

widened its objective from self-government for India to complete independence, although it was tacitly understood that it would accept dominion status or independence within the British Commonwealth. This is what ultimately happened. Gandhi's emergence also saw the conversion of the Congress from a Western political institution dominated by Westernized Indians into a national organization controlled for the most part by Indians with deep indigenous roots and comprising a mass membership reaching down to the peasants and workers. The weapon of revolutionary action was Western, but the Mahatma cloaked it in a typical Indian garb. Nonviolent noncooperation echoed an ancient Hindu practice, the practice of "sitting dharna"—that is, a system whereby a creditor or an aggrieved person sat at the doorstep of his debtor or oppressor and fasted until death or until he received redress. The virtue of the practice lay in the fact that it inflicted no physical injury on the wrongdoer but only on the aggrieved. On the other hand, many Westerners find it difficult to distinguish this practice from moral blackmail. Moreover, it could be effective only if both sides observed the rules of the game. Here India was frankly fortunate in having the British as rulers.

Gandhi was drawn to the idea of nonviolent resistance by the writings principally of Tolstoi and Thoreau, though two thinkers, Ruskin and Emerson, were also to influence his thought in other directions, notably in the ideals of simple living and of dedicated service. His first letter to Tolstoi was written from South Africa in 1909. He had been vaguely attracted by Tolstoi's ideas while studying in England between the years 1889 and 1891, and his Vaishnavaite upbringing, with its ascetic, protestant, and humanizing influences molded his outlook in the same direction. However, it was not until he went to South Africa that these ideas assumed definite shape and found positive expression. On his return from England in 1891, Gandhi met in India another man who was to influence his thinking considerably—the Gujarati poet and philosopher Rajchandra Rajjivbhar, by whom he seems to have been confirmed in his belief in continence, though even as a student in England he had gradually been drawn to the practice of self-denial and self-suppression.

The idea of adopting satyagraha as a political weapon appears to have taken concrete form around September, 1906, when Gandhi first advocated it to the Indian settlers in South Africa in protest against the Asiatic Law Amendment bill which subjected Asians to many humiliating restrictions and requirements. To Gandhi it seemed to have the dual virtue of teaching his countrymen to shed fear and master hate. Almost a year elapsed before the bill passed into law, when a body known as the Passive Resistance Association was formed to offer satyagraha. It was the first demonstration of its kind, and did much to give moral muscle to the Indian movement of resistance. Gandhi was sentenced to two months' imprisonment, although some of his associates were given six months' hard labor.

By 1909 when he wrote *Hind Swaraj*, a brochure which contains the gist of his political, economic, and social philosophy, Gandhi had crystallized for all practical purposes his views on life and living. He was then forty, and his experiments in truth, as he was to describe them later, had covered a span of nearly twelve years beginning with his return to South Africa in December, 1896, when he had come back from India accompanied by his family. In *Hind Swaraj*, which is primarily an indictment of "modern civilization," the Mahatma interprets satyagraha as "the gospel of love in place of that of hate. It replaces violence with self-sacrifice. It pits soul force against brute force." He extols the virtues of abstinence and asceticism. Gandhi incidentally had been observing brahmachari (sexual abstinence) since 1906, though he had attempted to practice sexual restraint for some six years before that. At the time that he took the vow of celibacy, he also took the vow of poverty, not so much, it would appear, as a condemnation of property but as a protest against inequality. He performed his first penitential fast much later, in 1913.

In his early days in South Africa Gandhi had been accustomed to wearing Western dress and to living as became a successful lawyer. He invariably traveled first class, and a letter he wrote to Dadabhai Naoroji from London in November, 1906, carries the address of the then fashionable Hotel Cecil, now demolished. As a boy he had eaten meat secretly on a few occasions in the belief that the meat-eating Englishman derived his strength from this habit. But he soon recoiled from it, as he did from smoking, which he also practiced secretly. His family were orthodox vegetarians. While a student in England he had worn Western dress, tried to play a violin, and had even attempted ballroom dancing.

When exactly Gandhi turned away from Western or modern civilization it is difficult to determine. He probably did so not long after taking the vow of celibacy and poverty, perhaps somewhere around 1907, though a photograph taken two years later in London shows him in Western clothes. Certainly by the time he set up his settlement known as Tolstoi Farm, some twenty miles from Johannesburg, his habit of life was completely Indian. This was around June, 1910, when he began to wear the clothes of an ordinary indentured laborer, later adopting, on his return to India in 1915, his native Kathiawadi* costume. Only in 1921 was he to adopt his famous loincloth.

In a letter to a friend summarizing the contents of *Hind Swaraj*, Gandhi, while asserting that there was no insuperable barrier between East and West, also declared that there was no such thing as Western or European civilization but modern civilization, which was purely material. It was this modern civilization, and not the British people, that was ruling India through the railways, the telegraph, the telephone, and other abominations. Gandhi

* A costume commonly worn in the district of Kathiawar, whence Gandhi came.

described Bombay, Calcutta, and the chief cities of India as "real plague-spots," and lumping together all aspects of modern civilization—medical science, doctors, the legal system and profession, English education, industrialization and machine-made goods—roundly condemned them.

The Mahatma's views as propounded in *Hind Swaraj* are both negative and inconsistent, for although as a humanist he is at pains to distinguish between Western and modern civilization it is obvious that the two are synonymous. Indeed Gandhi in the explanatory letter to his friend admits this. "East and west," he writes, "can really meet when the west has overthrown modern civilization almost in its entirety. They can also seemingly meet when the east has adopted modern civilization but that meeting would be an armed truce, even as it is between, say, Germany and England, both of which nations are living in the Hall of Death in order to avoid being devoured, the one by the other." It might be pointed out, and not by Westerners alone, that while denouncing the railways, the telegraph and telephone the Mahatma made good use of them then and thereafter.

"The Hindu mind is myself," Gandhi once observed. Although nonconformist in many ways, the mainsprings of his thought were essentially Hindu, and to him, for instance, nonviolence was not so much a social as a religious doctrine. He describes modern civilization as "irreligion," and his reaction against it is accompanied significantly by an idealization of the ancient traditional Hindu culture. In *Hind Swaraj* while attacking English education he urges the revival and study of Indian languages, with religion as the central core. As a shrewd British observer* comments, "He wants the old type of society and must therefore keep the religion which for ages has bound it together and supplied its theory of things."

To Gandhi, Hinduism was a system of unique merit, far

* Philip Spratt in *Gandhism* (Huxley Press, Madras, 1939).

superior to the ancient civilizations of Babylon and Rome, which had perished while Hinduism, because of its spiritual content and basis, had survived. According to the Mahatma the ascetic regime of his ashram at Sabarmati, later transferred to Sheogaon near Wardha, owed its inspiration to the shastras, the sacred religious and legal textbooks of the Hindus. Some of his critics regarded him as a Christianized Hindu. Gandhi had reverence for the Bible and was attracted by the Sermon on the Mount. But while he was influenced greatly by Christianity in his younger years, his roots were always in Hinduism, in his own society and religion. In his later days he turned decisively away from the West.

The result of his teaching, with its strong bias against modern civilization and culture and its simultaneous stress on the need for political independence, was to create a sort of intellectual schizophrenia, a split approach to political and economic problems. Gandhi regarded himself as primarily an Indian, but his political appeal was largely religious and mainly Hindu. He identified morality with religion, being more concerned with individuals than with society as a whole, and thereby gave politics a basis free from sectarianism. But undoubtedly his political thought was colored by a religious outlook, and despite his nonconformity in certain spheres he was strongly attached to his religion. He did not disbelieve in idol worship and accepted caste, but he was passionately opposed to untouchability. He believed in rebirth but not in conversion. He did not approve of the Untouchables being converted to Islam or Christianity nor did he want non-Hindus to be Hindus. A man, he insisted, must remain in the religious fold he was born into.

Not all these views commended themselves to the educated Indian who until then was the spur and spearhead of the political movement. But Gandhi's teachings were in line with traditional Hindu thought, and the idea of asceticism and renunciation appealed instinctively to the Hindu masses and to those classes with strong indigenous moorings who were also permeated with a sense of tradition. One unfortunate result of the Mahatma's attempt to give politics a religious hue was gradually to antagonize the Moslems and to deepen their suspicion that his politics was steeped in Hinduism. It was ironic, since Gandhi was no religious conservative and in reality sought to secularize Hinduism.

The combined role of prophet, priest, and politician is difficult to sustain. Though Gandhi's thoughts, being amorphous, gave his teachings a semblance of width, they appeared to lack depth. This was probably because his ideas stemmed more from feeling than from thought, and thereby lacked an intellectual synthesis. The Mahatma's knowledge betrays great gaps, and his habit of eclecticism led him to pay heed to what suited his outlook and to ignore the inconvenient. He acknowledges this frankly. "It was my habit," he writes in his autobiography,* "to forget what did not appeal to me and to model my behavior according to what did appeal to me." As a result his thought, though it very seldom lacked clarity, often lacked cohesion and presented itself as a ramshackle intellectual structure with no system or form. Much of his thinking was pragmatic, and he was content to move step by step as the occasion demanded. This made him seem at times confused and contradictory.

Nehru's early reactions to the Mahatma, which lingered throughout their association, reflect the impression Gandhi made on a Western-educated Indian. "Sometimes," Nehru writes in his autobiography, "his language was almost incomprehensible to an average modern." Gandhi's views on machinery and modern civilization frankly made little sense to the class of educated Indians of which Nehru was typical. They were irked by Gandhi's habit of giving politics a religious flavor, and felt that

* *My Experiments with Truth,* by M. K. Gandhi (Navjivan Press, Ahmedabad, 1927).

the Mahatma's definition of private wealth as a trust was both unrealistic and out of date. To praise poverty and suffering and to laud asceticism for its own sake seemed to them an exercise in excessive idealism. It was medieval and revivalist. It was also masochistic.

Nehru overcame his opposition to the Mahatma's views by rationalizing those opinions which he could not easily accept, and was able by his example to persuade many other Westernized Indians to forget their inhibitions and antipathies and to follow the Mahatma. With Nehru they were drawn to him by his insistence on active resistence to a wrong. However impractical his theories might seem, they noted that his methods were often practical enough to yield results. He had a habit of arguing his point gently but with unusual earnestness, and they noticed also that he generally got his way. Generally he also proved right. The results showed that the Mahatma had more political insight than they had suspected him of possessing, and they came to the conclusion that he could deliver the goods.

Other qualities impelled them to him. Gandhi combined courage with an unusually sensitive conscience, and could communicate both to many of his followers and associates. Through courage he taught them to shed fear and hate, and by appealing to their conscience he infused them with some of his sense of dedicated service. He was all things to all men, and had the gift of keeping men of diverse views and temperaments together. "He had a part of everybody's faith in him and also his own self-discipline," Nehru notes.

None the less the authoritarian streak was strong in the Mahatma, and more than one of his close coworkers* has noted that he was intolerant of independent thought among them and would brook no attempt on their part to impinge on his leadership. Toward opponents Gandhi was scrupulously polite. But he could be stern within his own circle, sometimes to the point of

* *Mr. Gandhi As I Know Him*, by Indulal Yagnik (Ahmedabad).

being cold-bloodedly harsh. Personally he made no attempt to establish contact with the educated Westernized middle class whose ways of life and thought were antipathetic to his and from whom he increasingly drew away. If they chose to follow him it could only be on his own terms. Like Nehru, they had to subordinate their own independent thinking to the greater good, as Gandhi conceived it, of the country.

Many of them chose to do so. In doing so they, more than any other class, helped Gandhi to give the national movement an Indian character and cast. By persuading them to draw their strength and inspiration from India and to cease being magnetized by the West, the Mahatma impregnated the British-created middle class with Indian ideas and ideals. This was his greatest revolution, for within less than three decades he had succeeded in erasing much of the influence of Western thought and methods and of implanting, instead, pride in indigenous ideas and instruments of progress. Satyagraha and swadeshi represented the political and economic facets of an Indian philosophy which, combining both, sought to give a moral stamp to the nationalist movement.

The paramount advantage which India derived from this method was that when the British withdrew, leaving the country independent, if partitioned, there was no vacuum such as had existed in the hundred years before the establishment of British rule. Indian ideals had developed to replace those of the British, and in the process distinctive Indian methods of advance had evolved. But the Gandhian technique also left many difficulties and problems in its train. Although Western civilization was largely at a discount and Western education not rated as high as it was in the pre-Gandhian era, the educated middle class, while more assertively Indian in outlook, was still susceptible to the influence of Western ideas and learning, which to it signified a more speedy and practical way to progress.

Thus was engendered the intellectual schizophrenia to which

we have referred and which developed a split approach to economic and political problems. From the Gandhian upheaval a new class of leaders had emerged, the majority comprising small-town lawyers, doctors, and social workers with a leavening of urban intellectuals, politically conscious peasants and workers, students and, not least important, a vast array of women. The entry of women into political life was among the Mahatma's distinctive contributions. In so far as all these elements broadened the base of the national struggle, their emergence into active life was beneficial. While the battle for freedom had lasted, a sense of dedicated service to the country had imbued them. But with the achievement of independence a new spirit emerged, and with it a conscious elevation of this new class as a patriotic elite corps entitled to the prizes of office and to the perquisites which prison-going seemed automatically to confer on them. They had invested in patriotism and they now demanded their dividends.

Gandhi was in no sense class conscious. He was in fact far less class conscious than the average middle-class Indian, and his antipathy to the latter was primarily, as we have noted, because of the average middle-class Indian's Westernized education and way of life. Although the Mahatma was more at home with peasants and artisans, particularly the former, his scheme of life had a place for all sorts of people, including the princes, capitalists, and the professional middle class. After all, he himself came from that class, as did the leading political figures of his time, notably Motilal and Jawaharlal Nehru, Vallabhbhai Patel and Jinnah, then a nationalist but famous later as the founder of Pakistan.

The new class which Gandhi brought into being, broad based as it was in the life of the country, became after independence, by the sheer weight of its numbers and augmented by the weapon of adult franchise, the ruling caste. One result was a distinct lowering in the quality of public life and in administrative standards.

Under the influence of Gandhi's teachings the old middle class, even those who followed the Mahatma, were caught in a vise. While those who did not actively participate in the Congress movement retained outwardly an English style of life, they developed at home a more Indian way of living and thought. With those who followed the Mahatma the external and domestic manifestations became Indian. But in the case of both, their minds and faces while turned inward were not wholly oblivious to outside influences.

Nehru belongs to this category. His heart was with the Mahatma but his mind remained largely his own, and even in Gandhi's lifetime he did not hesitate to reveal the intellectual differences which divided them. In this he reflected the doubts and hesitations which continued to oppress the educated Westernized Indian even in independent India. The old battle between the modern and traditional had still to be waged and won, but on a different battlefield.

Nehru, though the symbol and spearhead of the Congress-created new class, really does not belong to it. In a curious way his idea of modern methods and objectives approximates closely to Gandhi's conception of modern civilization as being neither Eastern nor Western, the basic difference between them consisting in the fact that while Nehru is attracted by the modern, Gandhi was repelled by it. By modern methods Nehru means methods suited to the conditions of India in modern days. Inevitably this brings him into collision with the traditional forces represented by the majority of the new class. But simultaneously it also faces him with the opposition of the majority of the old middle class, who are not enamored of his strongly socialistic bias at home or of his refusal to walk consistently in step with the West abroad. Nehru is thus caught in a double vise. As Gandhi's heir and simultaneously as a modern-minded Indian his invidious situation was perhaps inevitable. It represents the paradox which confronts modern India—to compromise with the past while moving boldly from the present into the future.

Could this paradox have been avoided had Gandhi not stepped onto the Indian stage? It is dangerous to be dogmatic, but on a careful consideration of actualities and potentialities it is possible that it could. Swaraj and swadeshi were ideals long before the Mahatma lighted on the Indian scene, and had the British-created middle class continued the battle for freedom on modern lines India, like Japan, might have staged its own Meiji revolution. Before Gandhi came, the internal battle for political leadership was waged between the liberal moderates such as Gokhale, Surendranath Bannerjea, and Phirozeshah Mehta and the militant revolutionaries represented by Tilak, Lala Lajpat Rai, and Aurobindo Ghose. Had the British Government responded with rapid constitutional reforms, the hands of the liberal moderates would have been strengthened and the transition to political freedom accelerated. Indeed, independence might have come earlier had not Gandhi intervened.

Between 1858, when India was transferred from the East India Company to the Crown, and 1920, when the Mahatma established his ascendancy over the Congress, there were four measures of political reform. The first was the Indian Councils Act of 1861 which provided for the inclusion of a few nominated nonofficials to the legislative council of the governor general and established similar councils in the presidencies of Bombay, Madras, and Bengal; next came the Indian Councils Act of 1892, seven years after the establishment of the Congress, which slightly enlarged and liberalized the composition and functions of these councils. In 1909 another installment of reforms increased the numerical strength of the councils, extended the right of interpellation, and also permitted members to move resolutions on the budget. Nonofficial majorities were conceded in the provinces, and one Indian member was appointed to the executive councils of the viceroy, the governors of Bombay and Madras and later of Bengal. Two years earlier a couple of Indians had been appointed to the secretary of state's council. The Act also introduced the system of communal electorates and election on a limited franchise. In 1919 the Government of India Act, based on the recommendations of the secretary of state, Mr. Edwin Montagu, and the viceroy, Lord Chelmsford, was passed, and this further extended Indian membership on the viceroy's executive council and on the executive councils of the provincial governors. The nonofficial element in the legislatures, central and provincial, was increased, and a system known as dyarchy, which made a certain number of ministers responsible to the legislatures in the provinces, was introduced.

Thus in the thirty-five years between the establishment of the Congress and Gandhi's active advent on the scene there had been four measures of political reform. It is perhaps not without significance that though India achieved independence some twenty-seven years later, there was only one measure of political reform —the Government of India Act of 1935 which was only partially implemented—in this span of nearly three decades. On the other hand the same period was punctuated by four satyagraha struggles and some individual civil-disobedience campaigns. Until Gandhi came, political agitation was confined overwhelmingly to the educated classes. It is the Mahatma's distinctive contribution that he made the masses politically conscious. Whether the ultimate result was hastened by these campaigns alone or also by external developments, such as the Second World War, the Japanese conquest of Southeast Asia, which included an attempted invasion of India; and the return of a Socialist Government to power in Britian in 1945 is open to debate. Certainly the Government of India Act of 1919 as much as the achievement of freedom in 1947 owed not a little to the two world wars, neither of which was of India's doing.

This is not to minimize the Mahatma's achievements but to assess and appreciate them in a context wider than that of India. Gandhi in fact had very little to do with the 1919 Act, for the Home Rule Movement, conducted primarily by Dr. Annie Besant during the First World War, made little appeal to him, being confined to the middle and upper classes and having in view a Western parliamentary type of government, from which he recoiled. Though he had initially given qualified support to the Act, he later characterized it as "a whited sepulchre." It is important, however, to remember that his first noncooperation movement in India was not directed against the Act but was provoked by another measure, the Rowlatt Act,* which contained drastic provisions against the liberty of the individual. Subsequent happenings, particularly the Jallianwala Bagh massacre at Amritsar in the Punjab when hundreds of unarmed men, women, and children were fired upon and killed, precipitated the Mahatma's satyagraha campaign in 1920.

One immediate result of the Congress decision to embark on nonviolent noncooperation was a further exodus of the moderates, including Jinnah, from the organization. The earlier dissidents, who numbered among them Surendranath Bannerjea, had organized themselves as Liberals by the end of 1918. Jinnah, though still a nationalist, now worked more closely with the Moslem League, with whom he was to achieve Pakistan when India was partitioned. Thus Gandhi's introduction of the new political weapon of satyagraha, while it unified and invigorated vast masses of the people, also created new dissensions and intensified old cleavages. It drove away the moderates, many of them highly educated, patriotic individuals, from the Congress fold and deepened the rift between the Hindus and the Moslems. Only in the first noncooperation movement was the Congress able to

* Named after the late Sir Sydney Rowlatt, a judge of the British High Court.

draw popular Moslem support by advocating the Khilafat cause opposing the Treaty of Sèvres which dismembered the Turkish Empire at the end of the First World War. Thereafter Hindu-Moslem relations, despite the Mahatma's efforts, deteriorated swiftly.

Some Hindu critics of Gandhi have alleged that by mobilizing the Moslems for the Khilafat cause under the Congress flag the Mahatma unwittingly infused a new and militant energy into the Moslems which later they turned against the Hindus. The fact remains that as Congress militancy grew, the Moslem League waxed in vitality, for to the vast mass of Moslems the ceremonial, symbols, and slogans increasingly associated with Congress activities under Gandhi's paternal Hinduism came to be invested with a distinctly Hindu flavor. By identifying morality with religion and religion with politics, the Mahatma unfortunately helped to strengthen this Moslem fear and suspicion. The "ifs" of history are intriguing, if irksome. Had the Congress rejected the weapon of noncooperation, would Jinnah have remained within it, fulfilling Gokhale's prophecy that here was "the apostle of Hindu-Moslem unity"? In that event, would Pakistan have materialized?

Other questions pose themselves. Once the Congress was dubbed an extremist body with no great faith in Western political institutions, it became increasingly difficult for the British raj to negotiate with that body, faced as it was with the threat of civil disobedience on the one hand and the distinct possibility on the other that given a further measure of political advance the Congress with its mass support would rout the moderates and the liberals and, having captured the legislatures, would make the new constitution unworkable. In that context the Congress under the aegis of Gandhi might fairly be charged with delaying rather than accelerating political progress. In the three decades of the Mahatma's dominance, only one measure of political reform, as we have seen, was introduced, and that too was only partially implemented.

The Government of India Act of 1935 which was enforced on April 1, 1937, envisaged an all-India federation comprising the Princely States and the newly formulated autonomous Governors' Provinces. Provincial autonomy came into operation in June, 1937, when the Congress, having staged a spectacular victory at the polls, agreed to head the governments in six provinces, eventually extended to eight. This gave the party control of eight of India's then eleven provinces, the non-Congress units being Sind, the Punjab, and Bengal, where coalition ministries were formed. At this stage Jinnah seemed genuinely anxious that the Moslem League should cooperate with the Congress and work provincial autonomy "for what it was worth." True, the league had fared none too well in the elections, but the Congress would have been wise not to have aggravated further the sense of grievance, frustration, and isolation smoldering in the Moslem masses and leaders by spurning their cooperation. Possibly the Congress believed that the league, being at a tactical disadvantage, could be driven into the political wilderness. Whatever the reasons, the Congress, while expressing its willingness to invite Moslem representatives, including members of the league, to join its provincial ministries, insisted that they could do so only if they became members of the Congress party. Jinnah was furious. It was nothing, he exclaimed, but a trick of the "Hindu Congress" to suborn the Moslems. For him, it signified the parting of the ways. In March, 1940, the Moslem League at its annual session at Lahore declared that Hindus and Moslems constituted two separate nations and that India should be divided to provide separate homelands for each. Seven years later Jinnah was to lead his followers, like a Moslem Moses, into the Promised Land.

The all-India federation envisaged by the new Act was unacceptable to the Congress and the league, though for different reasons. While the league feared that a strong federal government at the center might render nugatory the autonomy of the Moslem majority provinces, the Congress was opposed to a federation which gave the princes representation and influence beyond what their political status entitled them to, and which thereby virtually mortgaged the center to the British authorities. On their side, the princes were reluctant to trust their future to a party like the Congress, which was generally dubbed extremist and which regarded them as archaic feudal relics propped in authority by the British. The Congress was right in feeling that the princes, over-represented at the center, would throw their weight invariably in favor of the British raj. But it is possible that had the Congress consisted of less extreme elements, the princes might have been prepared to adjust their own position in a federal government and thereby have helped to establish an all-India federation before the outbreak of war. Had this been achieved, would Pakistan have been practicable? The overwhelming bulk of the princely order would then probably have clung to federation as an insurance against any attempt to divide and destroy them.

Gandhi's economic ideas were also a deterrent to clear thinking and positive action. Analyzed in detail they emerge, as many of his ideas do, as cloudy, contradictory, and confused. With Ruskin he was opposed to the idea of class struggle, but his attitude to Indian capitalism was none too tender. "India," he once wrote, "lives in her 750,000 villages, and the cities live upon the villages. They do not bring their wealth from other countries. The city people are brokers and commission agents for the big houses of Europe, America and Japan." He disliked both capitalism and industrialism because in his opinion they injured the peasants and village craftsmen. Yet simultaneously he supported the demand for tariffs and protection of Indian industries and accepted large capitalist contributions to his political and social funds. During his noncooperation movements he often asked the peasants to cooperate with their landlords and to pay them their rents, although he had no hesitation in denouncing the riches accumulated by the landlords as moral turpitude. He wanted above all things "a return to simplicity," to the India of pre-industrial days; but as Mrs. Sarojini Naidu jocularly but not incorrectly exclaimed, "The money it costs India to keep the Mahatma in poverty!"

This curious mental ambivalence which often gives the Mahatma's speeches and writings a lawyer-like subtlety and a perplexing casuistry of mind extends to other fields. It even encroaches on the domain of nonviolence where he sometimes betrays a tendency to equate expediency with principle. At the time of the Boer War he had not yet adopted nonviolence as a fundamental creed, but his sympathies were with the Boers, particularly with the Boer farmers whom he greatly admired for their industry and independence. He was aware of the widespread feeling that the war against them was not justified. Yet he unreservedly supported the British against the Boers, using the strangely insensitive argument that if the Indians helped the British and they won, the latter might look more kindly on the former. In 1914, some years after advocating the virtues of ahimsa to the Indian settlers in South Africa, Gandhi actively worked for the British cause in the First World War, recruiting on behalf of the Allies and organizing Red Cross relief. According to Mrs. H. S. L. Polak, wife of one of his oldest British friends and his close associate in South Africa, he was with difficulty prevented from offering himself as a combatant soldier.

These postures do not square convincingly with a devotion to nonviolence. They were to recur later, during the Second World War and even after independence. As the veteran congressman the late Maulana Abul Kalam Azad, who was Gandhi's colleague over many years, revealed in his autobiography,* the Mahatma, who until August, 1942, when the entire Congress Working Committee was imprisoned, had argued with his colleagues that if the only way of achieving Indian independence was to participate in the war he for one would not adopt it, stated on his release in 1944 that the Congress would cooperate with the British war effort if India were declared free. Azad also wrote that it was understood that the resolution passed on July 14, 1942, by the Working Committee a month before their arrest implied that the civil-disobedience movement they proposed to launch would be nonviolent only as long as Gandhi and the Congress leaders were free to function but that if the Government arrested them the people would be free to adopt any method, violent or nonviolent. Azad did not disclose whether the Mahatma was aware of this implication. Presumably he was. After independence Gandhi approved of the air transport of Indian troops in defense of Kashmir.

The reasons Gandhi gave for this basic *volte-face* were interesting but not always convincing. He explained his attitude in the Boer War, as also in the First World War, by claiming that as a loyal British subject—as indeed he then was—he was not expected to consider the rights and wrongs of the war. There were, the Mahatma argued, two courses open to him—cooperation or complete opposition. Lacking the power to oppose, he had to cooperate. It is an interesting illustration of what might be called his attachment to the absolutes and his dislike of being quiescent on important issues. For, in this instance, he might simply have kept quiet. Gandhi defended his action in recruiting for the British during the First World War on a plea which seems more dialectical than direct. "We are regarded as a cowardly people," he explained. "If we want to be free from that reproach, we

* *India Wins Freedom* (Orient Longmans).

should learn the use of arms." But that surely knocks the bottom out of his own plea for nonviolence. Elsewhere he suggested that the Arms Act which forbade Indians to hold arms without license is objectionable because it is nonviolence by compulsion when the will to nonviolence is absent! On the other hand, the Mahatma's approval of the dispatch of Indian troops to Kashmir seems consistent with his approach to nonviolence in an independent India. Writing in his weekly journal *Young India* on September 13, 1928, he conceded that when freedom came India would not adhere strictly to nonviolence, although simultaneously he affirmed that "I should not take any direct part in any war." "I do not say," he noted in an earlier article in the same journal, written on September 29, 1924, " 'eschew violence in your dealings with robbers or thieves or with nations that may invade India.' "

Yet these nuances in his complicated being, however much they may have mystified and irked the average educated Indian, flit like fitful shadows across the sunlit stretches of his personality and character. Gandhi was not a saint. He was a great human being with many shining virtues but also with some of the foibles and quirks of ordinary men. Those who knew him remember him for the radiance and strength he shed around him. Insignificant though he was physically, there was something kingly about him. He had the majesty of the meek.

With the coming of partition Gandhi must have realized that his life's mission had very largely failed. He had labored for the unity of India and for peace and concord between its many races and religions—most of all, since it was a symbol of his cherished faith for Hindu-Moslem unity. He had called on his people to shed fear and hate. Freedom had come, but it had come in a bath of blood with partition born of fear and hate, and brother slaying brother in an orgy of fratricidal killing unparalleled in human history. Many of his countrymen had followed him only to pay lip service to his ideals. He had shamed a goodly section of Hindu society into shedding practices such as untouchability, child marriage, and the degradation of women, but the realist in him must have recognized that he had only broken the crust of immemorial custom and that the hard core of orthodox traditional Hinduism survived with latent vigor. Even the Untouchables whom he had befriended and championed in the face of obloquy and attack had not always regarded him as their friend. The more politically conscious among them had questioned his motives, and their leader, Dr. Ambedkar, still continued to denounce him as a social reformer actuated by political considerations. Perhaps he himself had not always been consistent in the advocacy and practice of his tenets. But he had never asked others to do what he himself was not prepared to do. Yet very largely, he must have realized, his countrymen had failed him. They had also failed India.

Politically his ideal was the Indian village-state with each of India's 750,000 villages "organised according to the will of its citizens, all of them voting." He had envisaged the pyramid of his country's political structure as broad-based on the villages, with a grass-roots foundation far removed from Western parliamentary forms and the "evils" of urban industrialism. But industrialism abounded, and India appeared to have plumped for Western political institutions. The fashion for being English-educated, far from subsiding, threatened to grow, and the mounting indiscipline of India's youth, for which his own policy of associating the young with political demonstrations and movements was largely to blame, must have saddened him. India, he also realized, had not spun its way to swaraj through the charkha (spinning wheel) and khadi (hand-woven cloth), though the cult for both had spread. India had achieved freedom, but it was not the independent India of his dreams, plans, and hopes. All this must have grieved him and hurt him terribly. He was wounded in his own house.

I like to think of him in the last weeks of his life when, oppressed by the horror of the partition killings and separated by vital differences from some of his closest colleagues—a lonely, tired, enfeebled, and mentally anguished man—he yet insisted indomitably that justice should be done to all without fear or favor, to Hindus, Moslems, Sikhs, Christians, and all who sought the protection of India. In the general madness he kept his head. Against the wishes of his colleagues the Mahatma saw that the Indian exchequer paid to Pakistan the 120 million dollars which he believed were rightly its due under the agreed scheme of financial apportionment. He died as perhaps he would have liked to—in the cause of Hindu-Moslem unity and understanding, felled by the gun of a fellow Hindu.

This was Gandhi's finest hour.

V
The New Class

POSTERITY will probably rate Gandhi as one of history's magnificent failures. It would be a facile verdict, for though most of the Mahatma's objectives perished or were ignored within a decade of his death much of the spirit of his teaching survives and still permeates the Indian atmosphere. Above all, his idea of a *sarvodaya* society, with its emphasis on voluntary constructive work designed to create a moral impetus and to change the environmental forces outside the institutional political framework, is a distinctive contribution which still lives in Vinoba Bhave's *bhoodan yagna* movement for the voluntary renunciation of land and in other work and welfare agencies such as the All-India Village Industries Association, the All-India Spinners Association, the Hindustani Prachar Sabha, or Society for the Promotion of Hindustani, and the Talimi Sangh whose aim is to develop basic education.

From all this it is evident that the Mahatma was more interested in the purpose than in the mechanics of politics. He was in fact a poor political negotiator, as his well-known pact in 1931 with Lord Halifax, then Lord Irwin and Viceroy of India, proved; so also his performance at the second Round Table Conference in London shortly afterward, and his agreement at Poona with the

Harijan leader Dr. Ambedkar, in 1932. The Poona Pact was achieved at the cost, quite unfairly, of the higher-caste Hindus of Bengal, and electorally brought no advantage to the Congress; while the Gandhi-Irwin Pact was more concerned with social matters, such as the liberty to picket liquor shops and to manufacture salt, than with basic political objectives. At the Round Table Conference Gandhi failed inexplicably to reach a communal settlement with the Moslems when only one legislative seat was hanging in the balance, and his claim to represent the Harijans alienated Dr. Ambedkar and strengthened that leader's hands.

Gandhi was more a humanist than a politician. He was not particularly enamored, as we noted, of Dr. Annie Besant's Home Rule movement when he returned to India, and it is a curiously significant fact that he did not publicly voice a demand for swaraj until the Congress session at Calcutta in 1920. Even then he did it with some reluctance, for he had omitted reference to it in the resolution he had drafted only two or three days before the session. In *Hind Swaraj* he visualizes a society almost without government, with no police or army or other formal institutions. His sarvodaya society was conceived on the same model.

Therein lies Gandhi's failure, for the new class he created over nearly thirty years of undisputed leadership jettisoned his economic and political ideas within a decade of his death. To claim, as some do, that much of the moral spirit of the Mahatma's political teaching survives is valid. But it survives, as we have noted, not in the new class, which is concerned largely with the business of government and the perquisites of power, but in the old guard represented by leaders such as Vinoba Bhave and Jayaprakash Narayan who have kept conspicuously aloof from the administrative machine. One characteristic Gandhian doctrine which still influences a microscopic number of Congress leaders in the government, notably Nehru, is the Mahatma's creed of means and ends based on his insistence that the right ends could only be achieved by the right means. More than anything else this accounts for Nehru's attachment to democratic methods of government and his antipathy to totalitarian ways, though his own administration is not particularly sensitive to individual feeling.

As far back as 1931 Gandhi in a conversation with Nehru had outlined his idea of the role of Congress in an independent India. Nehru had then felt that the Congress should dissolve itself as a party. Gandhi had demurred. He believed that the Congress should continue as a party but that none of its members should accept a paid job under the state. If any one of its members wished to do so he should resign. In other words the Mahatma visualized the Congress as a party which would not take office or be actively associated with the administration of the country but would content itself with exercising moral pressure on whatever government happened to be in power. When independence came sixteen years later, Gandhi reiterated his views, urging the Congress to dissolve itself as "a propaganda vehicle and parliamentary machine," to cease to function as a political organization, and to convert itself into a Lok Sevak Sangh, or social-service body. The Congress, however, in the belief that it was the only organizational body which could run the administration, dissented from the Mahatma's view.

Gandhi probably foresaw the moral deterioration which would accompany the Congress party's active association with the government of the country and also anticipated the conversion of the new class he had created from a body dedicated to selfless service into a group primarily interested in privilege, power, and perquisites. This has come to pass, the Congress party as a whole being now more concerned with retaining political power and patronage than with intensive field work among the ignorant, still largely backward rural masses. The yogi is lost in the commissar.

By and large the new class has turned its back on most of

Gandhi's cherished ideals; and, ironically, it has done so under the inspiration of the Mahatma's chosen political heir, who is leading it and the country into a world based on modern idioms and instruments, away from the rural economics of the Mahatma and his spiritualized politics. It is probably right that this should be so, and also perhaps inevitable. But a doubt lingers and persists.

The comparative ease with which new mental attitudes have been induced in India over the past two hundred years is disturbing, for it suggests an intellectual insecurity with no stable moorings and still incapable of achieving a satisfactory synthesis between East and West, between Indian thought and Western endeavor. The Indian intellectual seems caught betwixt and between. The impact of the West culminating in the establishment of British rule brought into being an educated middle class attracted to Western ideas and methods. But Gandhi had little difficulty in persuading many from this politically conscious class to return to their indigenous roots, though he did not succeed in weaning them away completely from their attachment to certain aspects of modern civilization. In the process he created the new class approximating roughly to the more broad-based, radically revolutionized Congress party. With independence this new class, trained to be the servants of the country, became its masters, and in their new role cast overboard most of the Mahatma's teachings, advancing under Nehru's leadership to a more industrialized and planned socialistic society.

Can this class in turn be induced to change its mental attitude and connive at the conversion of India from a Socialist into a Communist state? Nehru's attitude to the rightist elements within the Congress party and outside is more hostile, clear, didactic, and defined than his approach to the leftists. He abhors and has denounced the economic conservatism and the social and religious obscurantism of many rightists. But while criticizing the Communists for their political opportunism and violence, he is generally more tender to the leftists. The danger of this ambivalent attitude is that it might in time generate a national frame of mind receptive to leftist ideas, and not easily able to distinguish between Socialism and Communism. With democratic Socialism it is necessary to stress equally democracy and Socialism. Nehru's economic policies are the result largely of his arrested economic thinking, for Nehru's economic thinking belongs to the late twenties and early thirties of this century, during which liberals looked on Socialists and Socialists on Communists through the golden haze typified by Harold Laski and the London School of Economics. The Welfare State need not necessarily be Communist or even Socialist, as Britain and the Scandinavian countries prove. As long as it rests on firm democratic foundations and strives to provide as far as practicable equal opportunities for all, why decorate or overweigh it with any particular ism?

India is not yet a democracy. It is a developing democracy, and the danger is enhanced in a country where democracy is on the defensive against the creeping paralysis of Communism on the one hand and of communalism on the other. The extreme left and right threaten the position of the middle-of-the-road Congress which under Nehru's leadership inclines toward left of center. Since independence India has held two general elections, and while in both of them the Congress has registered an impressive over-all victory it has lost ground increasingly to the Communists, though not to the communalists. One reason for this is that many right-wing congressmen, particularly in the Punjab, Uttar Pradesh, Rajasthan, and Madhya Pradesh, are for all practical purposes indistinguishable from members of communal organizations like the Bharatiya Jan Sangh.

For its successful functioning democracy depends on many factors—a healthy party system including not a single monolithic ruling party but also active opposition parties and groups; an informed electorate able to assess parties, personalities, and principles; and a vigilant public opinion reinforced by pressure groups at various levels, national, regional, and local. In India these prerequisites are in the formative stage and have still to develop. Because the Congress party was identified with the struggle for freedom, it came to be equated with the country and to represent, as it were, a monopoly of patriotism and the higher virtues. The glow has diminished more than somewhat over the past decade, but there are still congressmen who preen themselves on being the exclusive repositories of the national conscience, and as such entitled to a special status and reverence. In their eyes criticism of their party is tantamount to criticism of the country. It is near-blasphemy. Unfortunately, accession to power has accentuated this tendency and discouraged independent thinking along with bold and honest criticism. Gandhi identified good government with godliness. But some of his followers appear to see themselves in the image of Olympian deities. Even Nehru, highly sensitive to criticism of the socialistic pattern, has threatened to sweep away the apologists of private enterprise "with a broomstick." This does not foster the growth of a virile democracy.

There are many interesting, if disturbing, parallels between the Congress new class and the new class of the Communist system as vividly portrayed by Milovan Djilas.* Both had their base in an organized party, the only difference being that while in Russia the class had not taken root in the life of the nation, in India the new class had served the country during its subjection and ruled it on India's attaining independence. In both countries not every member of the party was a member of the new class, though this was so in India before independence. After the attainment of freedom the Congress new class was confined to the political bureaucracy or administrative hierarchy. In both countries the new class, comprising the monopolists of administration, grows

* *The New Class* (New York, Frederick A. Praeger, 1958).

progressively stronger while the party grows increasingly weaker. This is especially so with the Congress in India.

In the preindependence period when the Congress was not the government but the opposition, power was concentrated in the Working Committee which with the All-India Congress Committee (A.I.C.C.) represents the central organs of the party. Theoretically it still is. At the state level the key unit is the Pradesh (State) Congress Committee (P.C.C.). Above the P.C.C. is the A.I.C.C. which comprises one-eighth of the delegates of each P.C.C. and is formed by the P.C.C.'s voting their delegates separately. At the apex of this pyramid is the Working Committee which consists of the president of the Congress and twenty members chosen by the president from members of the A.I.C.C. The Working Committee functions through two subsidiary bodies, the Parliamentary Board which supervises the Congress ministries in the states and the Central Election Committee which screens Congress candidates for the central Parliament and also to some extent for the state assemblies. In theory, therefore, the Congress Working Committee is the party's most important decision-making body. "The basic policy of the party is laid down by the annual session," Nehru has explained, "and it is interpreted and implemented by the A.I.C.C. The Working Committee, as the executive of the Congress, is charged with carrying out this policy." In practice, certainly since independence, it is the central government, personified by Nehru, which both initiates policy and implements it. The new class has thus usurped the functions of the old Working Committee, and the prestige and influence of the president of the Congress have proportionately declined while those of the prime minister have increased. This tallies with Milovan Djilas's analysis that as the new class grows stronger, the party grows weaker.

Gandhi after independence foresaw that unless the Congress maintained its momentum and dynamism, purged itself of the lust for power for power's sake, and returned to its old standards of austerity, integrity, and service, it would lose its hold on the masses and, like the Marxist state, wither away. In December, 1947, a few weeks before Gandhi's assassination, a group of veteran congressmen who were also constructive social workers met the Mahatma and discussed with him the advisability of their sanghs (organizations) entering the government and using it for the purpose of building up a nonviolent social order. The group was headed by the then president of the Congress, Acharya J. B. Kripalani, now leader of the Praja Socialist party. Gandhi advised them against it. He did not, he said, want the constructive workers' organizations to be drawn into power politics and become a rival either to the Congress or to the government in the contest for political power.

"I do not want to take power in my hands," Gandhi told them. "By abjuring power and by devoting ourselves to pure and selfless service of the voters, we can guide and influence them. It would give us far more real power than we shall have by going into the Government. But a stage may come, when the people themselves may feel and say that they want us and no one else to wield power. The question could then be considered. I shall most probably not be alive then. But, when that time comes, the sanghs will produce from amongst them someone who will take over the reins of the administration. By that time, India will have become an ideal state."

He went on to warn them in words which have a curiously prophetic ring: "Today, everybody in the Congress is running after power. That presages grave danger. Let us not be in the same cry as the power-seekers. . . . Constructive work is not a strategy, or a technique of fighting. Constructive work is a way of life. It can be worked only by those men who have adopted it by the heart as well as by the intellect. . . . To set our own house in order is the first indispensable requisite, if we want to influence political power. If all the sanghs give a good account of themselves, work unitedly and in co-operation, without a jar or a jolt, it would be a grand thing. But they must not do it for the sake of popularity, or hanker for political power, even in their dreams. Soon we shall have adult suffrage. It is a good thing. But to regard adult suffrage as a means for the capture of political power, would be to put it to a corrupt use. . . . Today, politics has become corrupt. Anybody who goes into it is contaminated. Let us keep out of it altogether. Our influence will grow thereby. The greater our inner purity, the greater will be our hold on the people, without any effort on our part."

With the Mahatma's assassination in January, 1948, the constructive workers' organizations he had founded and directed tended to drift away from the Congress hierarchy, now absorbed in the administration of the country and in the many problems created by partition. Within the hierarchy, however, the tussle for power continued. Both the central government and the Congress Working Committee were divided in two camps with Vallabhbhai Patel heading the conservative group against the more forward policies of Nehru. The first three years after partition called for the new government's undivided attention to the urgent problems of consolidation and unity which indeed meant survival. In 1950, as we noted, a crisis developed within the party when the orthodox Babu Purushottamdas Tandon, a revivalist Hindu "of the old school," was chosen as the president of the Congress, with Patel's patronage, against Acharya Kripalani, whom Nehru favored but did not publicly support. Patel died in December of that year, and in the fall of 1951 Nehru forced a showdown by resigning from the Working Committee. Thereupon Tandon expressed his willingness to resign, and at a special meeting of the A.I.C.C. in September, Nehru was elected to replace him. For over four years, until January, 1955, when the mild-mannered U. N. Dhebar, Nehru's choice, succeeded him,

Nehru combined in himself the two posts of prime minister and Congress president, thereby simultaneously controlling the party and the government. Those four years created a Congress habit of mind which has led the overwhelming bulk of that party to look to the prime minister and not to the president of the Congress for political guidance. In February, 1959, Dhebar gave way as president to Nehru's daughter, Mrs. Indira Gandhi.

It would be misleading and unfair to interpret this as signifying the first step in the creation of a Nehru dynasty. There were no suitable aspirants for the job, which was offered to at least one state minister, who declined—a significant commentary on the waning prestige attached to this office. Mrs. Gandhi has matured politically in recent years, though she is generally regarded as standing left of what many deem her sufficiently leftist father. She has her own definite opinions and has shown a capacity for hard work. But inevitably the father image predominates in the public mind and cannot easily be erased.

If the Congress is to function as a democratic body and not as a monolithic front, the relations between the Congress Parliamentary party and the Working Committee on the one hand and between the top agencies of the party and Congress state and local committees on the other must be more clearly defined. Since 1955 the Congress president has functioned as no more than a glorified office boy of the Congress central government headed by the prime minister. This has weakened and blurred the nexus which should obtain not only between the Congress party and the Congress government but between the Congress president and the prime minister, as also between the Congress Parliamentary party and the Working Committee. The net result has been to weaken the party at the local or grass-roots levels, where its leadership is of poor caliber, and temporarily to strengthen the higher echelons represented by the Congress governmental hierarchy, or new class.

In the in-between cavity the Congress organization hangs like a floating kidney. But paradoxically it is here, at the state or regional levels, that there lies the promise of a true democracy developing, for it is here that opposition to the Congress by various parties and pressures from different groups have grown and are likely to increase. For a variety of reasons the Congress is particularly vulnerable in the states, where opposition to its policies has been mounted by widely separated groups—linguistic, communal, economic, and political. In the second general elections of 1957 the Congress lost votes to the forces of both the right and the left. In Kerala 60 Communists were returned, and formed a government with the help of five independents. A conservative coalition party, the Ganatantra Parishad, dominated by princes and landlords, won 51 seats in Orissa against 56 captured by the Congress. Elsewhere, in West Bengal and Andhra, the Communists secured 46 and 35 seats respectively, and in the Bombay State Assembly, helped by an alliance with the Samyukta Maharashtra Samiti, whose claim to a separate Maharashtra State inclusive of the city of Bombay they supported, the Reds raised their representation from one member to 18. In Bihar the Jharkhand party and the Janata party, both of whom espouse the cause of the tribal people, returned 55 representatives between the two of them. The Congress also suffered greater setbacks than they expected in Uttar Pradesh, where the opposition, comprising the Independents, the Praja Socialists, the militant Hindu-minded Jan Sangh and the Communist party, collectively returned 139 members. In Bombay the opposition, stirred largely by the linguistic issue and agitating for separate Maharashtrian and Gujarat states, secured 162 seats. The Congress was able to form governments in all the states except Kerala, but the opposition parties had succeeded in making some unexpected inroads.

Even in the first general elections of 1951–1952, although the Congress was able to form governments in all the states and the opposition parties did not fare particularly well in terms of parliamentary seats, the Congress failed to win a clear majority in Madras, PEPSU (Patiala and East Punjab states), and Travancore-Cochin (later known as Kerala). In Madras it secured only 152 seats in an Assembly of 375, while in PEPSU it returned 26 members out of 60. In Travancore-Cochin it won 45 seats out of 108, and for a brief period a short-lived government was formed here by the minority Praja Socialist party. Governmental instability and factional rivalries led to president's rule when the constitution was suspended for several months in the Punjab in 1950, in PEPSU in 1953, in Andhra in 1954 and in Travencore-Cochin in 1956. The figures for the first general elections reveal that though in the state assemblies the Congress won 2,248 seats out of 3,283, it secured only 42.2 per cent of the total vote.

On the national plane, however, as judged by its representation in the House of the People, the Congress continues to maintain its paramount position. In the first general elections of 1951-1952 the party polled about 45 per cent of the total votes cast but returned 362 members, roughly 74 per cent of the total of 489 seats. The Communists in the second general elections raised their representation from 27 to 29, but the Congress also increased its membership to 366. Congress success at the national level is due to various factors. Although independence transformed the party from a national movement into a political party, the critical internal situation and continuing crisis in the decade after freedom helped to perpetuate the national aura around the Congress. Nehru remained a national symbol, and at the higher echelons the top leadership is still good; while organizationally, owing to its longer experience and contact with the masses, the Congress has a country-wide advantage over the other parties. It has also been helped by the fact that the opposition is badly fragmented.

Failure to attract and recruit younger people largely accounts for the poor quality of Congress leadership at the local level. The old guard is concentrated mainly in the top leadership at the center, leaving an inferior tribe of leaders on the lower rungs. With a few rare exceptions, such as Bombay's Chief Minister Y. B. Chavan and the Finance Minister of Madras, C. Subramaniam, no new leaders have developed or emerged from the Congress ranks. Another factor which explains the growing Congress reverses at the state level is the accumulation of regional grievances, real or fancied, ranging from the urge for linguistic states to communal tensions, economic conflicts, and territorial disputes. This suggests that the average voter thinks on a dual plane—national and local—and is more directly concerned with regional grievances than with national issues. There is a threat to both nationalism and democracy implicit in this way of thinking, for while it encourages fissiparous trends and incites local factionalism, both of which are dangerous to the growth of a healthy nationalism, it also enables parties such as the Communists to espouse regional chauvinism and gain local adherents, thereby endangering democracy. If this trend develops, its cumulative effect will be to place national parties increasingly at a discount.

As long as the British raj remained the focal point of attack, the Congress continued to be the focal point of loyalty. But with the attainment of independence the Congress, reduced from a national movement to a political party, found the guns of other parties and groups turned away from the old focal point and trained on the new focal point, which was itself. The suddenness of independence took all parties, including the Congress, by surprise; and all found it difficult to adjust themselves easily to the new situation, for the Congress no less than the other groups discovered itself out on a limb. To the overwhelming majority of congressmen it seemed that their party, having spearheaded the battle for independence, was entitled on the attainment of freedom to a special status and special privileges. Moreover, possession constituting nine points of the law, they, as representing the administration in power at the time of partition and the British withdrawal, regarded the Congress government as a continuing entity entitled to govern until constitutionally replaced.

They were right, but they failed to realize that they were really in the same boat as the opposition groups ranged against them. With their own main target, the British Government, removed, they were now the main target of question and criticism inside the country. Like their political opponents, they had to adjust themselves to the new situation. In this they failed. Gandhi, as we have seen, counseled the Congress to shed its political trappings, continue its constructive work outside the apparatus of government, and operate as a moral pressure group on any administration which might assume power. But the Congress was in no mood to heed him. On the other hand the parties, groups, and units outside Congress were equally at sixes and sevens both among themselves and within their own individual camps. Even the Communists suffered from various internal stresses and strains after 1947 but were able to avoid an open split and to preserve an ostensibly united front. The other parties, notably the Socialists, gradually disintegrated into warring factions.

At all times, particularly in a time of crisis, it is the organized minority that wins against the disorganized majority. As the two general elections have demonstrated, the Congress did not command a majority of votes cast either at the center or in the states, though admittedly this yardstick is by no means infallible. In the first general elections, where the opposition parties polled quite 55 per cent of the total votes cast at the national level, as many as fourteen non-Congress parties entered the elections as national parties and 51 as state parties. Of the fourteen, only four qualified at the end of the elections as national, having received 3 or more per cent of the national vote. These were the Socialist party (10.6 per cent); the Kisan Mazdoor Praja party, or Peasants' party (5.8 per cent); the Communist party (3.3 per cent); and the Jan Sangh (3.1 per cent). Here again, although the Socialists polled the highest number of votes of the four they won only 12 seats as against 27 captured by the Communists. This was because the Communists concentrated in constituencies where their prospects were bright, while the Socialists unwisely dissipated their strength by running candidates in several constituencies.

Like the Communists the Congress was also subjected to internal differences after independence. These, as we have seen, came to a head in 1951, after which Nehru assumed charge of both the party and governmental machine, thereby enabling the Congress to contest the first general elections as a united team, with the blueprint of the First Five-Year Plan as its electoral program. The success of that plan saw the Congress facing the country again as a consolidated unit, but since the second general elections fissures have developed, notably at state levels. Internicine party and personal rivalries have left the Congress a house divided against itself in states spread over India north, south, east, and west, as also in the center, in Uttar Pradesh, the Punjab, Bombay, Andhra, Bihar, Orissa, West Bengal, and Rajasthan. While anti-Congress pressures grow at state levels, the Congress organization itself at the same levels shows signs of combustible internal fission which betrays at once the comparative poverty of local leadership, the widening gulf between the Congress hierarchy at the center and its representatives in the States and, most disquieting of all, the weakening link between the new class and the masses.

Of the opposition parties the Communists form the largest single group in the Lok Sabha, or House of the People, besides having for twenty-eight months controlled one state government, Kerala, and presently enjoying a considerable representation in the state assemblies of West Bengal and Andhra. Moreover, the Communist party has one or more members in each of the state legislative assemblies. That it owed its position in Kerala more to the deficiencies of the previous Congress administration than to any intrinsic virtues of its own is widely admitted. But habit is contagious, and a people inured to the spectacle of a Communist state government, even though now thoroughly discredited, may be tempted, if the Congress party deteriorates further, to extend the Red pattern to other states in the general elections of 1962, say, to Andhra and West Bengal. Growing Red influence in linguistically frustrated states such as Bombay, a bilingual unit where the demand for two separate Maharashtrian and Gujarati states is strong, can also not be ignored. It is likely that before the next general elections the Congress might itself steal the Communist thunder and divide Bombay State into two linguistic states. Present indications* are that this may happen very soon.

Since Kerala carries a warning to democracy, and is an object lesson in Communist tactics and control, it is worth scrutinizing in some detail. The same stresses, regional, religious, factional, communal, casteist, and personal, which are increasingly assertive at state levels throughout India, influenced the course of politics in Kerala and placed it finally in the hands of the Communists. How these factors, combined with the calculations of the Reds, led to a democratically governed state being converted by the democratic medium of the ballot box into a Communist-controlled area carries a warning and is an object lesson on the way the Marxists work and conspire to achieve power. In so far as it reflects faithfully these divisive forces and tactics, Kerala is a microcosm of modern India. Fissures within the party surfaced when on the eve of the Red government's dismissal in July, 1959, the National Council repudiated the Kerala chief minister's conditional acceptance of Nehru's suggestion that midterm elections might be held in the state. Thereby these Peking patriots confessed that in their own reckoning the people of Kerala would not reelect them. The Kerala Government also postponed the civic elections, well knowing the fate which awaited them.

Lying at the southern tip of the peninsula, with a long coastline

* Written in August, 1959.

looking out mainly on the west, Kerala covers an area of nearly 15,000 square miles and has a population of about 15 million. It is India's smallest state. A little over half of its male population and almost 32 per cent of its female population are literate, and with an over-all literacy figure of nearly 41 per cent Kerala heads the country's literacy list, having also the largest percentage of literate women of any state. This fact is interesting and important, since educated unemployment the world over represents economic waste and political unrest. Not that literacy in itself connotes education. In India the "educated" are officially defined as those with high-school education and better. On this basis a special study group appointed by the Planning Commission estimated the number of educated unemployed at around 550,000; and since it is computed that at the end of the Second Five-Year Plan (by 1961) there will be an additional 1,500,000 educated persons who will have finished their studies, jobs will have to be found for around 2,000,000 of them by then. In Kerala the density of population is a little over 900 per square mile as compared to the average country-wide density of 312. Between 1911 and 1951 the state's total population had almost doubled, and the rate of growth has not since diminished.

According to an inquiry undertaken by the Manpower Division of the Central Directorate of Employment Exchanges in May, 1957, the highest incidence of unemployment among women graduates was in Kerala. This in itself signifies little, since state statistics on unemployment are by no means precise and cover only the urban areas. Moreover, not all the unemployed register themselves. On the available figures it is estimated that about 25 per cent of the state's population are unemployed. The real problem is underemployment, many people having work for only a few months in a year or a few days in a month. Since 75 per cent of the population comprise agriculturists, and agriculture being a seasonal operation, this is not surprising. The really disquieting fact is that as many as 93 per cent of the unemployed graduates are men. The high standard of literacy is reflected in the number of newspapers. Though the smallest of the states in terms of territory and population, Kerala has a multiplicity of newspapers, the dailies numbering 25 and the weeklies 65. There are nearly 130 monthly magazines.

With the merger in July, 1949, of the two princely southern states of Travancore and Cochin, the Travancore-Cochin State came into being, lasting until November 1, 1956, when, following the report of the States Reorganization Commission, the new State of Kerala took its place. Kerala's boundaries were altered somewhat from those of the old state, the Malabar district (formerly part of Madras) being added to it and nine Tamil taluqs * being detached. This in turn changed the composition of the population for the benefit of the Communists. The suppression of non-Hindus and the Scheduled Castes, or Untouchables, was almost traditional in the old princely states, and in Travancore it led as far back as 1898 to a joint protest by the Malayalee community, notably by the noncaste Nairs and Ezhavas, against their exclusion from official jobs to the advantage of the high-caste Tamils. In this they were joined by the Christians and Moslems. The Travancore Government, while satisfying the Nairs, did not respond generously or even equitably to the claims of the Ezhavas and Christians, who as a result united in opposition. This invidious treatment continued, and when administrative reforms were introduced in the state in 1932 the Ezhavas, Christians, and Moslems were denied adequate representation in the legislature. Four years later these communities formed an organization which in 1937 was reconstituted as the Travancore State Congress with the cooperation of the noncaste Nairs, who were still aggrieved by the preferential treatment accorded to the Tamils and the Brahmans. The State Congress aimed at obtaining proportionate

* A taluq is a subdivision of a district.

representation for all communities in the legislature, the public services, and the state forces, and also pressed for adult franchise and responsible government.

In the following decade, until the attainment of independence, the State Congress, under the leadership of Pattom Thanu Pillai, was engaged in a continuous struggle against the government's repressive policies. The first general elections on the basis of adult franchise were held in 1948, four parties—the State Congress, the Travancore Tamil Nad Congress (T.T.N.C.), the Kerala Socialist party (K.S.P.), and the Communists—contesting at the polls. Of these neither the Socialists nor the Communists secured a single seat. Out of 108 seats the Congress won 93, the T.T.N.C. 14, and the Independents one. The first Congress ministry with Mr. Pillai as leader took office, but internal dissensions and rivalries soon split the party wide open, the Christians, Moslems and Scheduled Classes being particularly resentful over their exclusion from the government. Mr. Thanu Pillai was displaced by Mr. T. K. Narayan Pillai and left the Congress with fourteen dissidents to form the Democratic Socialist party, which later emerged as the Praja Socialist party. It was the beginning of a melancholy decline in the fortunes of the State Congress.

During Mr. Narayan Pillai's tenure Cochin was integrated with Travancore in July, 1949. This introduced a new divisive factor —regionalism, for the Cochin Congress Legislative party totaled a number which could not be treated indifferently or ignored. Their presence within the integrated Congress party led to new factions based on territorial rights of representation, Cochin clamoring for a seat in the government. Mr. Pillai resigned after twenty-seven months in office and was succeeded by C. Kesavan, who later reconstituted his cabinet to meet the Cochin group's demands.

A divided Congress party went to the polls in the general elections of 1951–1952. Of the 93 seats which the State Congress had captured in 1949, it was now able to retain only 45. The Socialists secured 12 seats, the T.T.N.C. eight, and the Communists, then officially banned* but masquerading as Independents, returned 25 members, securing 15.5 per cent of the total votes cast. They had benefited most from the caste, communal, factional, and regional conflicts which had split and weakened the State Congress. Within that body religious or communal rivalries continued to be keen, and communalism played a dominant part in the election of the parliamentary leader; a Christian, A. J. John, later to be governor of Madras, was chosen by a majority of two votes against his Hindu rival, Panampilly Govinda Menon. John was able to form a ministry only with the help of the T.T.N.C., and when that group withdrew its support on its demand being rejected for recognition as a separate provincial Congress unit with jurisdiction over the eight Tamil-speaking taluqs, the coalition government collapsed. In September, 1953, the State Assembly was dissolved, and fresh elections were held a few months later.

In the 1954 elections the Congress was able to retain 45 seats in a reconstituted Assembly of 117 members; but simultaneously the Praja Socialist party, having entered into an agreement with the United Front of Leftists (U.F.L.), a miscellaneous group composed of the Communists, the Revolutionary Socialist party, and the Kerala Socialist party, was temporarily in a key position. In order to keep out the U.F.L., the Congress entered into an alliance with the Praja Socialist party, which with Congress support formed a government under Pattom Thanu Pillai; but this uneasy partnership lasted barely nine months when the T.T.N.C.'s

* In the general elections of 1951-1952 the Communist party was permitted to contest elections except where it was violating the peace and attempting to overthrow the government by violence. During the elections the party was banned in only three regions—Travancore-Cochin, Hyderabad, and Andhra. This restriction was removed a few months later, and the Communists were free to contest elections throughout the country.

withdrawal of support brought down the ministry. Displaying a cynicism which was later to cost them dearly, certain Congress leaders now maneuvered to return to office irrespective of the wider interests of the state or the party. Having secured the support of the T.T.N.C. and two Praja Socialist members, these leaders assumed power under the leadership of Panampilly Govinda Menon. The impression this must have created on an electorate weary of the never-ending ministerial games of permutations and combinations for purely selfish personal and party ends had not a little to do with the coming of the Communists into power.

The overthrow of this ministry saw the proclamation of president's rule in the state in March, 1956, although the Praja Socialist party was assured of the support of various opposition groups, ranging from the Kerala Socialist party to the Revolutionary Socialists, and appeared to be in a position to form a government. This had two consequences. It put the Congress party out of countenance with the masses, who felt that it was unfairly preventing the formation of an alternate ministry, and simultaneously it united the leftist parties in their opposition to president's rule.

In this period of eight years since 1948 Travancore-Cochin had known three general elections (1948, 1951–1952, 1954), nine ministries, and 36 ministers. It also witnessed the rise of the Congress, which reached its apex in 1948, and thereafter its sharp decline until from 93 members in an Assembly of 108 in 1948 it was able to muster only 45 members in a House of 117 six years later. Nobody had done more to discredit the Congress than congressmen themselves. Riven by internal rivalries, they appeared to the electorate as cynical opportunists and place-men willing to do a deal with any party or person as long as it ensured their continuance in office. On the eve of the second general elections in 1957, the party was divided not only within itself but within its separate elements, Christians, Hindus, and Nairs, each of whom was to contribute in different ways to the victory of the Communists.

Communalism, fiercely rampant in Kerala, favored the Communists. With the reorganization of the state in November, 1956, the Christians, who were the mainstay of the Congress, were reduced from 31 per cent to 24 per cent of the population, while the Ezhavas and Scheduled Castes, dispossessed classes who were naturally inclined to the Communists, increased in strength. From 22 per cent the Ezhava group rose to 26 per cent, and with the Scheduled Castes they now comprise over 30 per cent of the population. Simultaneously the Nairs, who had also supported the state Congress but who had latterly cooled off toward that organization owing to its Christian predominance, were reduced from 23 per cent to 17 per cent. Moreover, a good number of Christians, disgusted by the ineffectual maneuverings of the Congress, actually voted for the Reds, as the Kerala Communist party secretary, M. N. Govendan Nair, gleefully acknowledged after the elections.

There was therefore widespread demoralization not only in the state Congress hierarchy but also among the party's rank and file. Here again Kerala mirrors the general course of trends in India where the Congress new class, having monopolized the administration, is becoming the central target of wide criticism and is rapidly losing touch with its rural workers and the masses. In Kerala too the Congress new class stepped in where the former princely rulers left off, and the suddenness of the transition affected them even more than it did the Congress generally in India; for in both Travancore and Cochin, apart from communal and regional stresses, the Congress organization was a ramshackle structure built round a group of personally ambitious, largely inexperienced individuals who in turn gathered around them other miscellaneous elements equally anxious to share the fruits of power. As a result discipline slumped at the higher levels, and there was no real affinity with the people.

The so-called leaders themselves represented various communal or regional interests and had no well-defined program for the welfare of the state. Politics was thereby reduced to a shoddy tactical maneuver to remain in office. The Congress leader, Panampilly Govinda Menon, wryly confessed at the time of his resignation in March, 1956, that the debacle which threatened his party was due to its own making and not to any positive action by the Reds. Even more rueful was Congress President Dhebar's declaration that he could not name a single prominent Kerala Congress leader who at one time or another had not intrigued to maneuver a minister out of office. Nepotism and corruption intensified this tale of woe. The field was ready for the Red harvest.

VI
Red Harvest

KERALA's Communist party was established in 1934, ten years after the formation of the Communist party of India (C.P.I.) and oddly enough in the same year as the creation of the Congress Socialist party (C.S.P.). In August, 1935, the Seventh Congress of the Communist International in Moscow advised the setting up of a united front in India, and thereupon the C.P.I. made advances to the Congress Socialists which the latter at first repulsed. In January, 1936, however, the C.S.P. agreed to establish a united front as between party and party and, further, decided to permit individual Communists to be members of the C.S.P. The Communists seized the opportunity with both hands. Not only did they infiltrate into the C.S.P. but they also entered the Congress party and the All-India Kisan Sabha (Peasants' Union).

By 1937-1938 the C.S.P. had two Communists as joint secretaries and two others on the Executive Committee. One of the communist joint secretaries was E. M. S. Namboodiripad, who was later chief minister of Kerala, and a founding father of the Kerala Communist party (K.C.P.). The C.S.P. decision was influenced largely by its general secretary, Jayaprakash Narayan, who was then a Marxist intellectual with no real understanding of contemporary Communism and its tactics. Jayaprakash was soon to realize his mistake, but by that time a number of Communists had succeeded in occupying vantage posts not only in the C.S.P. but in the All-India Congress Committee and the Pradesh State Congress Committee. With what now seems astonishing political naïveté, the Socialist party organizations in Andhra, Tamil Nad, and Kerala were allowed to be run by the Communists, and this had not a little to do with the subsequent consolidation of Red influence in South India.

As Namboodiripad writes in his book *The National Question in Kerala*,* a Communist League had been established in Trivandrum as far back as 1931–1932, but the Communist party only crystallized into being in 1934 with the formation of the All-Kerala Trade Union Congress. "This therefore," observes Namboodiripad, "may be considered to be the beginning of a stage in the democratic movement of our country—the stage of the struggle for proletarian hegemony." Initially the Kerala Reds operated as Socialists, though in 1934–1935 even the K.P.C.C. was dominated by leftists. They were to shed this cloak only in 1940, following the breakdown of the united front in 1939, when the C.S.P. in Kerala was openly transformed into the Communist party. The intensity and extent of the Red infiltration into the C.S.P. were demonstrated when four founder members of that party, Achut Patwardhan, Rammanohar Lohia, Asoka Mehta, and M. R. Masani, were compelled to resign from the executive in 1939 in order to get the party and the public to realize the gravity of the Communist menace.

Broadly, the Kerala Communists reflect the tergiversations and turns of the C.P.I., whose strategy since its formation in 1924 will now be considered.† Communism came to India shortly after the

* People's Publishing House, 1952.

† I have drawn here largely from two books, *Moscow and the Communist Party of India*, by John H. Kautsky (John Wiley & Sons, New York, 1956), and *The Communist Party of India*, by M. R. Masani (Verschoyle, London, 1954).

Bolshevik Revolution, the first link between the Communist International and nascent Indian Communism being the late Manabendra Nath Roy, who was expelled from the International by Moscow in 1929 and who much later founded the Radical Humanist movement in India. In the early stages the C.P.I. received its directions mainly from the British Communist party, principally through one of its outstanding theorists, Rajni Palme Dutt, a product of mixed parentage who had an Indian father and a Belgian mother. The Cawnpore conspiracy case of 1924, followed five years later by the Meerut conspiracy case in which three Britons—Philip Spratt, Lester Hutchinson, and Ben Bradley—were among the accused, immobilized the party, which from 1930 until 1935 was in the political wilderness. In this period the Congress, launching two mass movements in 1930 and 1932 under Gandhi's leadership, was active and for a time in the ascendant. There evolved from these several stresses and strains the united, or popular, front whose causes and motivations from 1936 to the outbreak of the Second World War we have traced and considered.

Earlier in 1933, the Communists had vainly attempted to embark on a program of drastic reorganization, but the process was short-lived, and around this time the party was proscribed by the British Government. Lenin had always advised Asian Communists to work with the national bourgeoisie, but the C.P.I., possibly under Manabendra Nath Roy's influence, had ignored that advice. Until the mid-1930's it was openly critical of the Congress and Gandhi, but events compelled a shift to the international party line and it then adopted the strategy of the united front. In a sense the Socialists by agreeing to the united front salvaged the Communists and gave them a new lease of life. History has a habit of repeating itself for the simple reason that men repeat their mistakes. In 1933 the Socialist party was divided between the Marxist leanings of Jayaprakash Narayan, then an intellectual adherent of the Communist International, and the Democratic Socialism of M. R. Masani, who in his student days had been a member of the British Labour party and the Independent Labor party (I.L.P.). Jayaprakash temporarily won but soon discovered his disastrous error. The attempt of the C.P.I. today to cloud the popular judgment by presenting itself as a party dedicated to Indian progress and ideologically not far removed from the Congress on the economic and even on the political plane, particularly in so far as it concerns foreign policy, is a repetition of the old united-front tactic in a new form. While not openly allying themselves with the Congress or attacking it, the Communists from within the legislatures and outside are imperceptibly edging the Congress into a position which might soon be indistinguishable from the Red stand. The Socialists paved the way for the Communists in Kerala. The Congress might do the same on an all-India scale with its advocacy of cooperative farming, its often unintelligent attacks on private enterprise, and its heavy emphasis on the public sector. This fits in with the so-called neo-Maoist strategy of the C.P.I. which sees cooperative farming as a steppingstone to collectivization and temporarily accepts the capitalist as one of the recognized four friendly classes on the model of Mao's China.

The Communist *volte-face* during the war, when it first resisted the conflict as inherently unjust, denouncing it as imperialist, and then supported the Allied cause when on June 22, 1941, Hitler attacked Russia, alienated the nationalists and confused the leftists. Namboodiripad in his book justifies it on the ground that the character of the war had changed and that it had "ceased to be an attempt of antagonistic imperialist groups to re-partition the world among themselves but a war to decide the future of the Soviet Union and through it of world socialism." Even he, however, confesses that the sudden turnabout had deleterious consequences for the Communists: "The right wing bourgeois leadership of the national movement, which had always appeared to the rank and file anti-imperialists as compromising, now assumed the role of uncompromising fighters against imperialism, engaged in a last-ditch battle with the enemy; while the Communists who had always been regarded to be the best fighters appeared as compromisers. The hitherto solid unity of the left elements was thus broken, a section of the leftists allying themselves with the right-wing Congressmen. Anti-Communism became the hallmark not only of the right-wing but sections of the left also. A new generation of anti-imperialists grew who genuinely believed that the Congress Party was a paid agent of British Imperialism."

For its prowar stand, as well as for its support of the Moslem League's demand for partition, the C.P.I. was expelled from the Congress in 1945. During the late 1940's and early 1950's the party appears to have received its instructions mainly from the Cominform, but more recently Moscow seems to be taking a direct interest in the C.P.I., which also looks increasingly to Peking. If the C.P.I. line has often been confused and contradictory, it is because it has not always understood Moscow's directions, which, owing to the Kremlin's earlier lack of interest in Asia, were not always specific.

According to John H. Kautsky, who has made a close study of Moscow's relations with the C.P.I., Communism adopts broadly three strategies in the underdeveloped countries—the "right" strategy, the "left" strategy, and what is now known as the neo-Maoist strategy developed during the Second World War.

The "right" strategy regards imperialism, feudalism, and fascism as the Communists' main enemies, and advocates an alliance of the Communist party with the anti-imperialist, antifeudal, and anti-fascist groups, both labor and bourgeois. It thus envisages first a bourgeois-democratic revolution to be followed by a proletarian-socialist revolution when the bourgeois elements have been either eliminated or detached from their old loyalties. Stated shortly, this strategy favors a united front "from above."

The "left" strategy considers capitalism and the national bourgeoisie as no less deadly enemies than imperialism, fascism, and feudalism, and therefore would skip the bourgeois-democratic revolution stage. This strategy seeks a united front "from below," preferring a direct appeal to the workers, the poor peasantry, and the petty bourgeoisie to leave the labor and bourgeois parties and work with the Communists, who must openly denounce the leaders of these parties as traitors to their followers.

The neo-Maoist strategy is more flexible than either of these two. Like the "right" strategy, it regards imperialism, feudalism, and fascism as the main enemies, and consequently allows for two separate revolutions. It also seeks an alliance of workers, peasants, petty bourgeoisie, and the anti-imperilist or national bourgeoisie (capitalists), as it has done in China. But unlike the "right" and like the "left" strategy, the neo-Maoist strategy advocates an approach to these groups "from below," that is, by not cooperating with the principal parties at the top but by mobilizing and uniting the rank and file against their erstwhile leaders. Thus, as Kautsky points out, "the Communist party itself now claims to be the true representative of the interests not only of the exploited class but also of the capitalists." This is the distinguishing mark of the neo-Maoist strategy. In any of these three strategies the means are flexible. They may be either violent or peaceful. The neo-Maoist strategy accepts the "right" strategy principle of the united front but adopts the "left" strategy method of a united front "from below."

In 1947, as Soviet relations deteriorated with the West, Moscow shifted its international line from the "right" to the "left" strategy. Nehru was denounced as "a running dog of imperialism," and at the so-called Southeast Asian Youth conference in Calcutta late in February, 1948, the Zhdanov line was adopted, leading to a series of violent insurrections in the countries of South and Southeast Asia. Burma erupted in April, Malaya in June, and Indonesia in September.

Simultaneously with this conference the C.P.I. held its second congress, also in Calcutta, when the Zhadanov line was confirmed and P. C. Joshi, advocate of the "right" strategy, was replaced as general secretary by B. T. Ranadive, who since 1946 had pressed for a militant policy of violent insurrection and guerrilla warfare. The adoption of the "left" strategy led to a trail of industrial sabotage and to terrorist excesses in the Telingana district of Hyderabad, Andhra, West Bengal, and Travancore-Cochin, where in 1946 the Reds had unsuccessfully attempted to capture two coastal villages, Vayalur and Punnapura, in Travancore. In West Bengal, Madras, Hyderabad, Travancore-Cochin, Indore, and Bhopal the state governments with the active support of the then Union Home Minister Vallabhbhai Patel reacted strongly, the Communist party being declared illegal in these areas, while some 2,500 Communists were held in detention. The upheaval was particularly fierce in Telingana where the peasants, directed by the Andhra Provincial Committee of the C.P.I., were responsible for some gross excesses.

Neither Moscow nor the C.P.I. at this stage seems to have appreciated the fine distinction between the neo-Maoist strategy and the "left" strategy, which they appeared to think was identical. While the "left" strategy was sharply antibourgeois, the neo-Maoist strategy allowed for two separate revolutions envisaging a stage of a united front with the bourgeois elements, but "from below." Nor was it identical with the "right" strategy, for while visualizing a period of temporary cooperation with the bourgeoisie it clearly laid down that this united front should not be "from above."

In June, 1948, the Andhra Provincial Committee of the C.P.I. had submitted an anti-Ranadive document to the Politburo advocating the neo-Maoist strategy, but Ranadive would have none of it. His strategy of a united front "from below" against the Congress had no room for the rich peasantry or any part of the bourgeoisie. He favored violence, but urban rather than rural violence. In July he attacked Mao Tse-tung openly, bracketing him with Tito and Browder, and denouncing the neo-Maoist strategy as "reactionary and counterrevolutionary."

But Ranadive's days were numbered. On January 27, 1950, an editorial in the Cominform journal advised the C.P.I. to take "the Chinese path" by mobilizing their forces on a broad united front to include all the anti-imperialist elements. In May and June, 1950, the Central Committee conferred, and Ranadive was replaced by Rajeshwar Rao, the leader of the Andhra Communists. The C.P.I. moved from the "left" strategy to neo-Maoism, but persisted with its violent tactics in Telingana. Only in April, 1951, did a statement of policy specifically reject the Chinese model of peasant guerrilla warfare; but it maintained the four-class approach, including the peasants, workers, petty bourgeosie, and the national bourgeosie in the united front, and while abjuring the use of violence in the prevailing circumstances did not abandon it in principle. Rao had proved himself no Mao, and was replaced by Ajoy Ghosh, the Telingana rebellion being simultaneously ended by a C.P.I. directive.

Including Ghosh, Rao, Ranadive, and Joshi, the C.P.I. has had five general secretaries since 1934. The first of this quintette was Dr. G. Adikhari. Among the veteran Communists is the Bombay leader S. A. Dange, in private a soft-spoken, pleasant-mannered man but in public a virulent orator and tub thumper. He was an accused in both the Cawnpore and the Meerut conspiracy cases, and in the last general elections was returned to the House of the People by a majority of over 90,000 votes, the greatest plurality accorded to any candidate in India. So far the Communist parliamentary group has had no decisive voice in the inner councils of the party, but it is beginning to reveal an increasing assertiveness on its own widely publicized plane.

The C.P.I. operates today according to the neo-Maoist strategy which the Kerala Reds also followed. From 1948 to 1951, when the Communist party in Travancore-Cochin was banned, the Communists worked underground among the rural masses, students, and trade-unionists. They spearheaded the cry for a separate Kerala which Namboodiripad voiced in his book *The National Question in Kerala* as far back as 1952. The Communists thus came to be regarded as the creators of Kerala in contrast to the Congress and the Praja Socialist party, who, realizing that they would be placed at a political disadvantage with the formation of this state, were lukewarm in its support. As we have already seen, the grievous sins of commission and omission of the Congress further helped the Communists to achieve power.

Interesting as a revelation of the neo-Maoist strategy which the Reds adopted is the Kerala Communist party's manifesto before the last general elections. In it the K.C.P. promised to sponsor some ninety-three specific measures ranging over the economic, educational, and social fields. It pledged not only agrarian reforms in a predominantly rural society but a 25 per cent wage increase, minimum wages for industrial and agricultural workers, and alongside nationalization of the British-owned plantations encouragement to private enterprise in order to step up the industrial development of the state, which the Congress had neglected. According to the Communist manifesto even the inadequate amount allocated for Travancore-Cochin by the First Five-Year Plan had not been fully utilized under the aegis of the Congress, and the Reds undertook to increase Kerala's earmarked allotment under the Second Plan from about Rs. 88 crores (nearly $175 million) to Rs. 200 crores ($400 million). The manifesto reflects the neo-Maoist strategy of including within its amorphous embrace the rural masses and urban workers on the one hand and the intellectuals and capitalists on the other. Each individually and all collectively were promised paradise on a platter. Politically the foreign policy of the Congress government, leaning well toward the left, facilitated the task of the Communists. The State Congress had proved itself completely ineffectual and moreover was ridden with nepotism and corruption. Internally it smelled to high heaven, while externally in the realm of foreign policy it flattered Russia and China by attention and praise.

The wonder is not that the Communists won in Kerala but that they did not win more decisively. This suggests that the C.P.I. is subject to more political pressures, internal and external, than the Congress party, and therefore labors under various initial disadvantages on which its opponents have failed to capitalize. Indeed, in its complete demoralization the Kerala Congress party sold the pass by allowing the Reds to adopt a superficially convincing posture as democrats able to deliver the goods and deliver them "honestly." Having once seized the leadership of the United Front of Leftists, the Communists, following the regulated recognized pattern, turned on the other leftist groups and destroyed them, both the P.S.P. and the Revolutionary Socialist party being unable to contend with their sustained fusillade. The Reds then claimed to be the only alternative to the Congress. And by an act of monumental stupidity, hoping thereby to draw away independent and wavering votes to itself, the Kerala Congress endorsed this interpretation. The result was disaster.

How did Communists fare in Kerala during their twenty-eight months in office? They soon found difficulty in maintaining the mask they wore at the polls, and despite the still divided, heterogeneous character of the opposition the Reds were not able to maintain convincingly their democratic postures. Coming to power by the ballot box, they attempted to confuse the electorate by automatically claiming a democratic character and status, thereby leading many even outside the state to hope that the new administration would reflect the "new look" which international Communism had assumed since Stalin's death in 1953. In their early months in office, Namboodiripad and his colleagues were careful to exude an air of sweet reasonableness. "What is our policy?" Namboodiripad rhetorically asked. "Our policy is to implement all that the Congress promised the people to do, and failed to do."

This seemingly innocuous soft line was peddled for some time. The Communists, it implied, wished and worked only for "peaceful coexistence" at home and abroad, but Namboodiripad himself, in an unguarded moment, disclosed his party's real strategy. Speaking to an American correspondent, he visualized the prospect of the Reds infiltrating into other states "by democratic means" and by the same methods entering the central citadel at Delhi. Clearly he saw Kerala as the Indian Communists' Yenan. "I believe," he remarked, "that at *first* there will be a coalition government in New Delhi with perhaps a large Congress bloc." The implication was that from a coalition this government would in time and by strictly democratic methods and processes be converted into a one-party Communist government. Had the Kerala Reds themselves not successfully undermined the United Front of Leftists and thereby isolated and immobilized the unsuspecting P.S.P. and R.S.P.? What could be done at a state plane could also be achieved at the national level. And it could be done through the parliamentary machine by democratic means. Why should the Reds resort to a violent revolution when they could achieve their purpose by a "voting" revolution?

This was their strategy. They failed to implement it, for once they attempted to put their ideas into practice they could not longer sustain their pose of reasonableness, their excesses finally welding even the heterogeneous opposition elements into a solid wall of defiance. The tendency to regard a Communist administration as some sort of Red colossus difficult to dislodge is common in democratic countries, too easily impressed or overawed by the unfamiliar. Yet the history of Communist rule demonstrates that these colossi have often feet of clay while their heads, wired to the Marxist juke-box, are afflicted by a hundred jangling discords. Because of his doctrinaire ideology or creed it is less easy for a Communist to think clearly than it is for a democrat. The history of the party is a history of divided, often confused, counsels, with much of the bizarre and not a little of the ludicrous. Nehru once labeled the Indian Communist party as "the most stupid among the Communist parties of the world."

In Kerala the administrative inexperience of the party soon exposed many chinks in its armor which a more competent opposition might have effectively pierced more quickly. The Red ministry was conscious of the fact that while elsewhere Communist administrations worked against a Communist background, in Kerala the Red government had to function within the larger framework of "a bourgeois system of democracy." This made its position peculiarly difficult and even vulnerable, with one eye on its Politburo and the other cocked on Delhi. "We have," confessed Namboodiripad, "to work within the frame of a system which includes several regulations and limitations which are not to our liking. But we will work within the framework of the Constitution and will try to utilise the provisions of the Constitution to amend the Constitution itself." While the Kerala chief minister spoke a constitutional language, safeguarding himself by holding up the constitution as a potential scapegoat and an alibi for his mistakes, his colleagues outside Kerala were more dogmatic and less constitutional. If the Congress did not allow the Kerala Government "to function properly," threatened Ranadive, the faith of the people in the ballot box would be lost. "We Communists have not changed," proclaimed Dange speaking on Kerala. "Let there be no mistake about it. We remain where we are." Even more specific was another Communist leader, P. Sunderraya, who observed that if the Union Government did not agree with the Kerala ministry's politics, the C.P.I. "would resort to other means." Here is the familiar Red dual tactic. Kerala to the Communists was no turning point to political respectability. It merely represented another shift of line.

To an electorate mindful of congressional corruption and maladministration—and it is difficult to deny this—honesty and efficiency were the hallmarks of good government. Realizing it, the Communist party promised both, but they were unable to achieve either. A major selling point in the Reds' electoral manifesto was the charge, partly justified, that the Congress had not even utilized fully the inadequate allotments earmarked for Kerala under the First Plan. This was especially so in regard to the development of agriculture and industry, where the accusation registered in a state whose most pressing problems are food shortage and unemployment. The Communists made extravagant claims for their performance in the first two years (1956–1957 and 1957–1958) of the Second Plan, but the figures showed that out of nearly eighteen crores ($36 million) allotted for the second year the Communists were able to utilize barely five crores ($10 million). In a clumsy attempt to cover their failure, the Communists blamed this on the administrative system they had inherited from the Congress, but it was hardly a convincing alibi. It would be more correct to attribute it to their own administrative inexperience and to their misdirected energy and enthusiasm in other channels, where zeal outran discretion.

The long list of lapsed budgetary provisions read out in the State Legislative Assembly was as embarrassing to the Communists as it was a godsend to the opposition. To extricate themselves from their embarrassment the Communists then allocated large sums for the development of minor irrigation schemes and power projects in an attempt to expend the allotted amounts by the end of the financial year. In their haste to do this, as well as for calculated political reasons, they omitted to comply with the normal procedures of preparing estimates, calling for bids, and having each scheme scrutinized carefully by financial and technical experts, their excuse for this being that these were dilatory procedures involving needless "red tape" by an ineffectual administrative machine. The Communist government also created a certain amount of resentment in the official ranks by countermanding the previous administration's directives to increase the salaries of higher grade officers. On the other hand the ministry upgraded the remuneration of the village officers, though their pay scales are not equal in the Malabar part of Kerala and in Travancore-Cochin. In fairness it must be said that the Communist ministers also reduced their own salaries to Rs. 350 ($70) a month and scaled down their allowances.

Instead of consigning the execution of these technical projects to experienced contractors, the Communists have devised what they described as an original method, the task of implementing the minor irrigation schemes being entrusted to a small committee of local officials who were required to choose the agencies of implementation from three bodies in the following order of priority—panchayats, or village committees, labor-contract cooperative societies, and ad hoc committees. Any one of the bodies chosen was required to provide some *shramdan*, or voluntary labor, and was advanced funds ranging from 33⅓ per cent to 20 per cent of the cost of the project.

The labor-contract cooperatives were the creation of the Communist government which sponsored their formation and which decreed that all "works" entailing a cost of Rs. 25,000 or less should be entrusted to them. Besides the advance funds made available to them, these "workers" were encouraged by share capital loans and working capital loans. No bids were called for, no sureties or bonds of agreement were required, and no stipulation was laid down as to the satisfactory completion of the work. This was a foregone conclusion!

In short, the cooperatives are Communist cells in transparent disguise. For *shramdan*, or voluntary labor, these organizations had no scruples in ordering the local police force "to volunteer." The policemen, dragooned into "voluntary" labor, were supplemented by other "volunteers" from the Communist Students Federation and the Communist party. The real purpose of the cooperatives was inadvertently revealed by the state revenue minister, K. R. Gouri, who in a reference to the toddy tappers' cooperative societies, another Communist creation designed to replace the toddy contractors who undoubtedly reaped a rich financial harvest as middlemen, declared that "the government has decided to entrust the toddy industry in the state completely to the toddy tappers' cooperative societies under a phased program of three years." These cooperatives, already buttressed by share capital loans and other forms of financial assistance, soon controlled one-third of the toddy industry, and it was estimated would control the entire excise revenue of nearly Rs. 2 crores ($4 million) from this industry within another two years. The Kerala Government next planned to extend these activities to the cooperatives in the coir and handloom industries. This despite the fact that the record of the cooperatives was by no means impressive, excise revenue showing an unaccountable fall while the illicit liquor trade grew. According to one estimate the state revenue has thereby suffered to the extent of Rs. 2,500,000 ($500,000).

Here obviously was one method of consolidating the influence and enlarging the party funds of the Communists, for it is no secret that a substantial proportion of the cooperative earnings finds its way into the Red coffers. A goodly proportion, it was alleged, also managed to be secreted in Marxist pockets. At the C.P.I.'s Amritsar session in the fall of 1957, the Tamil Nad Red leader P. Ramamurthy announced that the Communist party of India could mobilize a fund of Rs. 2,500,000 ($500,000). Later the Kerala Communist party declared its intention of collecting a fund of Rs. 300,000 ($60,000).

On the food front the Communists of Kerala ran into more trouble than they had envisaged. Kerala is notoriously deficient in foodstuffs; and with the increasing pressure of population, which is expected to grow by 1,500,000 by the end of the Second Plan, the position, already serious with a population of 15 million in an area of 15,000 square miles, will be precarious. Today the state is deficit to the extent of at least 1,200,000 tons of rice. During the First Plan period (1951–1956) food production in Kerala was said to have increased by some 346,000 tons, almost 19 per cent of the total plan outlay of Rs. 30 crores ($60 million) being expended on agriculture and community development projects. Of the Rs. 87 crores (about $175 million) allocated to Kerala under the Second Plan, the amount allotted for agriculture alone was Rs. 15 crores ($30 million), the target for additional food production being 350,000 tons.

The Kerala Government made much of its land-reform policy, which was in no way different in its antieviction laws and its provisions for fair rent and land ceilings from that in Congress-governed states such as Uttar Pradesh, West Bengal, Bombay, and the Punjab, but failed to expend even the limited Plan allocations granted to the state. In agriculture, over the last two years its utilization percentages were 9.68 and 16.23 in relation to the disbursements allowed. Rice, the staple food material, showed a price increase of 50 per cent within six months, thereby putting it almost out of reach of the common man. A major reason for this was the license permitted to so-called agriculture workers to hold to ransom the farmers, often petty owners of a few uneconomic acres graded as submarginal units. According to the authors of the Thirty-Year Master Plan, Kerala can achieve self-sufficiency within the next thirty years by raising an average of two and a half crops annually from the 1,900,000 acres available for rice cultivation in the state. But what hope or inducement was there for this with Communist-incited workers threatening even petty agriculturists? The Communists who had boasted that they could solve the food problem within twenty-four hours were hoist with their own petard. Their fair-price shops were a failure, and inevitably in their search for scapegoats they turned the Red spotlight on the constitution, which, they alleged, circumscribed them, and on the Central Government, which they accused of denying them adequate aid. Actually, according to Union Deputy Minister for Food A. M. Thomas, who comes from Kerala, out of the 257,000 tons of rice which the Central Government bought from Andhra, a surplus rice state, 196,000 tons were given to Kerala. In Kerala's own budget for 1958–1959 a crore of rupees ($2,000,000) was earmarked for food subsidy, but of this amount only Rs. 2,500,000 ($500,000) were expended.

Even more disturbing than this record of inefficiency is the dismal story of corruption, several irregularities in the Kerala Government's own rice deal with Andhra being alleged and proved. According to Kerala's deputy controller of accounts, C. Sankara Menon, the state government, by putting the purchasing transaction through a Madras firm whose manager, it was alleged, was a veteran Red and a schoolmate of the Kerala food minister, K. C. George, had incurred a loss of Rs. 153,000 ($30,600) on the purchase of 5,000 tons of rice, roughly equivalent to 68,000 bags. Mr. Sankara Menon, who had audited the accounts, declared before an inquiry commission subsequently appointed to investigate the affair that the Kerala Government had rejected a cheaper scheme to purchase the rice through local merchants. Here again the state administration had conveniently dispensed with the normal practice of inviting bids. These findings were later accepted and endorsed by an inquiry commission.

The Communists' administrative inexperience was pitifully exposed by the events culminating in violence and unrest on the tea plantations situated in the High Ranges. Soon after taking office in April, 1957, the state ministry ordered the police not to interfere in "peaceful" strikes and picketing but to intervene only in the event of violence. Simultaneously the government devised a labor charter applicable to field and factory workers, prescribing minimum wages, gratuities, and bonuses, the last being payable by industrial establishments irrespective of profit or loss. The Communists also encouraged the settlement of industrial disputes by what they described as "mutual consultations and negotiations." Prior to this, it was the practice that in the event of conciliation proceedings failing in a dispute the matter was referred to industrial tribunals for compulsory adjudication.

These directives, apart from demoralizing the police and the officials, led to an immediate deterioration in law and order, many Red workers at the lower level seizing the opportunity to vent old grievances on opponents or rivals. In some areas the Communists set up People's Courts which sat in judgment on those dragged before them. The Communists who had their own trade-unions dominated by the Red A.I.T.U.C. (All-India Trade Union Congress) also mounted an offensive against the other trade-unions led by the Congress I.N.T.U.C. (Indian National Trade Union Congress). This precipitated a clash between the two unions in the plantation estates, the majority of the workers being unwillingly dragged into the fray. Tension had earlier followed a demand by the workers for larger bonuses, gratuities, and Provident Fund contributions by the employers, as well as for more holidays with pay. But it eased when the plantation owners arrived at an agreement with the I.N.T.U.C. The settlement infuriated the A.I.T.U.C., which repudiated the agreement, incited one set of workers against the other, and threatened a general labor strike. In the violence which these developments unleashed, the police were compelled to open fire, resulting in some deaths and injuries to the demonstrating strikers. Kerala's labor minister, T. V. Thomas, thereupon denounced the police and declared that the strike of the Communist-led plantation workers was "perfectly justified." Such ministerial statements were not calculated to improve the law-and-order situation, and instances were frequently cited of local Communists attempting to browbeat and coerce district officials. As a result administrative standards slumped sharply.

The month-long Communist-led plantation strike caused a loss of 2.2 million pounds of tea, according to the planters. While the Kerala Government lost Rs. 1,450,000 ($290,000) and the workers incurred a heavy loss of wages, the Union Government dropped Rs. 1,600,000 ($320,000) in internal revenue and Rs. 4,400,000 ($880,000) in foreign exchange. It was an expensive venture all round.

To create a favorable climate for industrial development, industrial peace is vital. But this was conspicuous by its absence in Kerala, and consequently the state government was unable to make any headway in its development plans. Strikes and industrial disputes grew in number, over one million man-days being lost in 1958, while industrial disputes totaled 505 during the first seven months of the same year. In 1957–1958 only 165 new factories, most of them working on a small-scale basis, were registered. The same period revealed the total number of factories at 1,613 and the total number of trade-unions at 1,219.

For a Communist government the Kerala administration seemed unusually anxious to attract private enterprise, the reason being twofold. Only thus, said the Reds, could Kerala be industrialized, for the capital outlay on state-owned industries was small, totaling only Rs. 10,000,000 ($2,000,000), and the state's investment, excluding loans to private industries, was around Rs. 70,000,000 ($14 million). The Kerala Government's assurance that private capital would have "a safe, honorable, and permanent place" in the state attracted little response, the only outcome being a tentative agreement with Birla's to start a rayon pulp factory. The Praja Socialist party leader, Acharya Kripalani, was later to twit the Red government on its inconsistencies. In 1950, he remarked, the Communist party of India had described the country's Constitution as "a charter of slavery" but now they were swearing by it. The Reds talked of vested interests and yet they went on their knees before Birla and asked him to set up a factory in Kerala.

As a special case the Planning Commission has permitted the state government to invest Rs. 1,000,000 ($200,000) in the private sector. But the value of industrial production did not rise very much from the 1955–1956 figure of Rs. 200,000,000 ($40 million), which itself was low, while the disparity in agricultural and industrial development was revealed when in the same period agricultural production was valued at Rs. 1800,000,000 ($360 million). Meanwhile unemployment was on the upgrade, totaling nearly 170,000 job seekers by the end of 1958.

A measure which has provoked particularly fierce controversy in the state was the Education bill which under the justifiable plea of improving the teacher's lot in privately managed schools aimed at controlling the entire system of education and, through an approved panel of teachers and officially supervised textbooks, of indoctrinating both teachers and students. Since the privately managed schools, numbering nearly 7,000 out of a total of 10,000, are largely in the hands of the Christian community, the controversy assumed a dangerous communal complexion. The teachers' financial status, not only in Kerala but throughout India, certainly needs to be improved and safeguarded. Had this been the only motivation of the Education bill, no fair-minded persons would have objected. But the Communist motivations were deeper and wider.

The bill, as first drafted, required a panel system of government-approved teachers, from which appointments would be made to the aided or privately managed schools. No one whose name was not on the list could become a teacher in any government or private schools. The management of aided schools were required to make over to the government all the fees and other dues collected, the government giving these schools grants-in-aid which the ministry could adjust from time to time; and, if the government so desired, "for the purpose of standardizing general education or for improving the level of literacy" it could arbitrarily take over any category of aided schools. The bill also provided for government-appointed committees to prepare school textbooks, which again would be printed exclusively in the government press and distributed only through the school cooperatives.

The original bill with certain amendments was passed by the Kerala State Assembly and submitted to the president for his approval. In view of certain controversial aspects of this measure, involving among other things the issue of minority rights, the president referred the bill to the Supreme Court. The amendments in the bill at the select committee stage concerned the proviso for a panel system of government-approved teachers, which was deleted, these teachers now being required to be approved by the State Public Service Commission, which is government-appointed; a new clause that the provisions of the Act should not apply to schools other than government schools and those recognized and aided by the government, which meant that the management of an aided school was given the option to run it as a recognized school without government aid when the Act came into force; and finally another clause stating that nothing in the Act should affect the rights of minorities, including the Anglo-Indians.

In May, 1958, the Supreme Court held that some of the provisions of the bill seemed to conflict with Article 30 (1) of the Constitution relating to the rights of the minorities, and suggested that these might be amended. This was done by the Kerala State Assembly, and the Act, as amended, received the president's assent in February, 1959. The decision of Namboodiripad and his colleagues to implement the Act led to a counterdecision by the opposition to close down all nongovernmental schools as a protest. Opposition demonstrations reached their crescendo in June when the schools were scheduled to open after the summer vacation.

Yet as Nehru declared in the Lok Sabha debate after the dismissal of Kerala's Red government on July 31, 1959, and the establishment of president's rule under Article 356* of the Indian Constitution, the Education bill in itself did not spark the massive popular agitation against the ministry which began on June 10th and ended seven weeks later on July 31st when the Communist government was suspended. In this agitation which embraced the Congress party, the Praja Socialist party, the Moslem League, the Catholics and Nairs, estate owners and workers, at least fifteen people died in the police firings, and many thousands, including women and students, were arrested, some of them being brutally beaten up. The threat of the Vimochana Samara Samiti (the composite name under which the United Front of Anti-Communists was known) to invade the official Secretariat on August 10th and throw the Red ministers out finally forced New Delhi to act. In the Lok Sabha the home minister, Pandit Pant, explained that it was the combination of events in Kerala which made it inevitable for the Central Government to take action. At the end the Communists found themselves faced by an upsurge of the people, who were determined to oust the Reds if they did not leave voluntarily or if the Central Government continued to be reluctant to force them out of office. What compelled the Center to intervene was, in Nehru's words, "the enormous anger,

* Under Article 356 the president can by proclamation take over the government of a state if he is satisfied that it is not being carried on in accordance with the Constitution. The proclamation must subsequently be approved by both Houses of Parliament, and remains in force for six months. It can be extended for six months at a time, up to a maximum period of three years.

hatred, polarization and a tendency among the people to use knives." The prime minister, speaking among angry Red interruptions, disclosed that the Communist had themselves welcomed the Center's intervention, which was received with relief by them. Nehru's diagnosis was confirmed by Dr. K. B. Menon, the Praja Socialist member from Kerala, who after narrating stories of killings by the Communists said that if the Center had not intervened "we would not have fallen at the Communists' feet but rivers of blood would have flowed." The Communists, he added, should know that in Kerala it was the people and not the Center who had intervened.

The Communist members of Parliament, on their part, left their listeners with no illusions about the Red attitude to democratic practices under the Indian Constitution. "Democracy in this country," declared S. A. Dange, "if it is to be a democracy, must be a toilers' democracy. It cannot be an impartial democracy belonging to the exploiters and the exploited." In formulating police policy, added another Communist, A. K. Gopalan, all that the Kerala Government had sought to do was "to extend to the toiling people the protection hitherto enjoyed only by the vested interests." The Lok Sabha resoundingly endorsed the Center's intervention, the president's proclamation being approved by 270 votes to 38.

Not only Parliament but the country as a whole realized the real nature of Communist rule and the threat it posed to democracy and individual freedom. The Communists' acts and speeches implied that if large masses of the people were opposed to them, the Reds would not hesitate to enforce their rule even if it meant killing or imprisoning half the population. Kerala also made many of India's people realize that the Communist party had no roots in the country and that its members were the creatures of external agencies and influences—a conclusion which the Indian Communist party's attitude toward China's aggression in Tibet reinforced. Mrs. Indira Gandhi's disclosure that the Kerala Government had actually prepared school textbooks wherein Lenin and Mao Tse-tung were held up as world heroes while Mahatma Gandhi was ignored deeply offended Indian feeling. If the Reds owed no loyalty to the country, what right had they to expect the country's loyalty to them?

India's people now know that the extension of the Kerala pattern to other states and ultimately to the Center will spell the doom of democracy in India. Whatever party controls the Center rules India, provided the Union Government knows its mind and is prepared to act firmly, for the Constitution, though federal, has strong centralizing characteristics, the president having, as we saw, the power to suspend the government of a state in times of emergency and to establish president's rule. Though theoretically all the executive power of the Union of India is vested in the president, in practice, following the conventions established over the past twelve years, the president acts on the advice of the prime minister, whom, again theoretically, he appoints along with the Union ministers.

In certain eventualities, however, an anomalous situation could arise. If, for instance, the Communists were to capture three or more states it might be difficult for the Union Government, acting through the president, to suspend these governments should Delhi desire to do so. Moreover a situation might arise when the president could be a noncongressman while the Union Government was Congress, for the President is chosen for a term of five years by a special process, by the elected members of both Houses of the Indian Parliament and of the legislative assemblies of the states. Were the Communists to capture several states and secure substantial representation in the others and at the Center, they could, in the event of three or more candidates standing, return a non-Congress president who in turn might choose to ignore the precedents established since independence, and take every opportunity of embarrassing a Congress prime minister. This is possible, though not probable.

If the alternative offered to the voters is a choice between the Congress and the C.P.I. it might well be that an electorate voting on the basis of adult franchise would in time veer round to the Communists, though Kerala and Tibet have between them hit the Reds hard. It does not follow from this that the solution is a multiple party system, since the Reds, capitalizing on group factions and rivalries, could perhaps even more easily attain power through a division of opposition strength.

Since the Hungarian uprising in October, 1956, when Nehru was compelled to modify his pro-East bias in response to public protests in India, Delhi's foreign policy has shown no pronounced leanings to the East or to the West. On the other hand, the Government of India's internal economic measures, with a mounting offensive against the private sector, oppressive taxation at the higher levels, ceilings on landholdings and so-called cooperative farming—a convenient intermediate label which the Chinese Communists had earlier adopted for incipient collectivization—have made it increasingly difficult for the average Indian voter to distinguish between Communism and the Congress credo. In the interests of democracy, the necessity for a sharp distinction between the two systems is vital, but the likelihood of the Congress dividing into two parties, right and left, is slim in Nehru's lifetime.

It is possible that with Nehru's demission from the political scene the Congress, already straining at the seams, will burst apart—which will be a good thing for the country if the disruption results in the creation of two main parties representing the right and left wings. Their flapping can even now be heard, though faintly, inside the Congress auditorium. A three-party system—conservative, Socialist, and Communist—might yet enable India to achieve democracy.

For all practical political purposes the Socialists, divided hopelessly among themselves, are at a discount, and it is here that a new body of Socialists composed of former Congress workers could invigorate the old Socialist cause by bringing it the leaven of more seasoned experience and providing it with a rejuvenated faith. Since its foundation in 1934 the Socialist party has passed through three broad phases. The Congress Socialist party preserved its entity within the parent Congress body until 1948 when it organized itself as a separate group and later, with divided ideologies and little enthusiasm among the rank and file, contested the general elections of 1951–1952 with not too impressive results. In 1952 the Socialist party and the Kisan Mazdoor Praja Sabha (Peasants' party) merged to form the Praja Socialist party (P.S.P.) with Acharya Kripalani as its president and Asoka Mehta as general secretary. The P.S.P., however, was still plagued by internal differences and in 1955 it expelled one of its more prominent members, Rammanohar Lohia, who promptly formed a new group, the Socialist party of India. Lohia claims to have taken with him 30 per cent of the former party's strength, the active leadership of six state organizations, the bulk of the Socialist youth movement and one-seventh of its legislative representation. Nonetheless the P.S.P. in the general elections of 1957 fared fairly well, particularly in the state assemblies, where it increased its collective representation from 125 to 195. The growing opposition to the Congress at state levels, owing to various factors, more especially the linguistic agitations, largely accounted for this.

Apart from the Socialists and the Communists, opposition to the Congress on the national plane comes from the Hindu communal parties such as the Hindu Mahasabha, which has been under a cloud since Gandhi's assassination; the Bharatiya Jan Sangh, founded in 1951 by the Bengal leader, the late Dr. Shyama Prasad Mookerjee, whose death in June, 1953, greatly weakened the group; the Ram Rajya Parishad, perhaps the most orthodox of the communal parties; and the militantly revivalist Rashtriya Swayamsevak Sangh (RSS), which was also suspected of complicity in the Mahatma's murder. None of these communal groups has so far fared well at the polls; but should the recently formed Swatantra party* or any other rightist party develop, there is a danger of some of these elements joining hands with it and, while supporting its forward economic policies, pressing for a brake on social reform and demanding a more pronounced Hindu attitude and approach. If the rightist party of the future eschews these elements, it will gain greatly in internal and national strength. But the communal pressures are there and continue.

Thus the national parties fall broadly into three compartments, the first comprising the Congress, the K.S.P., the Socialist, and the Swatantra party, all wedded to the idea of a democratic secular state; the second represented by the Communists, who stand for a state on the Marxist model inspired by Moscow and Peking; and the third, composed of Hindu communal parties which look to Hindu tradition for their inspiration. Aside from these main units are various splinter groups with provincial, communal, and sectional interests or loyalties, such as the Samyukta Maharashtra Samiti and the Maha Gujarat Parishad (both of them linguistic groups in Bombay); the communal Sikh Akali Dal, the Scheduled Castes Federation, and the Dravida Munnetra Kazhagam; and sectional groups like the protribal Jharkhand party and Janata party in Bihar along with the proproperty Ganatantra Parishad in Orissa.

In a vast country like India, with a complicated economic and social pattern, the development of a multiparty system of numerous groups could create political instability in the states and even at the Center. This happened in PEPSU (Patiala and East Punjab States Union) in 1952 when local law and order broke

* See Chapter X.

down and president's rule had to be proclaimed. A multiplicity of groups contending at the polls, either at national or state levels, might precipitate confusion and could create chaos.

The Congress party, already disintegrating internally through personal and group rivalries at several state levels, will in all likelihood break up into two main parties with Nehru's withdrawal from the political scene. This will have one obvious advantage, for the present monolithic structure of the Congress almost makes it seem a democratic victory when an opposition group, even the Communist party, succeeds in beating its candidates at the polls.

Conversely, the establishment of a Communist government in Kerala has been an eye opener to discerning democrats, some of them bemused with the superstition that a Red regime was more efficient and honest than most democratic governments and produced quicker results. Kerala proved the contrary, providing a long-overdue corrective.

VII
Toward Unity

It is against a background of tradition, turmoil, and trial, of selfless and sometimes selfish endeavor, of farsightedness, folly, strife, and struggle that India's people and government have worked since independence to take the country onward to broader uplands and richer fields. The triumphs and setbacks of these twelve years are identified in and outside India with Nehru, for he has come to represent the symbol of all that a newly independent land strives through toil and sacrifice to achieve.

"India," affirms Nehru, "is a country of destiny." In a speech he made not many months after the attainment of independence, the prime minister revealed the vista along which he saw the future of the country. "Whether we are men or women of destiny or not," he declared, "India is a country of destiny and so far as we represent this great country with a great destiny stretching out in front of her, we also have to act as men and women of destiny, viewing all our problems in that long perspective of destiny and of the world and of Asia." This suggests an almost messianic approach to history, with India destined to play a decisive role in the development of human progress. But that is how Nehru views and visualizes India—a bridge between contending forces and peoples within and outside the country. Hence the primary need for the preservation of peace in and beyond India. Hence also the urgency for consolidation and unity within India.

These twin ideals have governed Nehru's internal and international policies since independence. They have expressed themselves in varied ways with a shift of emphasis which sometimes suggests a shift almost of purpose and direction. In the international field, as we have seen, Nehru has walked with more outward circumspection since Hungary, but at the national level he has tended more and more to move closer to Marxist solutions. This is particularly noticeable in the economic sphere, where with succeeding years his impatience at any criticism by the private sector of his Five-Year Plan shows increased irritability and vents itself in denunciations, often vitriolic, of private enterprise and big business.

The messianic fervor with which Nehru envisages India's role and destiny leads him to hustle the country along the Socialist path, at times barely distinguishable from the Communist, and to take it in his lifetime to a point of no return. His long-term objectives have always been clear, but in the short-term implementation of his targets his thought is apt to be cloudy and his methods confused. This explains his success as a strategist and his failure as a tactician. Nehru attempts simultaneously to move straight at and zigzag toward a target. The successful strategist gives him the reputation of a statesman, but his deficiencies as a political tactician dim the halo.

The contradictions which arise from the clash between the strategist and the tactician are reflected in almost every one of the policies and projects Nehru has pursued or implemented. On the international plane his genuine desire to be constructively helpful has paradoxically led him to be more often critical of the Western than of the Soviet bloc. In recent days he has attempted to counterbalance this impression by saying something critical of one bloc when he has to disagree with the other or, conversely, by being agreeable to one when he assents with the other. As a result India and Nehru have acquired a Janus reputation abroad.

The same contradictions arising from the same conflict are discernible in most of his internal policies. In the first five years of independence the paramount need, consequent on the problems of partition, was consolidation and unity. Both objectives have been achieved to a remarkable degree but neither has been completely fulfilled. Independence, with partition, brought with it some massively urgent problems which needed immediate attention, chief among these being the resettlement and rehabilitation of the refugees from Pakistan and the coalescing of India into a composite cohesive pattern comprising the government, princes, and people along with the capitalists, workers, and peasants; the setting up of a new Constitution for the country; and the redrawing of external frontiers and internal boundaries.

These were tremendous tasks for a new government as yet unused to authority and for a politically young people unaccustomed to independence. That the general framework of the politico-economic pattern should have been largely defined and settled within five years is impressive testimony to the resilience and resolution of India's people and government. This resilience and resolution derived as much from the long list of selfless patriots culminating with Gandhi as from the impress of British rule. Britain made India conscious of itself, and the Mahatma was to give this consciousness a new political awareness and purpose. It is curious to note how each of these inspirational forces, in many fundamental ways directly opposed to the other in outlook, temperament, methods, and objectives, was in a sense complementary, the one carrying the creation of the other a step or many steps further, though not always in the same direction. The British impact, as we have seen, brought Western concepts into the stream of Indian thinking, and with them new political, scientific, social, and economic ideas, humanistic values and ideals, rationalism and nationalism. By the creation of an educated middle class, nurtured on English learning and teaching, the British raj bequeathed to the country, when it withdrew, a qualified core of administrators and others capable of carrying on efficiently the day-to-day business of government and of helping forward the life of the people. Gandhi, as we also noted, by creating his own new class gave at least initially to an independent India a dedicated corps of political and social workers. Power was to sap the moral fiber and stamina of the overwhelming majority of these individuals, and as the higher echelons of British-trained Indian officials and administrators thinned there has been a perceptible slowing down in momentum and efficiency.

The early years of independence, despite the many problems with which partition overwhelmed India, as well as Pakistan, constituted a challenge to which the people and the government rose magnificently. Both realized it was a matter of stark survival. The most urgent and pressing of these problems related to the refugees, whose exodus and ingress involved over 12 million people in a two-way trail of blood and bestiality. Of this number some eight million came as refugees to India from West and East Pakistan, the majority comprising around six million Hindus and Sikhs coming from West Pakistan. The task of resettling and rehabilitating this vast uprooted population in a new environment called for enterprise, initiative, and understanding on the part of both the people and the government, which is why the final result represents a tribute and triumph for both.

By and large the problem is now under control, though in Bengal even after over a decade of independence a sporadic inflow of refugees continues intermittently from East Pakistan, adding greatly to the difficulties of a state government oppressed by overcrowding in Calcutta and other urban centers. Scores of improvised shelters are to be found here, though they also exist elsewhere in India, in cities such as Delhi and Amritsar. The perfervid clan spirit of the average Bengali, who finds it difficult to adjust himself to unfamiliar surroundings, complicates the task, to the mutual embarrassment of himself and the authorities.

But in most other parts of India communities such as the Sikhs, Sindhis, and Punjabi Hindus who formed the bulk of the influx from West Pakistan are reconciled to their new environment, and many of them have prospered and are happily resettled. In the early stages the huge dimensions of the refugee problem threatened to engulf and overwhelm the authorities. During this period the Central Government ran over 160 camps housing nearly a million and a half refugees, two of them being outside Delhi and accommodating some 150,000 people. After resettlement came rehabilitation, the process of integrating these unfortunate people into the economic life and pattern of the country, an undertaking which with substantial government aid to individuals and families has on the whole been satisfactorily accomplished. By the end of 1950 the refugee problem was under control, and since then progress has been sufficiently consistent and encouraging to reduce rehabilitation from a top priority to far down the scale of national urgencies.

The danger posed by the refugees was not only economic but political, for not unnaturally their enforced exodus embittered many, and for a while at least generated an irredentist outlook vis-à-vis Pakistan. The communal parties still count many adherents from among them, and significantly it was a Hindu youth, a refugee from West Punjab, who made the first unsuccessful attempt on Gandhi's life with a crude bomb, some ten days before the Mahatma was assassinated. The actual assassin was a militant Maharashtrian Hindu who resented Gandhi's efforts to protect the Moslems who had chosen to stay in India. These incidentally number 40 million, and constitute the third largest Moslem group in the world, being exceeded only by Pakistan and Indonesia.

Another aspect of the same process of consolidation and unity involved the integration of the princely states on the one hand and the consequent redrawing of the map of India to allow for new territorial alignments. We have seen how the princely order numbering some 562 rulers at the time of the British withdrawal were victims largely of their anomalous position which made them increasingly dependent on the British power as the rest of India advanced politically. Had the federal part of the Government of India Act of 1935 been implemented before the outbreak of the Second World War, India's political history might have been different, for federation meant the integration of the princely states into the federal framework while ensuring the princes not only their individual identities but also a not inconsiderable voice in the government of the country. The Act provided that when federation came into being the princes would have the right to nominate one-third of the members of the Lower House, or Federal Assembly, and two-fifths of the Upper House, or Council of States. For varied reasons, as we have seen, both the Congress party and the Moslem League were opposed to the federal part of the Act, which was never implemented.

When the British withdrew, their paramountcy over the princely states lapsed and so did their treaties with them. In theory each state became independent, but wisdom dictated that it opt for association with either India or Pakistan, which was the advice the then governor general, Lord Mountbatten, gave them. It is noticeable that the only three which hesitated to do so—Kashmir, Hyderabad, and Junagadh—brought trouble on themselves, and in the case of Kashmir, also on India and Pakistan.

A record of almost unrelieved misrule, combined with their heavy reliance on British authority in the face of a resurgent and assertive rationalism, forfeited the princes the sympathy of both the people and the politicians. When freedom came, they stood out as anachronisms in the body politic. The British had failed to persuade the states, except for a microscopic few, to modernize or liberalize their administrations, and with the removal of the raj the princes' lack of leadership and unity left them with no alternative to lining up with the new rulers.

The man responsible for effecting this revolutionary change with the minimum of dislocation was the then Union home minister, Vallabhbhai Patel. In July, 1947, a special States Department, headed by Patel, was set up to deal with the matter, and by August 15, 1947, when India became independent, all but three of the states within the country's geographical limits had acceded to India. The exceptions, as we have noted, were Kashmir, Hyderabad, and Junagadh. How did Patel achieve this? His tactics toward the princes were not unlike those of Mountbatten toward the leaders of the Congress party and the Moslem League before independence when he gave neither side time to think (or talk) and hustled both into freedom. Patel stampeded the princes into accession, his Standstill Agreements with them requiring them to accede only on the three subjects of defense, foreign affairs, and communications. This marked the first step in the process which was to lead finally to the merger of the princely states with the new India.

In these negotiations Patel displayed a characteristic combination of courage, skill, firmness, blarney, bluster, and bluff. He appealed to the princes' patriotism, warning them that the alternative would be "anarchy and chaos which will overwhelm great and small in a common ruin." He undertook to allow them generous privy purses and the full ownership, use, and enjoyment of all their personal properties, as distinct from state properties. But while he dangled these baits before the princes Patel was careful simultaneously to assure their subjects that they would have the same rights, liberties, and privileges as those enjoyed by India's citizens.

The states varied greatly in size and resources, and according to an ordained pattern integration took two forms—external integration, which meant the consolidation of the smaller states into sizable administrative units; and internal integration, which signified the growth of democratic institutions and responsible government inside the states, thus implementing the objective laid down in the first White Paper on Indian States, which "was the integration of all elements in the country in a free, united and democratic India." This meant that the rulers were deprived of effective power, though at first a few were appointed as rajpramukhs, or governors, of the enlarged units. Among the new states which emerged were Saurashtra in the Kathiawar district of Bombay; Rajasthan, Vindhya Pradesh, Madhya Bharat, and PEPSU. These five states unions, in which some 275 states were merged, were classified as "B" states. There were two other types of amalgamation. While some of the smaller states were merged and then joined to the former province of British India, others were consolidated into states unions and placed under the direct administration of the Central Government. Three states, Hyderabad, Mysore, and Kashmir, were allowed to retain their original form until the reorganization of 1956, being also categorized as "B" states. This arrangement resulted in twenty-seven states emerging out of some six hundred units, including the old provinces.

It was a tremendous effort in reorganization and reconstruction. For Patel to have achieved it within a year reveals his remarkable talent not only as an administrator but as a constructive statesman. The British in their day had also toyed with the idea of uniting the states into larger units so as to make for better administration. The imperious Curzon could have put it through, but the India Office in London faltered and procrastinated until it no longer possessed the power to impose its will. Had Patel lived another few years, the plight of the princes would have been better than that of mere gilded pensioners and he would probably have utilized their sense of tradition and their worldly experience more widely in the diplomatic and even in the administrative field. He would have tried to neutralize their feeling of frustration by canalizing their energies into positive work at home and abroad. In all likelihood he would have opposed the abolition of the rajpramukhs which the States Reorganization Commission recommended in 1956 and which the Government of India accepted in the following year.

Nehru's approach to the princes, as to all individuals and institutions whom he regards as vested interests, has always been basically doctrinaire and hostile. He has taken little trouble to conceal his contempt for personages who in his view are no better than archaic fossils and feudal relics suffering from a surfeit of overprotection and underdevelopment. To him the princes are anachronisms who could not possibly fit into a socialistic pattern of society. Yet the success of the landlord-dominated Ganatantra Parishad in Orissa and of some princely candidates in Rajasthan should induce second thoughts, for here is a potential nucleus for a militant rightist reorganization against the increasingly strident left. When and if the Congress party disintegrates, it might well be an inducement to fascism.

Gandhi's attitude to the princes would have been nearer Patel's than Nehru's, for Gandhi's India included all men; and, while insisting, as he did in his lifetime, that the peasant rated the highest priority and was entitled to the state's especial solicitude, he would not have treated the princes as a new depressed class, as pariahs and outcasts. He would have tried, like Patel, to harness them in the service of the country. This difference in attitude high-lights Nehru's basically different approach to men and matters. Lacking the Mahatma's organizational genius, which Patel shared, Nehru, unlike Gandhi, has little interest in individuals as individuals but prefers to deal with them en masse, one reason why he is more at home with vast masses of people than with a small group of persons, and one reason also why he is at pains to impregnate the people with his ideas, unmindful of the importance of building up an experienced cadre of men who would ultimately take his place. This habit of neglecting the individual for the mass explains the authoritarian streak in Nehru, whose political dogma postulates that what is good for the state is good for the individual. Gandhi would have put it the other way about.

Throughout history the masses have been alibis for demagogues and dictators. Nehru is neither, but sometimes he is perilously near both. The same masses whose wisdom and loyalty he lauds are those who at other moments he insists should be led. Everyone knows that the overwhelming bulk of the Indian people through no fault of their own are steeped in ignorance and poverty, both of which singly and together do not induce or encourage clear thinking. Yet Nehru and his colleagues, judging by a recent speech of Finance Minister Morarji Desai, who is generally believed to be right of the prime minister, would rather trust the judgment of the illiterate masses than heed the opinions of the educated few, which are sometimes more critical of the government's policies than New Delhi relishes.

In a speech at Ahmedabad in March, 1959, Desai, speaking at a high-school function, posed the question: Who are more responsible for the country's political stability—the illiterate masses or the educated few? And, answering the question, he plumped for the former. The reason he gave for his choice is illuminating and revealing. He found, he observed, that it was far more easy to convince the illiterate masses "about the true happenings and the situation in the country" than the educated. In other words, the masses were more readily prepared to accept what government spokesmen told them than the educated few whose skepticism presumably threatens the stability of the state. Carried to its logical conclusion this suggests that the vaster the illiterate masses, the greater the stability of the government. The obvious solution would then be to spread illiteracy as an insurance against political instability and to keep knowledge and education the privileged possession of a chosen few, doubtless the elite corps which constitutes the ministerial hierarchy and government, whose omniscience would thereby be safeguarded and protected against the vulgar criticism of the educated few. It is a curious argument, for it equates political stability with popular acquiescence in the doings and dictates of the government. It is also dangerously close to dictatorial thinking.

Nehru's treatment of the princes subsequent to divesting them of political power is an illustration of his strength as a strategist and his weakness as a tactician. To allow the princes to exercise special political powers, privileges, and prerogatives after independence would have been anomalous, and Gandhi, Nehru, and Patel rightly agreed that the princely order with its domains should be integrated completely in a democratic and independent India. But having done so, where was the necessity to ostracize them virtually from the realm of public service and deny the more civic-spirited among them equal opportunities with other Indian citizens to serve the country?

Similarly, while there is much to be said for the division of India into linguistic states provided the central control is effective, the manner in which this division was brought about created more stresses and frustrations than existed before. For this outcome Nehru is not entirely blameless, since his handling of the situation, alternating the direct approach with the zigzag tactic, confused the public and irritated those most closely affected by the result. Here the Congress party was caught largely in a dilemma of its own creation, for it was the first to give strong support to linguistic demands, doing so as far back as 1920 at its Nagpur session. Later it endorsed this resolution by reorganizing the regional units of the Congress on linguistic lines, and in the following years, until independence, it frequently reiterated its support for the principle. As the prospect of independence drew nearer, the attitude of the Congress to linguistic provinces changed in emphasis. In 1946 a congressional election manifesto declared that linguistic considerations would guide political divisions "not in every case but as far as it was possible in the circumstances of each case."

Henceforth Nehru grew increasingly enigmatic. "First things must come first, and the first thing is the security and stability of India," he announced in 1947. In 1948 the so-called Dar Commission was appointed to go into the question, and reported that it would be inadvisable to form provinces exclusively or even mainly along linguistic lines. Its recommendation was supported by a congressional committee headed by Nehru, Vallabhbhai Patel, and a leading congressman, Dr. Pattabhi Sitaramayya, but unfortunately this committee, influenced presumably by political and party motivations, added a rider that overwhelming public opinion should in any case be satisfied and that the creation of a separate Andhra State might be considered.

Not surprisingly, this set the linguistic ball rolling again. The cry for a separate Andhra State mounted and reached its climax after the first general elections of 1951–1952 when a Telegu congressman, Potti Sriramulu, fasted to death on this issue, thereby provoking a tremendous stir among the Telegu-speaking peoples of Madras State. Nehru yielded to the clamor and decreed a separate state for Andhra. In turn this began a linguistic chain reaction throughout the country.

In December, 1953, the Government of India appointed a commission to examine "objectively and dispassionately" the question of reorganization of states. At this time there was a threefold tier of states categorized as Part "A," "B," and "C" states. The Part "A" states, numbering ten, were composed of the former governor's provinces of British India with which some princely states had been merged. The Part "B" states, which totaled eight, included the five states unions we have already described plus the three states of Kashmir, Hyderabad, and Mysore. In the Part "C" category there were nine states, of a lower order than those in Parts "A" and "B," being carved out of the former chief commissioner's provinces to which some small princely states had been attached. The grand total was 27, which rose in 1953 to 28 when Andhra was created a separate state.

In 1955 the States Reorganization Commission submitted its report, following generally the linguistic principle with two major exceptions, Bombay and the Punjab, which were to remain bilingual states. The commission in effect recommended the creation of sixteen states and three union territories. But its calculated exclusion of Bombay and the Punjab from the accepted linguistic principle provoked a furor in both these areas which still smoulders. In Bombay the Marathi-speaking people had for long demanded a unilingual state with the city of Bombay as its capital, while in the Punjab the Sikhs had been clamoring for a Punjabi-speaking state.

Neither of these demands was conceded either by the commission or by the Government of India, which subsequently accepted the commission's findings, excluding Bombay and the Punjab from the linguistic principle but creating fourteen states instead of the sixteen recommended by the commission, and six union territories instead of three. Final action on the status of Bombay city was postponed indefinitely, a typical Fabian tactic of attempting to conquer by delay, which Nehru is prone too often to adopt in the face of opposition and difficulties. A "regional formula" for dividing governmental functions in the Punjab on linguistic lines was devised which, however ingenious it might look on paper, has proved disastrous in practice. The strategy was right but the tactics were wrong.

We have referred earlier to the three princely states of Kashmir, Hyderabad, and Junagadh which at the time of independence had acceded neither to India nor to Pakistan. Hyderabad and Junagadh had Moslem rulers, though the population of both was predominantly Hindu. In Kashmir a Hindu prince ruled a state overwhelmingly Moslem. On August 14, 1947, the maharaja of Kashmir, whose domain was contiguous to both India and Pakistan, signed a Standstill Agreement with Pakistan, but India was unwilling to enter into this commitment as it had no desire to encourage the maharaja to declare Kashmir an independent state. This was initially the maharaja's intention. Neither Junagadh nor Hyderabad were to prove as intractable problems as Kashmir.

Junagadh, a small state in the Kathiawar area, covers about 4,000 square miles, extending inland from the southern coast of the peninsula. It lies in Indian territory, though it is not far away from the southeast borders of West Pakistan. While a feudatory of the larger State of Baroda, Junagadh in turn received tribute from some minor feudatories in its territory, such as the sheikh of Mongrol and the ruler of Babariawad, both of whom had acceded to India. In September the nawab of Junagadh acceded to Pakistan, prevailed on Mongrol to renounce his accession to India, and sent troops into the territory of Babariawad in order also to "persuade" him. The nawab stationed troops in both Babariawad and Mongrol.

The Government of India, to whom these two territories had acceded, called on the nawab to withdraw his troops, but the request was ignored. Thereupon in November Indian troops entered Mongrol and Babariawad, and not long afterward the nawab fled to Pakistan, leaving the administration in the hands of his Moslem dewan (prime minister) who on November 8th formally invited the Government of India to assume the administration of the state. This was done, and in February, 1948, the Junagadh issue was submitted to a plebiscite in the state which resulted in an overwhelming majority in favor of India. Junagadh was merged in the Indian Union in January, 1949.

It cannot be denied that in the case of Junagadh both Nehru and Mountbatten committed themselves to the principle of a plebiscite where accession was in dispute. This was reaffirmed in the case of Kashmir by the same two principals in October, 1947, an undertaking which was constitutionally unnecessary but which, having been made, it was difficult to evade. Pakistan can hardly be blamed for attempting to pinpoint India on a principle to which in an unguarded moment it quite superfluously committed itself.

Hyderabad, like Junagadh, had a Moslem ruler, the nizam, at the head of a predominantly Hindu population. But for several reasons Hyderabad posed a problem far more formidable than that raised by Junagadh. It was the premier state of India, as large as France and situated deep in the heart of India. It covered some 83,000 square miles and had a population of over 17,000,000 of whom only 14 per cent were Moslems; but the nizam had dreams of enjoying an independent existence, and in this he was backed by some militant Moslem organizations in the state, notably the Ittehad-ul-Moslemeen, which had its storm troopers, known as Razakars, who were headed by Kassim Razvi, a fanatical Moslem educated at Aligarh University. Razvi claimed that Hyderabad was a Moslem state and that Moslem supremacy was based upon the right of conquest.

Hyderabad, having no geographical contiguity to Pakistan, could not accede to that country, but it was equally unwilling to accede to India. After prolonged discussions punctuated by Razakar demonstrations against India, the nizam in November, 1947, signed a Standstill Agreement for a year with India, giving to the Indian Government for that period control over defense, external affairs, and communications. About this time the nizam appointed Mir Laik Ali, a wealthy industrialist, as his prime minister. Laik Ali, who took the job only after consulting Jinnah, leaned heavily in favor of Pakistan, to whom the wealthy state of Hyderabad offered a loan. A currency ordinance discriminatory toward India was proclaimed, and the Razakars were encouraged to stage demonstrations against the Hindus, whom they also attacked.

India replied by imposing an economic blockade on Hyderabad, which was known to be buying arms abroad and gun-running military equipment by air from Karachi to Hyderabad. Inside Hyderabad the Razakars clamored for war. From the beginning of 1948 the Razakars had extended their activities from Hyderabad city to the rural areas, where oddly enough they were helped by the Communists, who characteristically attempted to exploit the Razakars' call to Moslem peasants and laborers to attack the Hindu landlords. Later, when Hyderabad was overwhelmed by Indian military forces, the Razakars were to turn over a large part of their arms and equipment to the Communists, who some months later staged a rising in Telingana, a district of Hyderabad.

Emboldened by the encouragement they received from the Hyderabad authorities, the Razakars, who kept the Hindu majority in a state of terror, began to carry on their depredations in Indian territory beyond the borders of Hyderabad. On September 7th Nehru in a speech to the Constituent Assembly revealed that the Razakars had made about 150 raids and forays into Indian territory and had attacked twelve trains on the border. They had killed many hundreds of people, abducted and raped women, and looted property worth over Rs. 10,000,000 ($2,000,000). They had also staged sporadic attacks on Indian troops stationed along the border or in enclaves of Indian territory within Hyderabad.

These violent incursions had their reaction in India, where the more militant-minded Hindus threatened reprisals on the 40 million Moslems resident in the country. Clearly the situation could not be allowed to deteriorate. Appeals to the nizam to control the Razakars were ignored, and the nizam instead appealed to the Security Council of the United Nations for aid in settling the dispute with India. The Indian Government opposed this reference on the ground that Hyderabad was not and had never been a sovereign state. As late as 1926 the British had categorically rejected Hyderabad's claim to an independent status. It could not legitimately be expected of the Indian successor government that it should automatically accept a position which its predecessor had rejected for good reason.

Meanwhile in India the public temper had reached a dangerously explosive point in the face of mounting Razakar excesses. The Indian Government decided to act, and on September 13th Indian troops converged on Hyderabad in a three-pronged attack christened Operation Polo. There was little resistance, Razvi himself taking no part in the actual fighting, and on September 17th the state forces laid down their arms and surrendered.

In February, 1949, the nizam entered into an agreement with the Indian Union on the lines of the agreements made with the princes. He was guaranteed all the personal privileges, dignities, and titles enjoyed by him within or outside the territories of the state before August 15, 1947, the day of Indian independence. The nizam was also guaranteed an annual privy purse of Rs. 5,000,000 ($1,000,000) and an additional sum of Rs. 2,500,000 ($500,000) yearly for the upkeep of his palaces besides a further $500,000 to be given annually as compensation for the income which he had lost from the Crown lands, now merged in the state. Generous monetary provision was additionally made for some of his relatives, including his two sons.

The state was placed for a time under a military administration, though the nizam was allowed to continue as head of the state. In January, 1952, Hyderabad participated in India's first general elections, and a popular government headed by a chief minister took office. The nizam, however, continued as rajpramukh, or governor, of the state. As we saw, the office of rajpramukh was abolished in 1956 and the states were reorganized on linguistic lines, Hyderabad passing out of existence with most of its territory shared by the enlarged states of Bombay and Andhra Pradesh, with the city of Hyderabad as the capital of the latter.

In the settlement of the disputes over Hyderabad and Junagadh, Vallabhbhai Patel, in whose homeland of Kathiawar the latter state lay, had been the moving spirit. Kashmir is Nehru's homeland, and although Patel had participated actively in the initial phases his death in 1950 left Nehru masterminding the Kashmir situation. It is doubtful, however, whether events would have taken a different turn in Kashmir had Patel lived a few years more, for on the basic issue he agreed with Nehru. He might, however, have handled particular problems, as they arose, differently.

Kashmir was Hyderabad in reverse, with a Hindu ruler at the head of an overwhelming Moslem population. Much of the blame for the Kashmir tangle and its subsequent, still-recurring repercussions must be laid at the door of its former ruler, Maharaja Hari Singh, a potentate congenitally incapable of making up his mind, weak, indecisive, selfish, and self-centered. In June, 1947, Mountbatten, then governor general of India, visited Kashmir and with the knowledge and consent of Nehru and Vallabhbhai Patel advised the maharaja that he was free to accede to either India or Pakistan, that he should make up his mind before August 15th, and that if he chose to accede to Pakistan this would not be regarded as an unfriendly act by New Delhi. At the same time the maharaja was clearly told that the Indian Government would under no circumstances recognize Kashmir as an independent state.

Hari Singh was unable to make up his mind, and excused himself from seeing Mountbatten again on the plea of illness. On August 14th, a day before partition and the declaration of the independence of India and Pakistan, Hari Singh signed a Standstill

Agreement with Pakistan, hoping to stave off the evil day of decision as long as possible. But events were to catch up with him. India declined his invitation to sign a similar Standstill Agreement, having already made it plain that New Delhi would not encourage the maharaja's dreams of independence.

Meanwhile Pakistan, not surprisingly, made every effort to persuade or propel Kashmir into accession to it. Hari Singh hovered, oblivious to the danger that partition would leave Kashmir suspended in midair with its soft underbelly of Jammu and Poonch exposed to the communal hates of the refugees pouring in from the two divided wings of the Punjab. Pakistan chose this moment to impose an economic blockade on Kashmir, an action curiously like India's vis-à-vis Hyderabad, though the Indian action came nearly a year later. Petrol, sugar, salt, cloth, and other consumer commodities which were urgently needed by Kashmir dwindled to a trickle. Hari Singh was in a quandary. Economically embarrassed, he was also politically threatened. For, having turned his Hindu Dogra troops loose on the Moslems who had rebelled against his authority in Jammu and Poonch, he was faced with an internal uprising. The situation was aggravated by the incursion of Moslem tribal freebooters from the Northwest Frontier who, crossing Pakistan territory with the connivance and active assistance of the Pakistan authorities, descended on Kashmir, looting, destroying, and pillaging as they went.

In this desperate predicament Hari Singh turned to India and appealed for troops to come to Kashmir's aid. Mountbatten was of the opinion that because India had no *locus standi* in the matter, New Delhi could not send troops to Srinagar unless Kashmir acceded to India. Hari Singh did so, and on the morning of October 27th a battalion was flown to Srinagar, arriving there just in time to save the capital. A huge airlift of troops over the tricky mountain defiles between Delhi and Srinagar followed, a feat of logistics which evoked Mountbatten's soldierly admiration. "It left our own SEAF efforts in the war standing," he observed to an aide.

Kashmir was eventually cleared, though not completely. When a cease-fire was announced one minute before midnight on January 1, 1949, the valley of Srinagar was freed of the invader; but Pakistan, which could not deny its complicity in the tribal raids, though it initially attempted to do so, still held an area of five thousand square miles along with Gilgit, northern Ladakh, and Baltistan, with a population of approximately a million people. In the early stages India had appealed to Pakistan not to assist the tribal raiders, but Karachi had ignored these plans, and New Delhi finally decided to refer the issue to the United Nations, which was done on January 1, 1948.

The point to note about this reference to the Security Council is that the Kashmir problem did not arise as a dispute about territory but as a complaint against aggression. The appeal to the United Nations was made under articles 34 and 35 of the Charter, according to which any member may bring any situation whose continuance is likely to endanger international peace and security to the attention of the Council. Some experts hold that India erred technically by invoking these articles, which appear under Chapter 6 of the Charter, entitled "Pacific Settlement of Disputes." In their view the more appropriate section is Chapter 7, which is specifically concerned with "Acts of Aggression." By invoking Chapter 6 India enabled the Council to traverse a wide field, which included charges by Pakistan of genocide against India, instead of pinpointing the issue to Pakistan's aggression against India.

Be that as it may, the issue, once a cease-fire was established, was the holding of a plebiscite. As we have noted, both Nehru and Mountbatten in the course of the Junagadh episode had committed themselves to the principle of a plebiscite where accession was in dispute. This was reiterated in October, 1947, when the maharaja of Kashmir acceded to India. There was no constitutional compulsion to do so, and indeed at the time of the Junagadh dispute the then Pakistan prime minister, the late Liaquat Ali Khan, had insisted that Pakistan had every right to accept the ruler's accession. "After all," he remarked to Nehru, "the ruler has the absolute right to accede without reference to the moral or ethnic aspects of the case." Perhaps at that time, early in October, 1947, the Government of India was more concerned with Hyderabad than with Kashmir. Had it accepted the principle of a ruler's absolute right to accede either to India or to Pakistan, New Delhi could not have objected to the nizam's acceding to the latter. Allowance must also be made for the immaturity of an independent government barely three months old.

Though they committed themselves to the principles of a plebiscite when the maharaja of Kashmir acceded, both Mountbatten and Nehru made the holding of this plebiscite conditional. Mountbatten's letter dated October 27, 1947, to the Kashmir ruler states that acceptance of the accession was provisional and that "as soon as law and order have been restored in Kashmir and her soil cleared of the invader, the question of the accession should be settled by a reference to the people." Nehru in several statements and speeches also reiterated these conditions—the restoration of law and order and the withdrawal of Pakistan from Kashmir territory. It has been argued by successive Indian spokesmen at the United Nations that though law and order have been comparatively restored, Pakistan still occupies a considerable sector of Kashmir territory and that unless it withdraws, a vital condition precedent to a plebiscite remains to be fulfilled. According to India the only absolute fact in the situation is Pakistan's aggression. The only conditional fact is India's promise of a plebiscite.

The plebiscite has still to be held. Despite the earnest efforts of various United Nations representatives, notably Dr. Frank

Graham and Sir Owen Dixon, no settlement has been possible, and as time goes on new factors enter the picture. India's present position appears to be that the situation has congealed on the cease-fire line and that unless the prior conditions are fulfilled the pledge of the plebiscite no longer holds. The maharaja's decision to accede has since been approved by the Kashmir National Conference, whose members support the present state government headed by Bakshi Ghulam Muhammad, as they did the previous administration led by Sheik Abdullah. By the Delhi Agreement of July, 1952, Kashmir enjoys a special relationship with India enabling it to have its own courts, public-service commission, and Urdu as the state language; it also possesses an elected head of the state called Sadar-i-Riyasat, the present head being Yuvraj Karan Singh, son of Maharaja Hari Singh, whose rule was ended in 1952. Kashmir has also its own constitution adopted in November, 1956, and Article 3 of the constitution unequivocally declares that the "State of Jammu and Kashmir is and shall be an integral part of India." When the constitution was implemented on January 26, 1957, both the Kashmir State Government and the Government of India announced that the integration of Kashmir into the Indian Republic was complete.

To have merged the princely states, redrawn the map of India, resettled and rehabilitated some eight million refugees, and restored a sense of unity and consolidation in the country within the space of five years was by any yardstick an impressive achievement. In the same period India drafted its Constitution, held its first general elections, and launched its First Five-Year Plan. In those early years the dedicated zeal of the government and the people carried the country forward at a pace which no one could have visualized when independence came. Beset with dangers and difficulties on many sides, the country battled its way to survival, infused with a grim will to live and to create out of the chaos and confusion of partition a new and better world.

Never has the strong fiber of India's people been shown to more resolute purpose.

No time was lost in devising a Constitution. Two weeks after India became independent, the Constituent Assembly, a body which had come into being in December, 1946, under the plan advanced by the British Cabinet Mission, appointed a drafting committee of seven which included leading lawyers like K. M. Munshi and Alladi Krishnaswami Iyer and gifted administrators such as N. Gopalaswami Ayyangar and T. T. Krishnamachari, who was later to be finance minister at the Center. The well-known leader of the Untouchables, also an eminent jurist, Dr. B. R. Ambedkar, was chairman, with B. N. Rau, later a judge of the International Court of Justice at The Hague, as constitutional adviser.

The Constitution, based primarily on the Government of India Act of 1935 and on Commonwealth models, provided for a democratic secular state guided largely by Western precedents and drawing heavily on those of Britain, the United States, Canada, Australia, and Ireland. Though the first draft was ready within less than six months, the Constituent Assembly devoted a year to discussing it, its labors entailing the examination of nearly 2,500 amendments out of 7,500 tabled. As it finally emerged, the Indian Constitution was an extremely long document containing much which in other countries is to be found in the statutory rather than in the constitutional law. Many, including constitutional lawyers, feel that it might be better were it briefer. During the past decade it has undergone some revisions, the amendments following certain decisions of the Supreme Court which related largely to land reform and other social measures. The Constitution, though federal, has strong centralizing characteristics which have led a British constitutional authority, Professor Kenneth Wheare, to describe it as quasi-federal, providing for "a unitary State with subsidiary federal features rather than a federal State with subsidiary unitary features." It was promulgated on January 26, 1950, when India was proclaimed a republic, being the first republic to be a member of the Commonwealth, and acknowledging the British monarch as head of that organization. This arrangement to enable republican India to continue as a member of the Commonwealth was reached at a Conference of Commonwealth Prime Ministers in London in April, 1949.

Though on the whole the Constitution has worked equably and well, it cannot be said to have always operated in practice on the accustomed lines of a democratic structure of government. The major decisions in India have not been made at the parliamentary level nor by the party in power but by a small group within that party. In the case of the Congress this is the Working Committee, which is dominated, as we have noted, not by the Congress president but by the prime minister, who according to the conventions established over the past twelve years is also politically more potent than India's president, though in theory all the executive power of the Indian Union is vested by the Constitution in the president. On the other hand Nehru and the Congress party are careful to work within the constitutional framework.

There is also a noticeable gap between the enunciation of certain fundamental rights in the Constitution and their practice. Thus, despite Article 17, which prohibits Untouchability, the practice prevails in many parts of the country. India's Supreme Court, which is modeled on the American prototype, has not been as successful in serving as a guardian of the Constitution, though it is undoubtedly the major shield of constitutional government. By amending certain provisos of the Constitution, the executive through Parliament has been able to whittle down the area of judicial jurisdiction. An amendment to Article 31, for instance, prevents the courts from judging what is reasonable compensation for expropriated property, though the very first paragraph of the same article decrees that "no person shall be deprived of his property save by authority of law." No wonder that Namboodiripad and his colleagues are hopeful of working within the Constitution to amend it for their own purposes.

Among the major achievements of the first five years was the holding of the general elections over some four months in 1951–1952. Adult franchise combined with the fact that almost 80 per cent of the electorate is illiterate made it a mammoth undertaking, the procedures of elections and other electoral details being first defined by the Representation of the People Act of 1951. These called for supervision by an election commission with a senior official, Mr. Sukumar Sen, as chief election commissioner. The electoral rolls, carrying over 173 million names of voters, were ready by the end of 1949 but had to be revised in the fall of 1951. Around 900,000 persons were required to supervise the polling, for which 600 million ballot papers, 2,600,000 ballot boxes, 132,500 polling stations, and 196,000 booths were prepared. Delimitation Commissions, with advisory committees, eventually set up 3,772 constituencies, 489 for the House of the People (Lok Sabha) and the remainder for the state assemblies. An elected M.P. roughly represented about 720,000 persons.

For the House of the People there were 1,874 candidates, while another 15,361 contested for the seats in the state assemblies. About 80 million persons, nearly 50 per cent of those on the rolls, voted. Some 85 parties were represented, and about 9,000 candidates forfeited their deposits. The elections went off without any major incident or disturbance; and though it cannot be claimed that every voter exercised his or her right intelligently or independently, the results showed that a largely illiterate electorate could exercise its franchise democratically given the minimum necessary conditions to do so. There was undoubtedly some confusion in the minds of the voters and also in the process of voting. But the over-all impression was distinctly favorable. An additional 20 million voters appeared on the lists for the second general elections in 1956, which went off smoothly.

The first five years of independence also saw the foundations of the Welfare State laid with the appointment of a Planning Commission in March, 1950, and the launching of the First Five-Year Plan in 1951. Four years were to elapse before the Congress party officially adopted the socialistic pattern of society at the Avadi session, but in Nehru's mind that goal was already defined. In a broadcast to the nation announcing and explaining the First Five-Year-Plan, the prime minister declared: "We have to aim deliberately at a social philosophy which seeks a fundamental transformation of this structure, at a society which is not dominated by the urge for private profit and by individual greed and in which there is a fair distribution of political and economic power. We must aim at a classless society, based on cooperative effort, with opportunities for all. To realize this we have to pursue peaceful methods in a democratic way. Democratic planning means the utilization of all our available resources and, in particular, the maximum quantity of labor willingly given and rightly directed so as to promote the good of the community and the individual."

How far India has succeeded in doing this we shall now examine.

VIII
Planning for Progress

In India, Kerala demonstrates that the difference between a revolution by consent and a revolution by coercion can sometimes be thin. Using the democratic process of the ballot box, Kerala's Communists have been able to capture a state administration and to pose as democrats. What can be done on the political plane can also be achieved on the economic. The economic objectives of Nehru and Namboodiripad in so far as both desire to establish a classless society are not markedly different, though the former would do it "in a democratic way" while the latter would not exclude the use of violence. But if Namboodiripad could also achieve his classless society by democratic means, why should he resort to violence?

As the Five-Year plans unroll their programs and patterns, the Communists increasingly and more vociferously come to Nehru's aid. The Nagpur resolution on land reform, with its concomitants of land ceilings, joint cooperatives, and state trading in food grains, provoked murmurs within the Congress party, but the Communists have acclaimed it rapturously. They have good reason for doing so, since in their reckoning Nehru is preparing today for their tomorrow. And as the difference between the Communists and the Congress, which is now committed to Socialism, narrows, the electorate, already confused, will soon be confounded. Not a few of them find it difficult to realize that for a totalitarian to be returned by democratic methods no more makes him a democrat than the possession of a vote by every adult citizen automatically makes a country democratic. With India moving toward the paradise of a classless society, the only difference between the Communists and the congressmen will be one of method.

Nehru stands for planning by persuasion, which is what every democrat in an underdeveloped country would endorse; for in a developing land like India, planning with fixed priorities and on a basis of regulation and coordination is imperative. India's economic problem is twofold—scarcity of capital and abundance of labor. To raise the first and utilize the second fully calls for a degree of governmental enterprise and planning greater than that subsisting in more developed countries. All this India, including its private sector, is prepared to accept and accelerate. But Nehru's increasing intolerance of criticism both by the private sector and his own followers draws him inevitably closer to the Communists and away from the democrats. It would seem as if the only thing he dislikes in the Reds is their resort to violence. Speaking at a function in Bombay in March, 1959, where a Soviet delegation to India was present and while the Indian Government was engaged in seeking Western aid for the Second Five-Year Plan, the prime minister observed: "Any association with Russia should not only be welcomed but eagerly looked forward to for a number of reasons."

When and where will the two systems, now converging toward each other, meet? For India the question is not academic. It is one which increasingly confronts thoughtful Indians disturbed by the growing trend away from democratic thought and practice, the repeated insistence on a "cooperative" society and on extending the cooperative principle from agriculture to industry.

At Nagpur the prime minister declared that the joint cooperatives envisaged by the land-reform resolution would be voluntary. But on a Congress member suggesting that if a majority of farmers in a village wanted joint farming the unwilling minority must be compelled to surrender their lands, Nehru raised no objection in principle to such coercion. All that he said was that this was a detail to be settled later! As in China, are these joint cooperatives to open the way to collectivization and communes? If the Communists succeed the Congress, they most assuredly will.

In themselves the two Five-Year plans which India has successively and on the whole successfully undertaken do represent planned economic development through democratic means. Their implementation, however, has called for sacrifices which rightly affect the more affluent sections of society; but in mulcting these sections and dunning private enterprise the Congress party, which has no qualms about accepting large contributions from these sources for its exchequer, has mounted a growingly virulent offensive against them which in some phases is indistinguishable from a witch hunt. It must be admitted that the overwhelming majority of Indian businessmen are not oppressed by notions of rectitude, and are often speculators on a large scale. But members of the Congress new class are themselves not exactly paragons of virtue. Congressmen in the Union Parliament while adjuring the country, particularly the private sector, to draw in its belt more tightly have not hesitated to increase their own parliamentary emoluments.

This difference between precept and practice, as exemplified by the Congress new class, has increasingly alienated that party from the people. The danger is that while the "have-nots" move progressively to the left, the "haves" are moving more to the right, leaving a chasm in which the Congress may easily founder. But the elimination of the Congress or a center party from the political scene would leave the country dangerously exposed to the Communists. In attempting to reform the country the Congress must reform itself. This is the only way out of the impasse.

Compared by Western standards, India's planning is on a modest scale. This is not surprising for a country whose annual revenue is less than that of General Motors or the budget of the City of New York. Even the 14.4 billion dollars earmarked for the Second Five-Year Plan represent, as Nehru graphically put it, "just eighty days' military expenditure of a great power." The prime minister pointed out: "This is in peacetime. In war it would be much more."

On the First Plan, which extended from April 1, 1951, to April 1, 1956, the government and private enterprise each expended just under Rs. 2,000 crores (approximately $4 billion) making a total outlay of $8 billion on the development program. Of the total amount about 90 per cent was met by India, the remainder being raised by foreign aid. The stress in the First Plan was on agriculture, and around 46 per cent of the public investment was reserved for increasing agricultural output and extending the country's irrigation and power projects.

The results, thanks to a fortuitous succession of good monsoons, were encouraging. While food-grain production went up by 20 per cent, national income over the five-year period increased by some 18 per cent. Through irrigation and land reclamation the area under crops was increased by 26 million new acres. Electric power output rose from 6,575 million kilowatts in 1950–1951 to 11,000 million kilowatts in 1955–1956. The production of cement over the same period was nearly doubled. Even allowing for a population growth of 5 million a year, this meant a gratifying all-round improvement, the per capita income rising over the five years from $53 to $56 per annum. At this rate it should take another four Five-Year plans to reach the per capita target of $100 a year.

An important feature of the First Plan was a dynamic rural

development and extension program which brought nearly one-fourth of rural India into its vitalizing range. This was the program for community development initiated on October 2, 1952, Gandhi's birthday, when fifty-five of these projects were launched. It represents an attempt in rural self-help covering many spheres of village life, including the building of local roads, embankments, schools and hospitals, reclamation of virgin and waste lands, helping the grow-more-food campaign and encouraging public health, education, and literacy. Sustained by liberal American funds, chiefly from the Ford Foundation, the community development projects have grown rapidly and on the whole encouragingly, depending in large measure on the quality of local leadership, enthusiasm, and perseverance. By the end of the First Plan, development schemes covered some 123,000 villages with a total population of 80 million.

The success of this program led to a supplementary undertaking known as the National Extension Service, aimed at creating a permanent organization for rural development which is linked with the administrative setup. Each service unit represents about 100 villages, and during the First Plan 1,200 such blocks were created, comprising 120,000 villages out of India's 550,000 villages. Of these blocks around 300 were taken under the intensive community program and 900 under the N.E.S. They have done much to bring the means and knowledge for self-help in agriculture, sanitation, public health, and literacy to the vast, illiterate rural masses of India. Here, more than anywhere, are the roots of Nehru's welfare State.

By the summer of 1955, chiefly under the direction of Dr. Frank Laubach, the celebrated American expert on literacy programs, over 14,400 adult education centers had been started, along with nearly 6,000 new schools, while another 1,600 old schools were given over to basic and craft training. As a result six million more children attended primary schools, while high-school and college education were also adapted to India's new needs.

A start was made with organizing health services, a concentrated drive being launched on the scourge of malaria which at one time annually afflicted 100,000,000 victims. Until 1951 a million died every year directly of the disease, while another million died indirectly. The initial emphasis was on prevention rather than on cure, and with the help of DDT, supplied by American Point Four, the incidence of the disease was gradually lowered. In 1955 the figure had been reduced from an annual average of 100 million cases to 25 million.

Alongside these activities was a program for reclamation of forest and waste land, over 400,000 acres being reclaimed by June, 1955, while another 155,000 acres were cultivated with fruit and vegetables. In the same period the villagers helped to construct about 12,000 miles of road and 600 miles of essential drains. By and large, distinct advances have been registered on many fronts "in terms of provision of basic amenities needed by the people—education, health and sanitation, water supplies, communications," as an evaluation report, made under the directions of the Planning Commission on the working of the Community Projects and N.E.S. blocks, testifies.

The problem of landless laborers has been acute almost from time immemorial, and land reform, beginning with the abolition of large estates, was adopted as a Congress policy at the Karachi session of 1931. Two years before that, at Nehru's persuasion, the United Provinces Provincial Congress Committee had declared that the existing land system should go and that the big landowners, known variously as zamindars or taluqdars, should be replaced by peasant proprietors. Around 1948 the Communists who had incited a peasant rebellion in Telingana raised the cry of "Land to the Tiller." Nehru's government found in the Fundamental Rights embodied in the Constitution, which guaranteed the right to property, an obstacle to its proposed land reform. It accordingly amended the Constitution, altering the procedure of compensation in case of acquisition but assuring the landlord of a fair compensation and also guaranteeing that no landlord would be deprived of his property except by process of law and on grounds of public interest. Since the responsibility for implementing land reform rests on the state governments, not all of whom are enthusiastic about it, progress has been slow, though the old system of zamindari landlordism whereby hereditary tax collectors for the British Government in time assumed ownership of the land itself has been abolished. But compensation had to be paid to them.

Congress agrarian legislation in some respects created more problems than it set out to solve. The problem was not erased but fragmented. One result, for instance, of the abolition of the zamindari system was the formation of smaller vested interests whereby cooperative societies became the handmaid of the propertied rural classes, who, being economically and politically stronger than the small peasant proprietors, established a corner in seeds, fertilizers, pumps, and other farming equipment. Nor were the land reforms followed by social or institutional changes designed to prop up the weak peasantry. The increase of population raised both the demand for and pressure on land. Kerala has nearly a thousand persons per square mile, while West Bengal has over eight hundred. Three-fourths of India's people subsist on the land, but Indian yields per acre are still among the lowest in the world—about one-third of those of Japan or China. When independence came, the landless laborers, drawn largely from the Untouchables, totaled some 48 millions, larger than the entire population of France.

The need for land reform is therefore vitally urgent. What form it takes is also vitally important, for once the pattern is set it will be difficult to break the mold. Communist support for the Nagpur land-reform resolution, as for most of Nehru's economic policies, is forthcoming because these tend to take the country forward on lines which favor the Reds and which set a pattern today which the Reds will find it comparatively easy to complete tomorrow. Just as the Communists have attempted to infiltrate into Vinoba Bhave's *bhoodan yagna* movement, they will certainly try to enter the lower cadres of the farming cooperatives, which will need a vast army of minor officials and functionaries to administer them. "The people's suzerainty is more important than judicial suzerainty," was a dictum Namboodiripad laid down recently while rejecting a judicial finding on the Kerala Government's rice deal with Andhra.* No doubt after infiltrating into the lower cadres of the joint cooperatives, the Communists will bend their energies to turn them into instruments of "the people's suzerainty." The Socialists, as we saw, inadvertently paved the way for the Communists in Kerala. Now it is the turn of Congress to precipitate the same situation—but on an all-India scale reaching deep down to the rural roots of the country.

In themselves the proposals embodied in the Nagpur resolution read innocuously. There is to be a ceiling on landholdings, state trading in food grains, and the establishment of service cooperatives over a period of three years with the ultimate intention of converting them into "voluntary" farming cooperatives. There is to be no compulsion, declared Nehru at Nagpur, though simultaneously, as we noted, he countered a suggestion that coercion should be applied by the plea that it was "a detail to be settled later." On February 19, 1959, the prime minister, addressing the Lok Sabha (House of the People) in Delhi, assured it that no legislation for joint farming would be introduced. On the following day the chief minister of the Bombay Congress, Y. B. Chavan, told a meeting of the Bombay Pradesh (State) Congress Executive that the state government would bring forward legislation on cooperative farming during the monsoon session of the legisla-

* See Chapter VI.

ture. As a prominent critic of the Congress inquired, "Whom is one to believe?"

The principle of land ceilings for the rural masses raises several questions which still remain to be answered convincingly by the Congress. If there is to be a ceiling on landholdings why not a ceiling on urban incomes? Nehru's reply is that a ceiling on urban incomes is not for the moment practicable (which is right), and in any case the rural ceilings planned to be imposed are on land, not on agricultural, incomes. But this is begging the question, since the quantum of land regulates the amount of income. The method also looks suspiciously like an attempt to squeeze surplus value out of the peasants, and industrialize the country on the proceeds. In some respects the Planning Commission seeks to out-Herod Herod. Some time ago the Andhra State Government tried to fix the ceiling on agricultural income at Rs. 5,200 (a little over $1,000) a year, but the Planning Commission objected on the ground that it was too high, and insisted on a ceiling of Rs. 3,600 ($720) per annum, that is, Rs. 300 ($60) per month for a family of five. This is the yardstick adopted by the Congress to regulate land ceilings. The incentive to the farmer to produce more is thereby lowered, and must affect the country's food output. It must also, by making it difficult for the peasant to maintain a viable standard, force him into the "voluntary" joint cooperatives.

In the long run, as experience demonstrates, state trading in food grains, even if it eliminates the middleman, benefits neither the producer, who gets less, nor the consumer, who often has to pay more. The state, being the monopolist, can regulate both supply and demand, and, following the example of Communist countries such as Russia and China, accelerate economic development by increasing production but forcibly holding down consumption. Thereby the surplus available for investment continuously increases. Though displacement of the middleman must drive many small traders out of business, it simultaneously increases the growing army of petty officials who will be required to administer state trading. Whether these functionaries can deal with the intricacies of business as swiftly and efficiently as those in the trade is doubtful. Lack of official storage facilities spells another form of wastage. The remedy, apart from being worse than the disease, could also prove lethal.

In a vast country such as India, where 70 per cent of the population depend for their livelihood on agriculture, where five out of every six live in villages, and where the farmer is indigent and often ignorant, institutions such as service cooperatives and multipurpose cooperative societies meet a real need. But joint or cooperative farming, whether voluntary or enforced, is a back-door method of introducing collectivization, for the peasant would have no property rights left when the boundaries of his farm were demolished. In Bombay and southern India, where the ryots have owned and tilled their lands from ancient days, attempts to enforce joint farming might be seriously resisted, leading to class conflict. In Nehru's home province of Uttar Pradesh the zamindari system has only recently been abolished and peasant proprietorship is a new phenomenon. Joint farming might be more easily implemented there. But the sense of ownership, even if new, is nonetheless always strong, and the seeds of class conflict could find as fertile soil in Uttar Pradesh as in Bombay and the South.

The net result of the agrarian policy of Congress will be to reduce food production, increase unemployment on the land, and take the class war to the villages. Alongside the new despotism of the army of rural bureaucrats there will come into being a new depressed class in the villages. They will be the joint creation of the Congress new class to whom a critic recently recalled Gandhi's well-known dictum that people in the cities would offer to do everything for the peasants "except get off their backs." The failure of collective farming in Soviet Russia and its revision in Poland and Yugoslavia carry a lesson for India. But the Congress Bourbons are evidently determined to learn nothing and to forget nothing. Both the prime minister and the president of the Congress, who is his daughter, have invited those congressmen who do not agree with the Nagpur resolution to leave the party. At least one prominent congressman, Professor N. G. Ranga, a member of the Lok Sabha and secretary to the Congress Parliamentary party, who is opposed to the Nagpur resolution, has resigned his post. Others, known to be equally hostile, have preferred to be silent. "I have a firm belief in the rightness of joint cultivation," Nehru told the Lok Sabha. "I shall go from field to field and peasant to peasant begging them to agree to it." Since the fields run into thousands and the peasants into millions, this will be a Herculean job. It is more likely that the "persuaders" will be less exalted and more forceful.

A dramatic type of land reform which has attracted the attention not only of India but of many countries is Vinoba Bhave's *bhoodan yagna* (land-gift sacrifice) movement described by Acharya J. B. Kripalani as "the greatest revolution since Gandhiji." Some describe Bhave as the only genuine Gandhite in India today. There are others, but no one symbolizes more vividly or faithfully the moral force of Gandhi, and in a sense even the Mahatma's personality and language. Lean, stringy, and ascetic, with a gift for phrase and telling analogy—reminiscent of Gandhi—Vinoba Bhave has a face which has been compared to that of Rodin's John the Baptist. He is frail but seemingly tireless, a small brown bundle of volcanic energy, with expressive eyes which can be luminous or stony, and the straggly, wispy beard of a prophet.

Vinoba Bhave's economic thinking, like Gandhi's, is elementary but fundamental. He attaches supreme value to the act of giving. When an old peasant woman told him that she had six acres of land and five sons and asked if he would become the sixth son and accept one acre, Vinoba replied: "Yes. Your one acre is as good as 100,00 acres in my eyes. It is a blessing of a mother to my humble mission."

The mission of bhoodan asks for the voluntary surrender of land from those who have for the benefit of those who haven't. Vinoba's mission was inspired by the pleas of a group of landless laborers, who were also Harijans, who begged of him for some land for cultivation. They wanted eighty acres. On that April morning in 1951 he was in a village in the course of one of his frequent walking tours, and surrounding him were the villagers, peasants and landlords.

Vinoba addressed them. "Brothers," he asked, "are there any among you who will give land to your brothers so that they may not die of starvation? They need only eighty acres."

One man stepped forward. "I will give a hundred acres," he said. It was the beginning of the bhoodan movement.

Since then Vinoba has roved India's countryside asking for the voluntary renunciation of land. He set his target at 50 million acres, and though over the years he has managed to collect only some 5 million acres his movement has lit a moral fire and loosed a fervor for nonpolitical constructive work which has drawn among others the former American-educated Socialist leader Jayaprakash Narayan.

Vinoba talks the language which Gandhi did, and his thoughts are in the Mahatmic mold. He regards money as an unstable commodity and prefers barter and labor: "I know that money, like God, is everywhere, and it is not easy to eliminate it from life. The currency that I want is labor, a currency the villagers have always used among themselves." He looks at the Five-Year plans much as Gandhi would have. There could be, he told the Planning Commission, no national self-respect unless the country was self-sufficient in food. What was the use of planning without ensuring full employment? The river-valley projects were all very well, but first things should come first. What the villagers needed is wells, and the commission should set about "digging thousands of wells in all parts of the country." It is how Gandhi would have talked and thought.

Of the five million acres he has received from some half-million donors, Vinoba has distributed some 500,000 acres. Much of the land he has received is of poor fertility and often not cultivable, consisting of grazing tracts and forests. The distribution is village-wise, and the villagers, on the basis of serving the neediest first, determine the order of priority, each family normally getting five acres. If there is not enough to go round, lots are drawn. A family holds the land in trusteeship and it cannot be sold, mortgaged, rented, or left fallow. If it is uncultivated it goes back into the common pool.

Though the government enters the picture as keeper of records, the work of distribution and administration of bhoodan land is carried out by voluntary workers who are not always numerically sufficient and sometimes inefficient through lack of experience. The economic value of bhoodan is therefore problematical, and the economic results have been disappointing. Only a small proportion of the land collected has been distributed, and much of it is hard to cultivate. But the moral fervor it has generated has been considerable, and some of Vinoba's utterances suggest that he lays more store by this: "The seers of old and the Gita counseled three things: Sacrifice, Charity, and Austerity. Of these, through bhoodan, I called for two—sacrifice and charity. But unless we insist on austerity the other two will not be fulfilled. It is for the workers to adopt austerity." And again: "I believe that the true good of one cannot clash with the true good of another. Nor can the good of one country go counter to that of another. I do not merely want people's land. I want also to win their hearts."

This is in line with the Gandhian tradition of thought, of

sarvodaya which enshrines the spirit of selfless service, voluntary and constructive, dedicated to work in a classless and castless society—not classless in the Marxist sense of the term but as typifying a society where prince and peasant, landlord, capitalist, farmer, and worker join in united labor for the benefit of all. Out of bhoodan have grown other movements such as *sampattidan* (gift of wealth), *koopdan* (gift of wells), *shramdan* (gift of voluntary labor), *jivandan* (gift of one's life, that is, personal service to a cause), and *baildan* (gift of bullocks)—all these tapering pyramid-wise to the apex of *gramdan* (gift of villages), representing communal ownership of village land and the establishment of Gandhi's concept of village democracy. These ideas have taken root in rural India, where they thrive in various degrees, nurtured for the most part by dedicated apostles of Gandhism who remain apart from the Congress new class. Off and on, some from the new class take part in these movements, but more often than not as a political flourish, with the apparatus of publicity aiding and abetting their activities.

Koraput, an aboriginal district in Orissa, is the heart of the *gramdan* movement where nearly 1,500 *gramdans*, or communal villages, have come into being, with the land owned by the village and each villager functioning as a trustee. The village land is donated wholesale, but after the gift is made the local council decides how much land each villager will retain for his individual and domestic upkeep, and in this division both the landlords and peasants participate. Whether the land will be cultivated on the principle of private trusteeship or on collective or cooperative lines is left to the villagers to decide. It is significant in view of the congressional Nagpur resolution on cooperative farming that the majority of villages and villagers, left to their own choice on the manner of implementing *gramdan*, have overwhelmingly plumped for private trusteeship.

Following the First Five-Year Plan, which was completed in

April, 1956, India embarked on a Second Five-Year Plan, extending from 1956 to 1961, and is now engaged on blueprints for a Third Plan. As we saw, the stress in the First Plan was on agricultural development and the extension of the country's irrigation and power projects. This was necessary since with the partition of India nearly half of all the irrigated lands of undivided India went to Pakistan, and at the time when the First Plan was initiated only a little more than one-sixth of the total farm land was irrigated. When the irrigation projects of the Second Plan are completed, it is estimated that more land will be under irrigation than in all of India's previous millenniums of history. The Second Plan aims at putting 21 million more acres under irrigation, besides increasing agricultural production by 28 per cent and food-grains production by 25 per cent. By 1961 it is hoped to have all of rural India, comprising some 325 million villagers, covered by the rural development program.

The great multipurpose river-valley projects such as Bhakra-Nangal, which will cover Punjab and Rajasthan; the Damodar Valley scheme which will benefit Bihar and Bengal; and the Hirakud project in Orissa, were conceived and planned even before independence by the British Government, as were also several state projects. Many of these are being executed with foreign aid and under foreign supervision. The largest of them, Bhakra-Nangal, which will be completed around 1960, has over forty American technicians supervising its construction, including Harvey Slocum and G. L. Savage, who have built some of America's greatest dams. Bhakra-Nangal has the highest-powered concrete gravity dam in the world, and on completion will irrigate some 3.6 million acres in Rajasthan and the Punjab through a 3,000-mile canal system. It is estimated to cost Rs. 160 crores ($320 million). A project which has attracted wide attention is the Kosi scheme designed to tame the wayward Kosi, "the River of Sorrows," from which Nepal, where a barrage will be constructed, and Bihar stand to benefit. Nepal is cooperating with India in this work. Other important irrigation and power projects are the Chambal, affecting Rajasthan and Madhya Pradesh; the Lower Bhavani in Madras; and Nagarjunasagar in Andhra.

What briefly are the aims of the Second Plan? Its stress is on the heavy and basic industries, particularly steel production and the fabrication of steel into producer goods, to which many feel the First Plan should have paid more attention. The Second Plan entails an over-all expenditure of $14.4 billion, of which the states and the Central Government will spend about $10 billion, over twice what they expended for the First Plan, with an additional $4.8 billion expected to be invested by private enterprise in industry, agriculture, and other development. The Plan aims at an 18 per cent rise in per capita income, which means a rise from $56 a year in 1956 to $66 in 1961. A 21 per cent increase in consumer goods is provided for, while primary schools for nearly eight million more children, some two million more homes, 12,500 additional doctors, and around 3,000 more rural health clinics are planned. Thereby increased national production and income will make it possible to save larger amounts for investment in national development, while at the same time living standards will rise. If this matures, 11 per cent of national income at the end of the Second Plan, as against about 7 per cent at the end of the First Plan, will be invested in productive output.

In order to achieve this goal, apart from the development of agriculture and irrigation, which we have noted, the Second Plan concentrates on the rapid development of industry, power, and transport, visualizing a 64 per cent increase in net industrial production. Intensive development of basic industries with a 150 per cent rise in capital goods production alone is envisaged, while three new steel plants at Rourkela, Bhilai, and Durgapur (established respectively with German, Russian, and British aid), representing 231 per cent more steel production, including doubled private steel capacity, figure prominently in the scheme. There will be a 100 per cent increase in electric power production and a 58 per cent growth in coal output. The railways are to be modernized and improved so as to carry at least 35 per cent more freight and 15 per cent more passenger traffic, while transport will be expanded with 19,000 more miles of surfaced roads, and ports, harbors, and shipping will be enlarged.

Broadly the Second Plan sets out to achieve four objectives by 1961. These are: (1) a 25 per cent increase of national income so as to raise the low living standards; (2) rapid industrialization, particularly the development of basic industries; (3) a large expansion in employment opportunities; and (4) reduction in inequalities in income and wealth, promoting thereby an increasing measure of economic and social justice for all groups. It will need many more Plans before India moves, in Nehru's phrase, from "the cow-dung stage" to the age of atomic energy, the pace of growth depending on how fast India can produce more—more of goods, services, machines, and food. According to present calculations it is hoped to double the production achieved by the Second Plan in fifteen years, that is, by 1971, and to raise it by 2½ times within twenty years.

But these calculations depend on a number of hypotheses being fulfilled. India lives in its villages, and the first priority is the development of agriculture and the lifting of living standards for the rural masses. Economically the country has still to cross the threshold which divides an underdeveloped from a developed land. Such is the nature of its economy that in planning higher production a balance has to be struck between large and small industries, between heavy industrialization, without which progress cannot be accelerated, and the ancient small and hand industries without which the vast reservoir of manpower cannot be absorbed and social stability ensured. Even in the United States one-fourth of production and employment depends on small industries, while the proportion for Japan from the same source is over one-half of its national production and around two-thirds of its employment. In India, as elsewhere, the fostering of small and hand industries is a vital part of balanced industrial growth. So low is the peak of production that it will be dangerous, if not disastrous, to lower it further—which is the threat that the joint farming visualized by the Nagpur resolution poses. The obvious solution is to develop India's industrial or semi-industrial potential, thereby relieving pressure on the land—one reason why the Indian Government's insistence on heavy industrialization in the Second Plan is justifiable. Along with this, in order to preserve a balanced economic structure, the Second Plan provides for intensive development of village and small-scale industries so as to increase their production by 30 per cent.

What the Indian Government aims at is a mixed economy combining the three elements of public enterprise, private enterprise, and in-between cooperative enterprise on the lines of Scandinavian countries such as Sweden. In this type of mixed economy the balance must inevitably be tilted in favor of the government, with the area of the private sector progressively shrinking. Although the private sector is estimated to spend some $4.8 billion during the Second Plan, which is 50 per cent more than over the First Plan, its proportionate share vis-à-vis the public sector has shrunk from 50 per cent in the First Plan to around 33⅓ per cent in the Second. The likelihood is that as the Plans develop, the private sector's share will progressively decrease, which appears to be the trend, judging from the mounting attacks leveled by Nehru and many congressmen on big business. The nationalization of life insurance in 1956 placed an amount aggregating some Rs. 306 crores ($612 million) in the hands of the government while simultaneously and arbitrarily depriving private enterprise of this windfall in premiums and assets. It is noteworthy that in a resolution sponsored by the All-India Congress Committee, expansion of life insurance, presumably as a compulsory levy, is mentioned as one of the ways of raising resources for the Third Plan. Steel seems likely to be nationalized, and cement as well. For all practical purposes the airways are nationalized. Rabindranath Tagore once compared India to a house with the upper floor occupied by the affluent and educated and the lower by the indigent and illiterate, with no stairway between. Nehru is attempting to build the stairway. But sometimes the manner in which he sets about it suggests that simultaneously he might bring down the roof.

There remain the two urgent problems of population and unemployment, the one linked with the other and each faced with the prospect of the rising graph of population on the one hand, with no immediate likelihood of a soaring graph of production and employment on the other. India's population, which is increasing at the rate of five million a year, constitutes an oppressively major problem. When independence came in 1947, neither industry nor agriculture was creating enough new jobs to relieve unemployment, the number of workers employed by manufacturing industries totaling under 2,500,000. Pressure on the land, far from being relieved, was increased, and in its wake came growing fragmentation, unemployment, and economic distress. Urban employment even today accounts for only a little over 5 per cent of workers, which means considerable unemployment and underemployment in villages and towns. During the First Plan the then finance minister, C. D. Deshmukh, placed the number of fully unemployed people at 15,000,000, though some reckon the total of those unemployed and underemployed at nearly 40,000,000. Allowing for the annual growth of population, some 2,000,000 more a year, or 10,000,000 over the period of the Second Plan, at a conservative estimate, will have to seek employment. Add to this the possibility of increased automation in the new large-scale industries, which will absorb less and less workers, and the menacing dimensions of the problem are appreciated.

The solution is obviously twofold—to increase production and control population. What is being done about the latter? As living conditions improve, along with better sanitation and health, the population graph tends to rise faster, and at the present rate of 5 million more a year India's population by 1976 should total around 500 million. What the country needs is not any Western form of family planning but one more adapted to its circumstances and needs, commensurate with low economic standards and widespread ignorance and illiteracy. Such a method will have to be cheap and easily understood, being preferably oral, with the minimum of mechanical or chemical devices. The Indian Government earmarked funds for family planning during the First and Second Five-Year-Plan periods and is likely to increase the allotments as the Plans progress. Unfortunately even the modest allocations made were for various reasons—including the disinclination of some states to encourage family planning—not fully utilized. Of the Rs. 6,500,000 ($1,300,000) set aside for this purpose in the First Plan period, more than half was unused. It is feared that in the Second Plan period the greater part of the allotted sum of Rs. 40,000,000 ($8,000,000) will similarly remain unutilized. Although the Family Planning Association of India has many enterprising workers, its record of results is by no means impressive. Surveys reveal a widespread desire, particularly in the rural areas, for some form of cheap contraceptive; but until now this has not been forthcoming, and the apathy of state governments, along with the ignorance and poverty of the masses, retards progress. There is undoubtedly some resistance to family planning from conservative Hindus and Moslems, as well as from Catholics, but the sheer logic of economic realities combined with greater official enthusiasm should prevail.

Owing to lack of finances and other developments, such as the closing of the Suez Canal in 1956 and a serious drought in 1957, the Second Plan has run into difficulties and has had to scale down its targets, though the hard core has been preserved. How it will finally emerge depends on factors some of which are incalculable and others adventitious. The Suez crisis, which inflated the costs of imported commodities, led the Indian Government in October, 1957, to authorize the withdrawal of its sterling assets in London, totaling $630 million, which represented about eight months' imports into India. Similarly the drought compelled India to import more food than planned, raising the Plan costs by 20 per cent. The total foreign-exchange requirements of the Second Plan were originally at least Rs. 1,700 crores ($3.5 billion), this sum covering both government and private development programs, and it was hoped to raise the amount by foreign aid and loans from organizations such as the World Bank. Not all these hopes have fructified. During the First Plan the United States provided around $300 million in aid plus a special wheat loan of $190 million and World Bank loans totaling about $30 million. To help finance the Second Plan the United States in March, 1958, agreed to lend India $225 million, and of this amount $150 million was to be made available by the Export-Import Bank, the balance of $75 million coming from the Development Loan Fund. But if India was "to save" the Plan, it needed, according to its finance minister who visited the United States late in 1957, immediate foreign credit totaling $600 million. This was not forthcoming, and in May, 1958, the Indian Government announced that the Second Plan would have to be cut down by perhaps as much as 15 per cent. For the remaining three years, until 1961, India needed $1.4 billion from foreign sources in order to salvage the Plan. Allowing for the loan of $225 million in March, the possible conversion to rupees of the 1952 wheat loan and additional aid from American and non-American channels, there still remained a gap of $900 million. In February, 1959,

India's Commissioner General for Economic Affairs put his country's requirements for the last two years of the Second Plan at $700 million. How much of this will be forthcoming is uncertain at the moment of writing,* but at the Washington discussions held under the auspices of the World Bank in March, 1959, American, British, German, and Japanese spokesmen, representing the five main "creditor" nations, indicated their countries' willingness to help. What the total quantum of such aid will be has still to be determined, though India is hopeful that it will be sufficient to enable the scaled-down Second Plan to achieve its 1961 targets.

Is a Marshall Plan of funds and food not possible for the economic development and political stability of Asian countries such as India, financed by Western Europe, North America, and the more advanced countries of the Commonwealth? The group of nations round the North Atlantic Ocean has been dubbed "the privileged aristocracy of world society," comprising some 16 per cent of the world's population and enjoying some 70 per cent of its annual income.† Owing to lack of trained manpower, the countries of Asia could absorb no more than three billion dollars of new capital per year, which is less than 1 per cent of the United States national income. According to Barbara Ward, the noted British economist, aid at the rate of one or two billion dollars a year over the next fifty years would salvage and preserve for democracy and freedom the majority of mankind who live there. Enlightened self-interest, at the very least, should induce this gesture.

Work has already begun on devising India's Third Plan. Though nothing has been made final, Nehru has indicated that the basic effort would be to provide for the maintenance of the

* April, 1959.

† Barbara Ward, *The Interplay of East and West* (London, George Allen & Unwin, 1957).

existing standard of living for the population, taking into account the steady increase in numbers, which was rising at the rate of around 1.9 per cent annually, and also allowing for some improvement in living standards. As the prime minister has often emphasized, one-year or five-year planning periods do not constitute arbitrary yardsticks. They must be rounded off by "perspective planning" that sees the goal far ahead toward horizons stretching out over ten or even twenty years. Various figures for the Third Plan expenditure have been mentioned, from Rs. 13,000 crores ($26 billion) and even a minimum outlay of Rs. 6,000 crores ($12 billion), the latter being a Socialist estimate. During the Third Plan period some Rs. 60 crores ($120 million) will have to be provided annually as interest on foreign debts, while another Rs. 420 crores ($840 million) will have to be repaid. Where is the money to come from? Here again various suggestions have been put forward, including heavier and wider taxation, an increase of the share of the rural sector in the total tax revenues, deficit financing, the scrapping of prohibition, which is estimated to cost the country about Rs. 30 crores (roughly $60 million) a year, pruning down of civil and military expenditure, the imposition of a salt tax which should annually bring in Rs. 15 crores ($30 million), more stringent collection of income tax where evasion loses the exchequer Rs. 200 crores ($400 million), and other expedients. But even allowing for these measures, a considerable sum, probably in the neighborhood of Rs. 2,500 crores ($5 billion) will have to come from foreign sources. Considering the low per capita income and the large annual increase in food consumption in a country where less than 20 per cent of the cultivable land is under irrigation and the remainder at the mercy of the monsoons, it may be necessary to tailor and streamline the Third Plan to more modest dimensions.

On the other hand India, with its rapidly rising population, cannot stand still economically. It must move—and move forward. It is rich in natural resources, particularly in iron, manganese, bauxite, coal, titanium, mica, and thorium ores. Its rivers are magnificently capable of being harnessed for hydro-electric purposes. It was left two valuable economic legacies by the British—an extensive railway system and the industrial triangle of Bengal-Bihar-Orissa. The key to progress is production—and more production; and the economic fate of India may well be determined in the crucial decade covering the Second and Third plans.

IX
Foreign Policy

THE Tibetan uprising against the Chinese in March, 1959, high-lighted the overtones and undertones of India's policy of nonalignment, and aroused sharp criticism of Nehru's mildly middle-of-the-road attitude toward Peking. This criticism was expressed at home and abroad. As on Hungary, Nehru's later statements were less equivocal. Clearly he did not want India to be dragged into the cold war on this issue. Expatiating on the difficulties of his position at a press conference shortly after the Dalai Lama had crossed the Indo-Tibetan frontier on March 31st, the Indian prime minister explained that he was faced with the problem of balancing and adjusting the three major factors involved. These were first and foremost the security of India; second, the desire to have friendly relations with China; and third, "our strong feelings about Tibet."

Elaborating on the last, Nehru explained that India as the land of the Buddha, "the greatest Indian who ever lived," had a special attachment to Buddhist Tibet which "affects some deeper chords in our hearts." He spoke of "this tremendous bond," and went on to say: "We do not want Tibet economically or socially to be backward. We want it to progress." The position which China occupied vis-à-vis Tibet, he explained, was that of a suzerain authority, not a sovereign, and suzerainty was "obviously less than sovereignty."

Tibet's autonomy had been recognized by the former British Government in India and, according to Nehru, also by Chou Enlai, who had assured him of this when the Chinese prime minister visited India in 1956. When Nehru himself went to Peking in 1954, Mao Tse-tung had assured the Dalai Lama in the presence of the Indian prime minister that Tibet would enjoy autonomy which "no other Chinese province enjoyed in the People's Republic of China." This assurance had earlier been incorporated as a major article in the Sino-Tibetan agreement of May, 1951, whereunder Tibet was guaranteed full regional autonomy and the Chinese Government undertook not to "interfere with Tibet's political institutions and internal administration." Though under this agreement Tibet returned to Chinese authority, Peking promised that there would be no change in the religious structure or the position and authority of the Dalai Lama, who is both the spiritual and the secular head. In return for China's control of foreign relations and defense, Peking recognized Lhasa's right to control its political and internal affairs.

In a sense the Communist Chinese claim that Tibet is a part of China is as much a legacy from the Manchus and the Kuomintang as the Indian Government's plea that while China is the suzerain authority Tibet is an autonomous area derives from the former British Government in India. At the first Asian Relations Conference in March, 1947, the Indian sponsors in New Delhi had put up a huge map of Asia in the auditorium showing the boundaries of Tibet clearly demarcated from China. The then Kuomintang representative had protested vigorously, declaring that Tibet was a part of China, and in order not to ruffle his susceptibilities the Sino-Tibetan borders as shown in the map were actually erased. The Chinese, it is true, have always claimed sovereign rights in Tibet, but from the fall of the Manchus in

1911 until the Sino-Tibetan agreement in 1951 the Tibetans enjoyed *de facto* autonomy, the Chinese Government being unable in this period to exercise even suzerain rights. During the last war Tibet opened its own Foreign Affairs Bureau, and Lhasa did not "throw in her forces on the side of China," thus "asserting and maintaining her complete independence."

Shortly after assuming power in October, 1949, the Communists in Peking invited the Tibetans early in 1950 to "accede peacefully," backing up this "peaceful" plea by stationing an army not far from Chamdo in eastern Tibet. The Tibetans thereupon sent abroad a seven-man mission which arrived in India; but it was refused permission by the British authorities to proceed to Hong Kong, since both Britain and India had recognized Peking. The Tibetan mission accordingly stayed on in India; and in the second week of September, with the Indian Government's permission, it got in touch with the first Communist Chinese ambassador to New Delhi, but the talks ended inconclusively on October 1st. At the suggestion of the Indian Government, the Tibetans subsequently agreed to proceed to Peking to negotiate directly with the Communist Government; but on October 25th, the day the mission was to have set out for China, Peking sent its troops into Tibet. This was done, according to the New China News Agency, to "liberate three million Tibetans from imperialist aggression, to complete the unification of the whole of China, and to safeguard the frontier regions of the country." On October 27th New Delhi announced that a note had been sent to the Chinese Government on the previous day expressing "surprise and regret" at the invasion of Tibet and deploring the fact that Peking should have sought a solution of its problems by "force instead of by the slower and more enduring methods of peaceful approach." The Chinese Government in its reply dated October 30th in effect told the Indian Government to mind its own business. It declared that Tibet was "an integral part of Chinese territory" and that the matter was "entirely a domestic problem of China and no foreign interference will be tolerated." The Chinese note also asserted: "The Chinese People's Liberation Army must enter Tibet, liberate the Tibetan people and defend the frontiers of China. . . . With regard to the viewpoint of the Government of India on what it regards as deplorable, the Central People's Government cannot but consider it as having been affected by foreign influences hostile to China in Tibet."

New Delhi spiritedly rebutted these allegations. It "categorically repudiated" the charge that the Indian Government's attitude was affected by foreign influences hostile to China, and it advised Peking "to settle the Tibetan problem by peaceful negotiations, adjusting the legitimate Tibetan claim to autonomy within the framework of Chinese suzerainty. . . . Tibetan autonomy is a fact," the note added, "which the Chinese Government were themselves willing to recognize." Peking in its reply repeated the claim that "China possessed sovereign rights in Tibet," and accused India of "blocking a peaceful settlement" in Tibet in order "to prevent the Chinese Government from exercising its sovereign rights in that country." Speaking later in Parliament, Nehru reiterated India's desire that the question should be settled peacefully by its two neighbors. He was mildly sarcastic on China's talk of "liberation." It was not clear, he said, from whom the Chinese were going to "liberate" Tibet.

On November 18th the delegate from El Salvador to the United Nations formally called upon that body to condemn Communist China for its "unprovoked aggression" against Tibet. This appeal was referred to the General Assembly's steering committee. It was shelved indefinitely, the main reason being that opinion was divided on Tibet's international status. In the view of most international jurists, Tibet is a half-sovereign state enjoying a status analogous to that of Southern Rhodesia, which is a self-governing colony of Britain. On this analogy Tibet would be regarded as under the protection or suzerainty of China.

It is possible that India's strong reaction to China's rape of Tibet in 1950, along with Nehru's friendly advice to Peking to "settle peacefully," influenced the Communists into the seemingly generous settlement embodied in the Sino-Tibetan agreement of May, 1951. Events since then have proved that despite the agreement and the bland assurances of Mao Tse-tung and Chou En-lai, the Chinese had decided to absorb Tibet. Since 1951 Tibet, despite local feeling, has increasingly become a province of metropolitan China. The first years of Chinese rule were devoted to apparently innocuous activities such as road building and the establishment of some welfare services. But very soon the Communists set out to open up Tibet—for themselves. Many thousands of Chinese were settled in a land whose people have never regarded themselves as Hans. Airfields were built at four pivotal centers, Chamdo, Kantse, Dam, and Jyekund, and two national highways linking Tibet with China were constructed. Scores of Tibetan youth were taken to China for indoctrination, euphemistically termed "education." The next step was to "integrate" Tibet, the country being divided into three administrative zones and a separate military area. The central and western districts were placed under the administration of the Dalai Lama, fourteenth of his line, who is regarded as a God-king. The Shigatse area was put in charge of the Panchen Lama, normally only a spiritual leader who is deemed to be the incarnation of Amitabha, "the Boundless Light." The present Panchen Lama, who is the tenth of his line, was arbitrarily appointed by the Chinese Government in 1949, without waiting for Tibetan decision or recognition. His predecessor, who had been expelled by the thirteenth Dalai Lama (1876–1933), had fled to China, where he died in 1937. The present Panchen Lama is thus a ward of the Chinese, and their creature. Tibet's eastern region is controlled by a Chinese soldier, General Chang Kuo-hua. Under the aegis of the Chinese military and administrative commission which was admitted by the terms of the agreement, "reforms" were then inaugurated on the familiar Communist lines. These included attempts at land reforms and the taxation of monastery lands. In April, 1956, Peking set up the preparatory committee for the Tibetan autonomous region—a Sino-Tibetan body designed in time to take over authority. The nationalization of temple lands sparked off the first major revolt in Tibet, spearheaded by the traditionally warlike Khambas, while almost simultaneously there was unrest in the Chinese province of Szechwan, where many Khambas reside. Early in 1957 the Communists at Lhasa decided to beat a strategic retreat following a visit from Peking by General Chen Yi, the present foreign minister, who advised the local authorities to defer the reforms until 1962, which marked the end of the Second Five-Year Plan, and then only "if the upper strata had been won over." Part of the Chinese garrison was simultaneously withdrawn.

Apparently "the upper strata," including the Dalai Lama, continued to resist the reforms, and rumors of trouble in Tibet filtered and rumbled across the Indo-Tibetan border as far back as May, 1958. Trouble erupted to the surface when the Dalai Lama was peremptorily ordered to report himself "unescorted" to the Chinese authorities. His failure to do so led to a bombardment by Chinese artillery of Tibetan monasteries occupied by the rebel lamas which, apart from loss of life, entailed the vandalistic destruction of valuable manuscripts and religious relics.

If Peking's first invasion of Tibet in 1950 had roused Indian ire, the brutal suppression in March, 1959, of the country-wide Tibetan revolt—the Chinese admitted it was not localized in Lhasa—moved Indian indignation to fever pitch and generated a surge of anger, hostility, and suspicion against Peking. Were these the apostles of *Panchshila* and "peaceful coexistence" with whom India had been inveigled into signing a Panchshila pact, whose five principles* were ironically enough first enunciated in the preamble to the Sino-Indian agreement on trade with Tibet in April, 1954? Later in June of the same year they reappeared in the course of a joint statement signed by Nehru and Chou En-lai when the Chinese prime minister visited Delhi. For the first time Indians realized the vigor, vitality, and violence of the Chinese mind.

Late in 1950, shortly after China's first invasion of Tibet, Nehru had declared that any aggression of the Indo-Tibetan border would be resisted. The same principle, he stated, would apply to the Nepalese-Tibetan border. Delhi proclaimed its determination to do so by guaranteeing the integrity of the Himalayan border states of Nepal, Sikkim, and Bhutan. Who could the transgressor be? There is only one—China. Today, as the Indian people realize, the Han hordes are on their borders. The Chinese have still to accept the MacMahon Line, a result of the Simla conference of 1914 which defined the frontier between India and Tibet for about 850 miles east from Bhutan, following a spur of the Himalayas through the north and northeast borders of Assam to a point where China, Tibet, and Burma meet. China admittedly did not ratify the Simla Convention, but Panchshila implies a two-way obligation incumbent on China no less than on India. Yet maps issued by Peking show parts of Assam, now held by India, as Chinese territory; nor are informed Indians ignorant of the Chinese irredentist urges voiced by Sun Yat-sen and repeated by Chiang Kai-shek and Mao Tse-tung. Mao's list of territories belonging to China—he cites them in his brochure *The Chinese Revolution and the Chinese Communist Party*, published in 1939—includes Korea, Formosa, the Ryukyu islands, the

* Panchshila means Five Principles. They are (1) mutual respect for each other's territorial integrity and sovereignty; (2) nonaggression; (3) noninterference in each other's internal affairs; (4) equality and mutual advantage; and (5) peaceful coexistence and economic cooperation.

Pescadores, Port Arthur, Burma, Bhutan, Nepal, Hong Kong, Macao, and Annam. Even as late as November, 1948, a year after India had obtained independence, the Chinese high priest of Marxist dialectics, Liu Shao-chi, cited India, Burma, Annam, the Philippines, Indonesia, Indochina, and South Korea as "semi-colonial countries" which needed to be "liberated" by the Communists.* Nehru might relevantly ask in this context, as he did on Tibet, "From whom?"

The revulsion of sentiment provoked in India by China's latest attack on Tibet was deep-seated, however Nehru might have attempted publicly to conceal national feeling. Tibet, like Hungary, was an example of Communist imperialism with one important difference. In Hungary it was a question of oppression and butchery by one European country on another. In Tibet it was the same equation but Asian, on a par with the prewar Japanese aggression mounted against China. In Asian eyes imperialism until recently has always had a color connotation, being associated with the domination of a white race over a black, brown, or yellow one. Hungary demonstrated that it could be white versus white. Tibet proved, as the Sino-Japanese War did, that it could also be Asian versus Asian, with Asian Communists claiming the right to lord it over other Asians. Though China reckons the Tibetan people as one of its "five nationalities," the Tibetans, like the Cambodians, are culturally and spiritually nearer to the Indians than to the Chinese. The Soviet Russians wish simultaneously to make slaves and Slavs of others. Chinese chauvinism would impose the rule of the Hans like the Huns of yore.

Tibet is an ideal base for aggression against India, and the Chinese establishment of military bases and airfields in southern Tibet, along with a network of roads leading to the borders of Bhutan, has not gone unnoticed in India. Except for a brief period

* In his book, *Internationalism and Nationalism.*

during the rule of the Cholas (A.D. 850 to A.D. 1150), Indian expansionism has never sought political control, as Chinese expansionism has, but has been primarily cultural or commercial. India's chief export to Tibet has been Buddhism, which in Tibet has taken the form of Lamaism. That is why the spiritual authority of the Dalai Lama is not confined to the three million Tibetans living within the 580,000 square miles of their country, but extends to Bhutan, Sikkim, Kashmir, and the Chinese provinces of Sikang, Sinkiang, and Mongolia, where Lamaism is practiced and where another two million Buddhists reside. Though the Panchen Lama also exercises spiritual authority, the fact that the present incumbent of that office is a Chinese nominee has detracted from his influence. Incidentally, the first Panchen Lama was created by the fifth Dalai Lama, who bestowed this title on a revered tutor.

On the international plane, as we have noted, Nehru has been more often and more openly critical of the Western than of the Soviet bloc, though since the Hungarian tragedy he has moved circumspectly, balancing his criticism of one side with a frown on the other, or being blandly polite to both. Tibet provides the latest illustration. While showering his sympathy on the Tibetans, Nehru has not been openly critical of the Chinese but has gone out of his way to express India's friendship for China. Shortly after the Dalai Lama had been granted asylum, and the Indian prime minister had stressed the "tremendous bond" which links India and Tibet, he spoke of the two-thousand-year-old bond which also binds India in friendship with China, and in the context of a Communist country referred somewhat incongrously to the "great link" being the Lord Buddha. Nehru also emphasized that during those two thousand years India and China had never been at war.

India's policy of nonalignment is correct, being in consonance with the country's traditions, geographical situation, and political and strategic needs, and has the support of the overwhelming majority of the people. But a policy of nonalignment, if justly pursued, should not express itself in fierce condemnation of the Western bloc when its actions are wrong and in equivocal language when the Soviet bloc goes off the rails, as it did over Hungary and Tibet. Apologists for these equivocal tactics explain them on the ground that one is expected to talk frankly to friends and more circumspectly where strangers are concerned. There is an obvious answer to this argument. In the first place, while one is certainly expected to talk frankly to friends one does not normally rebuke or castigate them in public. One does so privately. In the second place, where a doubt exists one usually gives the benefit of the doubt to a friend. Moreover, where the right is demonstrably on one side and the wrong on the other, nonalignment does not require a country to equivocate. The balance between aggressor and aggressed cannot justly be held even, which is India's stand vis-à-vis Pakistan over Kashmir.

One reason for the Indian Government's circumspection over Tibet, apart from the obvious need to be cautious with an aggressive neighbor, is the Sino-Indian agreement of April 20, 1954, which governs India's relations with Tibet. In this document New Delhi for the first time recognizes Tibet as the "Tibet region of China," thereby recognizing Chinese sovereignty, as distinct from suzerainty, over that area. The Simla Convention of 1914, under which the Tibetans accepted Chinese suzerainty, was repudiated by them on the ground that it was never signed by the Chinese Government. Subsequently, under the Sino-Tibetan agreement of May 23, 1951, Tibet accepted Chinese suzerainty, while Peking recognized Tibet's autonomy. In the flare-up of March, 1959, both sides have repudiated this document, the Tibetans claiming to be independent and the Chinese presumably intending to assert their sovereignty. For India to have accepted the description of Tibet as "the Tibet region of China" comes ironically from a country which has rightly protested against the description of Goa as a "province of Portugal." It might even be questioned whether India was justified in glibly accepting the principle of China's suzerainty over Tibet as a legacy inherited from the British when other imperialist legacies were summarily brushed aside or ignored. On that basis the status of the Indian princes who had treaty relations with the British raj, safeguarding their rights and privileges, should have been respected. Moreover the Simla Convention of 1914, as we have seen, whereunder the Tibetans recognized Chinese suzerainty, was repudiated by the Chinese themselves, who never signed the document, and thus left the Tibetans morally and constitutionally free to reassert their independence. But India's action in accepting the British legacy in Tibet, while it might be excused on a narrow legalistic interpretation, is not morally justified. Nor, as events have proved, was it desirable in India's own national interests.

If in practice Nehru's policy of nonalignment has occasionally deviated from the straight and narrow path, the policy is governed by principles which have an instinctive appeal for India's people, who regard their country as a major bridge between East and West, whether these terms signify the two blocs or the Occident and the Orient. As the largest democracy in the world, India is also the biggest non-Communist state in Asia, and the policy of nonalignment has given it an influence in international councils far beyond what its actual strength, in military and economic sanctions, would seem to warrant.

Beyond the mountain ranges that guard India's frontiers are the two leaders of the Communist world—Russia and China. Including Nepal and Bhutan, India has the longest border of any non-Communist state abutting on a Red domain. Moreover, in the Northeast Frontier area and in the Ladakh sector of Kashmir there are what are known as "floating frontiers"—factors which collectively and cumulatively make India's geographical and strategic situation very vulnerable despite the natural barrier of the Himalayas, now no longer impregnable. India must perforce move warily.

However one might sublimate a country's foreign policy, it is inspired basically by enlightened self-interest. India is no exception. Shortly after the country became independent, Nehru in a speech to the Constitutent Assembly declared: "Whatever policy you may lay down, the art of conducting the foreign affairs of a country lies in finding out what is most advantageous to the country. We may talk about peace and freedom and earnestly mean what we say. But in the ultimate analysis a government functions for the good of the country it governs and no government dare do anything which in the short or long run is manifestly to the disadvantage of that country. Therefore whether a country is imperialistic or Socialist or Communist its foreign minister thinks primarily of the interests of that country."

India's interests demand a sufficiently long period of peace to enable it to give its newly won political independence an economic substance and reality. Its abhorrence of the cold war which at any moment might explode into an atomic conflagration stems largely from this paramount urge, which leads Nehru to ride the razor's edge of coexistence. In a sense this policy is itself a compromise between India's philosophical traditions and political necessities. The Buddha upheld the doctrine of the middle way, which he called the Noble Eightfold Path. Jainism preached ahimsa, or nonviolence, the emperor Asoka repeating it in his rock edicts and Gandhi proclaiming it in a new idiom rooted in an old faith many centuries later. It has been left to Nehru to tread a path midway between tradition and necessity.

"There is always a great difference between a prophet and a politician in their approach to a problem," he observed in a speech he made in March, 1949, referring to Gandhi. "We had the combination of a prophet and a great statesman; but then we are not prophets nor are we very great in our statesmanship. . . . There is the grave danger, on the one hand, of denying the message of the prophet, and on the other, of blindly following it and missing all its vitality. We have, therefore, to steer a middle course through these."

The compulsive need for sustaining this tightrope act leads Nehru into equivocal postures which initially drew the criticism of the Western world and which are now ironically attracting the fire of his own countrymen. His constant stress on moral and ethical values is resented by the West as an implied rebuke to their alleged lack of them. Yet Nehru in talking of morality and ethics attempts more to explain his policies to his own countrymen in terms of their traditional background of thought and teaching than to mount a moral pedestal and castigate the West. On the other hand, many Indians have noted the inconsistency in Nehru's hesitation to denounce unequivocally China's aggression on Tibet on the plea that this can only aggravate the cold war. For surely the same plea was relevant during the Anglo-French aggression in Suez which Nehru rightly did not hesitate to condemn in the most unequivocal language.

If more recently Nehru's foreign policy has evoked increasing criticism in India, it is largely because Indian political thinking in the twelve years since independence has matured, and while still desiring peace will not have it at the price of security. Thoughtful Indians no longer equate colonialism with color. They have grown up politically, awakened first by the Soviet aggression on Hungary and later by Chinese brutality in Tibet. No longer is imperialism identified with the West alone, a hangover from the bad old days when Europe infiltrated into Asia and the Portuguese, Dutch, French, and British contended for power in India. Although Indian liberals long before independence came were strongly critical of the tsarist regime for its authoritarian acts of commission and omission, the hostility and suspicion directed by the British Government in India to tsarist Russia's expansionist schemes made Indians look with kindlier eyes on Russia, the more so when the rule of the Bolsheviks replaced the rule of the tsars. "The continued friction that we see today," Nehru wrote as far back as 1927, "is between England and Russia, not between India and Russia. Is there any reason why we in India should inherit the age-long rivalry of England against Russia?" Indians also noted that when the Bolsheviks came to power, they voluntarily liquidated the special privileges which the tsarist government had claimed in countries such as Persia and acted with equal generosity toward Turkey and China. It must also be remembered that America was not then the principal Soviet foe. It was Britain.

Russia therefore in Indian eyes had no stain of original sin to wipe out as the West had. This is why Asian revolutions have been directed primarily against the West and against all that the West represented, for Western imperialism or assertive nationalism roused an answering nationalism in Asia. Colonialism and capitalism appeared to Asia as two faces of the same coin, Western imperialism, and made the task of the Communists proportionately easier. The withdrawal of the West from Asia has coincided with an increasingly assertive nationalism on the part of Soviet Russia and Communist China and has altered old perspectives and focuses. India is no longer hostile to Britain and is proud to be a member of the Commonwealth. On the other hand, with independence it has grown acutely aware of the threat which Russian and Chinese expansionism poses. China is strung along India's frontiers, and Russia is not far away. The Communists are knocking at the door of India which leads into the hinterland of Asia. As Lenin observed long ago, "The outcome of the [Communist] struggle depends in the last account on the fact that Russia, India and China comprise the gigantic majority of the population of the world." Russia and China know this. But so does India today.

Will these new and increasingly insistent factors influence a change of emphasis or direction in India's foreign policy? Basically it is unlikely that the country will abandon nonalignment, for the closer proximity of the Communist menace from across its frontiers induces caution and the need to move circumspectly. But there will undoubtedly be a change of emphasis, a disposition to look on the West with more understanding and regard, and less readiness to take the Communist bloc at its word, along with an inclination to examine its motivations and methods more searchingly. The extent of the shift in emphasis will depend as much on the West as on the East.

China's repression of Tibet which provoked some 20,000 Tibetans to rebel* angered and disturbed India. It proved that Panchshila was not worth the paper it was written on, and the incongruous coincidence of the Dalai Lama's categorical declaration that he left Tibet and came to India of his own free will alongside Chou En-lai's insistence that he was abducted by the rebels and came "under duress" was not lost on India. What value could one attach to the pious promises and pledges of the Communists? In the first statement he made on April 18th at Tezpur, the Dalai Lama referring to India as "the Land of Enlightenment, having given birth to Lord Buddha," submitted a dignified account of the reasons and events which led him to leave Lhasa, and in confirming the aggressive character of the Peking regime, and its calculated disregard for Tibetan autonomy to which it was pledged, made a deep impression on the minds of millions of Indians, including members of the Congress party. The national committee for helping Tibetan refugees which was sponsored in Delhi includes the former Congress party president U. N. Dhebar. These developments cannot but influence a shift of emphasis in India's foreign policy—provided the West does not blunder.

* This figure was given by Chou En-lai in his speech to the People's Congress at Peking on April 18, 1959.

The habit of the West of taking Asia for granted is what has particularly riled Nehru and India. It provoked the Asian conference at Colombo where Burma, Ceylon, India, Indonesia, and Pakistan—the so-called Colombo Powers—convened in April, 1954, and later led to the Afro-Asian conference at Bandung in December, 1954, the prototype for other, similar conferences to follow. Shortly before India became independent, at the Asian Relations Conference in March, 1947, Nehru had insisted that in all matters concerning Asia, decisions should be taken only after consulting the free countries of that continent. He repeated his plea in an address he gave before the United Nations General Assembly at Paris in November, 1948:

"May I say, as a representative from Asia, that we honor Europe for its culture and for the great advance in human civilization which it represents? May I say that we are equally interested in the solution of European problems; but may I also say that the world is something bigger than Europe, and you will not solve your problems by thinking that the problems of the world are mainly European problems? There are vast tracts of the world which may not in the past, for a few generations, have taken much part in world affairs. But they are awake; their people are moving and they have no intention whatever of being ignored or of being passed by. It is a simple fact that I think we have to remember, because unless you have the full picture of the world before you, you will not even understand the problem, and if you isolate any single problem in the world from the rest, you do not understand the problem. Today I do venture to submit that Asia counts in world affairs. Tomorrow it will count much more than today."

More than anything else the traditional Western attitude, a relic of colonial days, has irked and irritated Nehru, and has made him look with kindlier eyes on Russia and China. More recent developments have compelled some rethinking: a similar onus also rests on the West to do its own rethinking in the altered context of events. Nehru has deprecated any talk of India as the leader of Asia, being conscious of the tremendous economic problems and challenges which face it. But this does not make him less aware of the fact that geography, territorial area, and population give his country a pivotal place in Asia. Speaking before the Congress of the United States in October, 1949, Nehru confessed that there might not be much in common between the Chinese and the people of the Middle East nor between the lands of Arabia, Iran, Southeast Asia, and the Far East, but he went on to declare, "Whichever region you take, India inevitably comes into the picture." The problems of all these countries impinge on India, whose geographical situation makes it a link between the New World and the Old, looking westward to Europe and the Atlantic Ocean, eastward to China and across the Pacific to the Americas, northward to the Soviet Asian republics, and southwest to Africa. Across the Indian Ocean to the southeast are Australia and New Zealand.

"India," said Nehru, "becomes a kind of meeting ground for various trends and forces and a meeting ground for what might roughly be called the East and the West."

What India's foreign policy primarily aims at is the enlargement of "the area of peace" or the extension of the nonaligned forces throughout the world so as to prevent or at least to delay the cold war generating into a hot war, and simultaneously to create a buttress and buffer against encroachment by either bloc in Southeast Asia. It cannot be claimed that this policy has succeeded, though the overwhelming majority of Indians are agreed that it is a policy consistent with their country's interests, and also consistent with the interests of world peace and of both blocs. But there can be no denying that the policies of both blocs have contracted "the area of peace" and, in Nehru's words, have brought the possibility of world war "right up to our door."

In India's eyes two developments have contributed most to this result. The latest and in many ways the most dramatic was the Chinese aggression in Tibet, which we have examined. The other is American armed aid to Pakistan, which really holds the key to the success or failure of Nehru's foreign policy, and in a menacing sense counterbalances the Communist thrust in Tibet by a reinforced threat, aided by a Western power, on India's equally vital western and eastern flanks. This is the dilemma which faces India, for howsover the Americans or Chinese might explain their actions the net result, as far as India is concerned, is to bring both blocs converging on her frontiers, thereby not merely contracting "the area of peace" but increasing the possibilities of global war.

Washington, it is true, also offered military aid to India which New Delhi, in consonance with its foreign policy, refused. No responsible Indian questions America's motives in proferring such aid to Pakistan, which, according to the State Department, is provided for defense against Communist aggression. But Pakistan has not concealed its intention of deploying it primarily against India. Karachi's membership in SEATO and the luckless Baghdad Pact, both of which are anathema to Nehru, further complicate the difficulties of India's situation and add to the complexities of its foreign policy. Here again Pakistan has made no secret of its resolve to use both these forums primarily for propaganda hostile to India, a maneuver which has sometimes acutely embarrassed Britain and the United States.

Here the West, like India, is caught in the contradictions of its own policies. It cannot afford to ignore a country which proffers the hand of friendship, even if Western policy permits Pakistan to clamber onto a bandwagon from which to snipe at India. At the same time the West cannot but be aware that the policy of lending military aid to various countries in Asia and the Middle East, with whom it is also associated through security pacts, far from creating a sense of security and stability, generates a widespread imbalance which in turn produces dangerous stresses and strains. This is being demonstrated in the Middle East, as well as on the Indian subcontinent where the one factor —Indo-Pakistan understanding—which spells stability for this important area is being undermined not only by the errors or lapses of the two countries concerned but by the mistaken if well-meant policies pursued by the West. In effect the West is sabotaging its own safety and imperilling the peace of the world.

Nehru has characterized the importation of Western arms into Asia as "a reversal of the process of liberation," since it means the West's reentry into Asia militarily by the back door. This is bad enough, for to Asia it signifies the conjuring up, genielike, of the old hobgoblin of colonialism. It portends much more. Simultaneously the back door is being prized open for another type of "liberation"—made in Moscow and patented by Peking. India, as we have noted, is high on the list of countries to be "liberated" by China, and now with Peking at the door the danger is more immediate and imminent. An altercation with Pakistan might give Peking an excuse to "liberate" India. Conversely, if the West, having provided Pakistan with military aid and equipment, kept aloof in the event of an Indo-Pakistan clash India might have no alternative to turning for military equipment to Russia and China. On Kashmir, Russia has been unequivocally on India's side, though China has been reserved.

India's relations with Pakistan are thus of central importance not only in the context of its foreign policy but for world peace and Western stability and strength. A strong India would provide a firm bulwark against an aggressive China. But a strong India united with a strong Pakistan would be an even surer shield against Communist attack. It is not in the interests of the West to reestablish colonialism, for were it to do so it would help to establish Communism.

Many things have bedeviled Indo-Pakistan relations since 1947. Some ascribe the continued tension to the inherent conflict between two contrary concepts of life—the Hindu and the Moslem; but the presence of some 40 million Moslems in India appears to contradict this, though undoubtedly, as we have seen, the Hindu outlook differs markedly from the Moslem. Others see it as a lingering legacy of the bad blood which subsisted between the Indian National Congress and the Moslem League, the former being identified with independence in India and the latter with the achievement of Pakistan. But here again the Moslem League is virtually defunct with the establishment of military rule in Pakistan, while in India the Congress party represents a rapidly wasting asset. There is the resentment left by the many problems created by partition—the treatment of minorities in the two countries, claims to evacuée property, economic hardships, and frontier incidents. But by and large the two major problems which divide India and Pakistan are Kashmir and the canal waters.

At the moment of writing* it appears as though a settlement might be reached, through the good offices of the World Bank, on the canal-waters dispute. This dispute relates to a division of the waters of the Indus Basin, through which six rivers flow, the three western rivers, the Indus, the Chenab, and the Jhelum being in the lower reaches on the Pakistan side, while on the Indian side are the rivers Beas, Ravi, and Sutlej. The latter carry about 30 million acre feet of water as against 120 million acre feet carried by the western rivers. In addition there are some canals in Pakistan which before partition received about 10 million acre feet of water from the eastern rivers, and two of these canals depended for their supplies on works now situated in India.

In 1948 it was agreed that India would divert a good share of the water from the rivers running through Indian territory, while

* April, 1959.

Pakistan, with India's financial assistance, would make alternative arrangements for the water it required by more efficient use of the waters available in West Pakistan, supplemented by a series of link canals. The implementation of this agreement, however, bogged down in a dispute over details. In 1952 both countries agreed to accept the good offices of the World Bank for a solution of the problem, and two years later the World Bank made certain proposals which India accepted in principle as a basis of discussion. These envisaged the availability of the entire flow of the three western rivers to Pakistan for its exclusive use except for a small volume of water for Kashmir. Similarly the entire flow of the three eastern rivers would be available for India's exclusive use except that for a transitional period, estimated at five years, India would supply to Pakistan "her historic withdrawals from these rivers." During the transitional period Pakistan would construct the "link canals" it needed to replace these supplies. Each country would construct and pay for the works located in its territory, but India would also bear the cost of link canals in Pakistan needed to replace supplies from India "to the extent of benefit derived by her therefrom." This was expected to amount to between Rs. 40 crores ($80 million) and Rs. 60 crores ($120 million). India might also be required to pay for provision of storage facilities which would inflate her bill still further.

According to the World Bank's proposals Pakistan will receive 80 per cent of the available water in the Indus Basin for the use of 30 million people residing on some 39 million acres of which 21 million acres are irrigated land. India will get the remaining 20 per cent to serve some 25 million people on 26 million acres, only five million acres of which are irrigated. Actually what Pakistan draws today from the three eastern rivers allocated to India is less than 10 per cent of the total quantity which it uses for irrigation. These "historic withdrawals" total around 10 million acre feet of water, and already Pakistan has constructed link canals capable of replacing nearly 5 million acre feet. Karachi is thus dependent on Indian supplies for less than 5 per cent of its total requirements. India meanwhile needs water for its multipurpose river-valley development and irrigation schemes and cannot wait indefinitely until Pakistan works out plans for replacement. New Delhi has agreed to extend the transitional period to 1962 when the Rajasthan Canal Project and other projects in India will be ready to utilize the diverted waters.

The canal-waters dispute is essentially a human problem, economic but not political, and capable of solution given good will and understanding. The signing of a transitional *ad hoc* agreement between the two countries in Washington on April 18, 1959, raises hopes of a permanent settlement.

Kashmir poses a more intractable issue, emeshed in political, economic, strategic, and emotional imponderables. These we have already considered.* Obviously India regards Kashmir as a closed chapter with the problem congealed on the cease-fire line. Addressing Parliament on March 19, 1957, President Rajendra Prasad categorically declared: "Jammu and Kashmir State is and has been a Constituent State of the Union of India since October, 1947, like other states which acceded to the Union." The conditional promise of a plebiscite given to Kashmir, India argues, is no longer valid, since it depended on the fulfillment of certain prerequisites, none of which has been implemented. India's offer was a proposal and not a commitment, and no individual or government which makes a conditional offer can be expected to wait indefinitely on the sweet will of the other party, particularly in a situation which has altered greatly over the years. Kashmir abuts on three countries, Russsia, China, and Afghanistan, a consideration very much in the forefront of Nehru's mind. Less than a week after India's intervention in Kashmir, Nehru re-

* See Chapter VII.

ferred to this state as "a frontier territory adjoining great nations and therefore we were bound to take an interest in the developments there." China's invasion of Tibet brings the Communists to Kashmir's eastern border of Ladakh, while its northern frontier is already exposed to them. Were Pakistan to precipitate trouble at this juncture in Kashmir, both India and Pakistan would be left more vulnerable to the Red threat. In New Delhi's reckoning American armed aid to Pakistan, first extended by Washington in February, 1954, has altered the complexion of affairs and noticeably influenced that country's aggressive attitude toward India. Moreover, the safety of the 40 million Moslems residing in India would be jeopardized were Pakistan to embark on a new adventure in Kashmir, while similarly the lives of the 10 million Hindus staying in Pakistan would be imperilled. A conflagration in Kashmir might see the horrors of partition reenacted throughout the entire subcontinent.

A plebiscite in the circumstances which obtain in Kashmir will not be a purely political procedure with the voters faced as in an election with a choice between two or more candidates. Pakistan's propaganda on Kashmir is based on the claim that as a Moslem-majority state Kashmir belongs to it, and the plebiscite will thus pose a loaded question charged with communal and religious dynamite. In short a plebiscite in Kashmir will provoke more problems than it solves. Much is made of the right of self-determination. "Let the people decide," says Pakistan, and in this it is supported by its allies. But the plea comes strangely from a government which has not let its own people decide on anything, including who should rule them and how, for the past twelve years. Pakistan has had no general elections since independence, while India has had two.

The paradox of Pakistan is that, demanding to be divided from India, it finds itself divided by India, with its eastern and western wings separated by a thousand miles of Indian territory. Of its

80-odd million population some 56 per cent reside in the eastern zone, divided from the western by language and, before the establishment of military rule, by contending claims for representation in the government, legislatures, armed services, and civilian administration. This has created a dual frustration complex—externally against India and internally between the two zones. If the internal conflict has momentarily been resolved by the military government of General Ayub clamping down the lid on both zones, the external frustration vis-à-vis India remains. Tormented previously by a plague of politicians, Pakistan was politically instable, with one ministry succeeding another, a fact which made it difficult for India to arrive at any settlement with its neighbor. The temptation to dangle Kashmir as a distracting bait when internal stresses proved unduly strong was one which a succession of weak and incapable governments found it hard to resist. Military rule has undoubtedly imported an element of stability in the country's government, but a military administration which believes that government is too serious a matter to be left to politicians might do more than dangle Kashmir as a bait. It might be tempted to reach out for it.

India's own interests demand strong and stable neighbors—but also neighbors friendly toward it. An aggressive China and a hostile Pakistan are liabilities, not assets, and add increasingly to the difficulties confronting New Delhi. The simultaneous pressures exercised by the two countries, one linked to Moscow and the other to the West, can only strengthen, even harden, India's policy of nonalignment, however much Indians might be disillusioned over the magic of Panchshila and peaceful coexistence. For, ironically, if Tibet proved the impracticability of the lamb coexisting with the wolf, Indo-Pakistan relations also demonstrate that the beatitudes of Panchshila and the bliss of coexistence demand a bilateral acceptance of obligations and rights.

The question arises whether Indian public opinion, stirred by the events in Tibet, will project its thinking on Panchshila and coexistence from what might be described as a local incident to the international plane. Will it regard with equal skepticism those who preach coexistence between the two blocs, and, having discovered its impracticability when one side purloins the other's nickel to hit the jackpot, question the wisdom of nonalignment? China does not confront India merely across two thousand miles of mountainous frontier, for Sino-Indian rivalry and competition run like a jagged spine throughout South Asia. If Tibet could not coexist with China inside China, will India and China be able to coexist inside Asia? Enlightened self-interest compels India to pursue a policy of nonalignment which safeguards its own primary interests and also ensures a longer period of global peace. What the democracies represented by the West need now more than ever is some breathing space. The Tibetan tragedy should see some shift of emphasis in India's foreign policy, but if that shift is finally to crystallize into active support of the democratic world the West must show more sensitivity and farsightedness than it has.

and nine schedules is the lengthiest and most intricate Constitution in the world. But India's parliamentary government is based more on statute than on convention, which is where it differs vitally from that of Britain.

In a curious way convention is less flexible than statute, the latter being amenable to alteration by a parliamentary majority, as the changes in India's Constitution within the past twelve years demonstrate. What is there to prevent the Communists altering the Constitution to suit their purposes as the Congress has done in order to push through its land reforms, and similarly to claim that they operate through parliamentary processes? While the structure of India's government approximates closely to that of the Western parliamentary democracies, it does not in practice function along the same lines. Personalities tend to count more than principles, and policy is determined basically not by the agencies of government but by the party in power, which today happens to be the Congress.

Even within the Congress party, as we have seen, the major decisions are not made by the party as a whole but by Nehru, who is sometimes assisted by a handful of close associates. It is this functional difference which leads many in the West, to the irritation of not a few in India, to inquire persistently, "After Nehru, what?" Will a new personality, equally strong and overwhelming, emerge to direct the government and keep it stable on the lines he visualizes? If not, will the constitutional pattern remain democratic, or assume a distinctive form more suited to Indian ways of life and thinking? The answer depends on whether Nehru during the past twelve years has set a mold which cannot easily be altered or shattered. In other words, has his sense of hustle infused India's people with a habit of mind which will maintain the country on the same economic, social, and political keel?

Undoubtedly Nehru has created in independent India a certain climate of thought. But it is open to debate whether this habit of mind is strong or compulsive enough to sustain the country on the lines he has planned and adopted. If those of his immediate lieutenants who pay lip service to his ideas and ideals while he is politically active and alive deviate from them or denounce them when he is no longer there, the chances are that the country, beset by doubts arising from confusion of thought and lack of confidence in the new Congress leadership, might look for direction elsewhere.

Gandhi's new class, or political elite corps, perished largely with him. But the country had sufficient confidence in the Mahatma's political heir to give Nehru its dedicated devotion and support. The men who now surround Nehru, as we noted at the outset, are far below him in stature and prestige. India's people could follow Nehru as confidently after independence as they had followed the Mahatma before freedom, since to them, both signified a talisman and an ideal. But who will there be in India tomorrow to embody either of these images?

Individually there is no one. But collectively a group may emerge to continue governing the country vigorously and on defined democratic paths. If with Nehru's demission from the political stage the Congress divides into two groups, the likelihood is that the leftist group in conjunction with the Socialists outside the Congress party will eventually emerge the stronger. As long as the Congress keeps together as one party, the only alternative to it in the eyes of the majority of the electorate is the Communist party. This assessment represents the prevailing position, and is one reason why the creation during Nehru's lifetime of a Center party, right of the Congress, would provide a buttress for democracy during the fluid in-between period through which India is passing. The chances for the establishment of such a party are small at the national level, though the success of the Ganatantra Parishad in Orissa and the encouraging support which the tribal Jharkhand party was able to muster in Bihar, Assam, and Manipur during the last general elections of 1957 portend the increasing emergence of groups to the right and left of the Congress at various state levels. Constitutionally this would create an interesting situation, for while party groupings at the Center would be on British or American lines, they would approximate closer to the former French pattern of group rule in the states.

One inevitable result would be the elevation of the president's authority vis-à-vis the prime minister's. As we have noted, the president under the Constitution is empowered with far greater executive authority than he in fact exercises. But in all spheres of constitutional and administrative rule the personality and prestige of Nehru have proved overwhelming, overshadowing the authority of every other holder of office from the president downward. With Nehru's withdrawal from the political scene and the growing pressure of non-Congress groups in various states, the fulcrum of power would tend to be identified with the president rather than with the prime minister, since in theory all the executive power of the Union of India is vested in the former, and the likelihood of his exercising it more assertively will increase in the changed circumstances.

Although the Indian Constitution stipulates that "the Ministers shall hold office during the pleasure of the President," it also lays down that "the Council of Ministers shall be collectively responsible to the House of the People." Nonetheless the president of India enjoys a status and can exercise powers above that of the British sovereign, though technically he has no constitutional means of implementing any decision he might wish to take. Obviously much hinges on the personality of the president who in future years, like Nehru today, might exert an authority outside the strict ambit of the Constitution. According to Article 77 of the Constitution, "all executive action of the Government of

India shall be expressed to be taken in the name of the President," who in fact enjoys extraordinary powers which he might or might not choose to exercise vis-à-vis the prime minister, a personage whom under the Constitution he appoints. This implies that where the choice of a prime minister by the Congress Parliamentary party does not coincide with that of the president, he may withhold his approval and compel the party to think again. The president has also powers to promulgate ordinances while Parliament is not in session, and in a "state of emergency" he can assume the government of any province under the provisions of the Constitution. These provisions operate when peace and security are threatened by internal or external forces; when the country's financial credit and stability are jeopardized; or when a state government cannot be carried on within the stipulations of the Constitution.

The vital question therefore might well be: "Who will succeed India's highly respected President Dr. Rajendra Prasad?" instead of the familiar query: "Who will succeed Nehru?" No apostolic succession prevails so far as Nehru is concerned, for his confidence in India's future rests on the people rather than on the politicians, who include his own associates. Yet for two obvious reasons the voice of the people is likely to be subordinate to that of the politicians. For one thing, the latter control the political machine whose mechanics they comprehend and can direct more effectively than the electorate can. Second, the electorate is too ignorant and illiterate to imbibe deeply the principles which Nehru has preached and which he has attempted to put into practice over the past twelve years. Ask an average Indian peasant or worker to define the distinction between Socialism and Communism, or for that matter between the Congress and the Socialist parties, and he would find considerable difficulty in doing so.

The imprint of Gandhism, built and maintained over three

decades, has for all practical purposes vanished within a decade. How long will the impact of Nehruism survive? As we have seen, it was comparatively easy for the British to fill the intellectual vacuum of the hundred years between Aurangzeb's death and the early establishment of their own rule with new ideas imported from the West, and to create a middle class impregnated largely with a British outlook and British ideas. But Gandhi was able to harness the same middle class for his own patriotic purposes and to overthrow the raj with the help mainly of a British-created class. Simultaneously the Mahatma fashioned a distinctive elite corps of dedicated Congress workers who with independence and the acquisition of political power converted themselves into the new class which today rules India. Gandhi by charging the Indian atmosphere with an Indian idea was able to neutralize the menace and magic of Communism, though admittedly in this he was assisted by the prevailing circumstances which impressed on Indian minds the folly of exchanging one foreign ruler for another. The question arises: If the Mahatma's teachings could survive for barely a decade, how long will it take to efface the secular impact of Nehru, who has nothing intrinsically Hindu in his ideas, which again are geared to what his critics characterize as purely materialistic concepts?

Nehru's reasons for his major sin of omission, that of neglecting to build up a younger generation of leaders as Gandhi did, carry little conviction. His contention is twofold—that he would rather have India's people understand and imbibe his ideas than himself build up or nominate a successor; and that in order to do so speedy progress is imperative. The first contention would be valid were the masses able to follow the major distinctions even if they did not understand the finer nuances between political and economic creeds. Although it might be argued that the electorate displayed a considerable sense of acumen and judgment in the last two general elections, there is no knowing how the individual vote will shift as the major group compulsions change. For in India today the electorate by and large votes not so much on an individual as on a caste, communal, or local basis, exposed to and influenced by its immediate rather than by the national environment. True, local grievances and problems also at times influence national elections in other countries, but the major motivations operating in India are of a group, not an individual, character. The group mainly determines how the individual votes. Speed again is not the essence of the matter, though it is an important factor, for too great hustle generates mistakes which need to be revoked or remedied, and too many changes induce in turn a disposition for change. This lack of stable political moorings has characterized India's history from very early days, and once again the instability not only of the illiterate masses but of the intelligentsia might irrevocably rock the boat.

The mantle of the Mahatma descended at his death on a single individual, and not on the people as many had hoped. Interposed between that individual and the people is the new class which plans to remain in power, though divided at the higher echelons within itself and subject to increasing pressures from the right and the left. A group rather than an individual will in all likelihood direct the government after Nehru's demission. Since a group implies an association of individuals broadly in agreement, and since the Congress party even now has members inclining either to the right or to the left, two groups are likely to emerge led by individuals whose political leanings accord with those of their followers.

Right of Nehru are the ailing Dr. Rajendra Prasad and the present home minister, Pandit Govind Vallabh Pant, while the former strong man of Bombay, Morarji Desai, now finance minister, perambulates in the vicinity of the throne. In the wings is another Bombay personality, S. K. Patil, once boss of that city's

Tammany Hall, and presently minister for food and agriculture in the Central Government. These four men represent the hard core of the Congress right wing, though each is inclined that way for somewhat different reasons.

Patil is the most bluntly forthright of the four, being temperamentally and politically an upholder of authority sustained by strong-arm methods, impatient of Socialism and implacably opposed to the Communists. He is also the youngest of this group, being fifty-nine. Patil is an able organizer and a forceful speaker, skilled in the mechanics of party politics, with an ability to muster and mobilize the popular vote when the elections come round. But in ministerial trappings in Delhi he is less conspicuous and less at home than he was on his stamping ground in Bombay. Patil is marking time, holding his political horses until he is sure which way the national juggernaut will run. Whether he will ultimately emerge as a front-rank national leader is debatable. Undoubtedly he has the guns but he lacks some of the ammunition. He is ambitious, persistent, forceful, not devoid of guile or cunning, ruthless when the occasion demands it but with a perspective and judgment more sure at state levels than on a national plane. His advantages are his comparative youth, which should enable him to outlive most of his rivals, his infinite capacity for calculation, and his more newly derived virtue of patience, which persuades him not to reveal his hand until he is fairly sure which way the cards are stacked or falling.

What of the other three? Like Patil, Morarji Desai comes from Bombay, once described as "the Cinderella of India," since for many years in British days it was unrepresented in the Central Government. Desai, who is sixty-three, is widely regarded as the most likely successor to Nehru. For one thing he is younger than either Rajendra Prasad, who is seventy-five, or Pant, who is seventy-two. Desai is able and a strong administrator, but he is apt to talk too often in terms of first principles and inclined to confuse personal fads with individual morals. An ardent prohibitionist, he eyes those who imbibe alcohol, however mildly, as moral lepers, although simultaneously he appears to see nothing wrong in consorting with big businessmen, many of whom are addicted to vices that are more antisocial than drinking. As a Congress party man in preindependence days, he was nearer to Vallabhbhai Patel than to Gandhi. Like Patel he is authoritarian and autocratic, but unlike Vallabhbhai he lacks resilence, farsightedness, and imagination. His handling of the Maharashtrian-Gujarati linguistic dispute while chief minister of Bombay might have high-lighted his capacity as a strong administrator but it dimmed his reputation as a statesman. The years have possibly mellowed him, and he is capable on occasions of a sweet reasonableness which because it is unexpected can be disarming. But basically he remains a politician, not without guile and with a single-mindedness of political purpose not easily discernible from personal ambition.

Desai would make an outstanding home (or interior) minister, for he is not averse to hitting heads (despite his professed nonviolence) and hitting them with uncanny accuracy, resolve, and effect. He was sixty-two when he first left India, and though his visit to the United States, Britain, and Europe in 1958 opened a new vista on men and affairs it is possible that he saw it with more closely blinkered eyes and static mind than he might have done had he gone abroad earlier. Morarji's main defect is that he is his own yardstick, expecting others to conform to his often rigid views rather than accommodating himself to the differing opinions of others. This constitutes his major handicap both within India and outside. Nonetheless he is a man of considerable personal charm, when he chooses to turn it on, and of mental alertness. Despite his parochialism he remains among the more outstanding personalities in the line of direct succession to Nehru.

Pant, like Prasad an ailing man, is politically more acute and perceptive than Morarji Desai; and, coming from Nehru's home state of Uttar Pradesh, he is in a better position to read his master's mind and accommodate his views accordingly. Temperament inclines him to the right economically and communally, but long training in political dialectics, with consequential calculation, now keeps him nearer to the left. Less inflexible than Morarji, he will echo dutifully whatever Nehru says, and provide seemingly convincing reasons for not wholly convincing policies. Pant is a superb parliamentarian but in a sense even more parochial than Desai, for quite apart from never having traveled abroad, he has rarely moved inside India beyond the charmed orbit of Uttar Pradesh and New Delhi. He is a man of massive common sense but too addicted to power to assert it effectively.

Gentle in mien and manner, seemingly modest, with a rustic façade which conceals an urban political mind, Rajendra Prasad might in the event of Nehru's early demission from the political scene succeed him as prime minister. It is well known that he successfully resisted Nehru's efforts to displace him twice as president when Jawaharlal would first have preferred to nominate the veteran C. Rajagopalachari and later Dr. Radhakrishnan, the present vice president, to this post. Prasad, realizing that he could carry with him the national and state legislatures which elect the president, resisted the prime minister's move. And Nehru wisely resiled. Within the Congress Parliamentary party, which elects its leader who might be prime minister, Prasad could probably reckon on attracting more votes than either Pant or Morarji. He is the most Hindu of the three, more traditional and conservative. Socially, religiously, and economically, he would take India to the right. Prasad, emulating Nehru, has recently been journeying abroad, and despite the asthma which afflicts him he moves around India, devoting some months of every year to sojourn in the south. Prasad has knowledge of India but little appreciation of foreign countries and policies.

With S. K. Patil virtually out of this political rat race, the main contenders for the prime minister's post would be Prasad, Pant, and Morarji Desai, with the last exercising an advantage owing to his being the youngest of the trio, and also younger than the prime minister. Yet several decisive factors might ultimately rule him out. Morarji is vastly unpopular in Maharashtra and even in his home ground of Gujarat. Nor does his astringent reputation make for popularity in most parts of India. A Nehru laying down the law might be tolerated as long as he lives, but not a Morarji Desai who publicly gives the impression of being a law unto himself and to others. Two handicaps affect equally Prasad and Pant. These are age and ill health, Pant being afflicted with Parkinson's disease and more recently stricken with a mild attack of thrombosis.

There is therefore the possibility of a comparative dark horse emerging as Nehru's successor, and many see him in the person of the present minister for commerce and industry, fifty-five-year-old Lal Bahadur Shastri, who also comes from Uttar Pradesh. Politically and personally Shastri is very close to Nehru, but he lacks an assertive personality, being of diminutive stature and a retiring disposition. He remains, however, the best compromise choice, particularly if one or other of the contending trio chooses to exercise more decisive political direction as the president.

If on Nehru's demission the Congress rightists succeed in controlling the party machine, the dominant group will probably comprise Prasad, Pant, and Morarji Desai, with S. K. Patil and the fifty-nine-year-old minister for parliamentary affairs, Dr. Satya Narain Sinha, who hails from Bihar and is very much to the right, in close tow. Lal Bahadur Shastri, despite his present leftist leanings, would probably work in conjunction with this group. A government inclined right of center would then emerge.

Since the Congress left wing commands no outstanding personality, the likelihood in the event of a party split would be a move to coalesce with the Socialists led by J. B. Kripalani and Asoka Mehta as a counter to the right. Kripalani, a former Congress party president and veteran Gandhite, has a volatile disposition and, like Cassius, a lean and hungry look. His mental cerebrations are unusually active, and he possesses a vigorous pen and an acridly forceful tongue. On the other hand he is inclined to be impulsive, and lacks political judgment. But no one suspects his personal bona fides or his dedicated devotion to the country's good as he sees it. Kripalani is a well preserved seventy-one. The more youthful Asoka Mehta—he is only forty-eight—is a politician, pamphleteer, and economist with a live social conscience; he is an earnest student of public affairs, and constructively progressive in his approach to most problems. Of all the Socialists he is probably nearest to the Congress left wing, and would find little difficulty in adjusting himself to his new alignments. Whether Kripalani and Asoka Mehta could together attract and mobilize public support sufficient to enable a Congress Socialist group to hold office is doubtful, for neither commands the mass appeal nor exercises effective control of the party machine, as do the more politically experienced leaders on the right.

Much will depend here on the attitude of the attractive but elusively enigmatic Jayaprakash Narayan. He was the founder-secretary of the Socialist party, though he is now actively associated with Vinoba Bhave's bhoodan movement. Jayaprakash, who is fifty-seven, was born in Bihar and lived in America for seven years in Iowa and Wisconsin, where he studied sociology and worked as a farm hand to pay his way through college. Gandhi is said to have introduced him to Nehru at the memorable Lahore session of the Congress in 1929 over which Nehru presided, and both men took immediately to each other. Before and after independence Nehru has more than once declared in private that Jayaprakash is a future prime minister. There is little doubt that Nehru would very much like him to attain that office.

Jayaprakash, once a Marxist, is now firmly convinced that the roots of true Socialism and Indian progress lie in Gandhian philosophy and that the key to real advance rests in the villages and the land. Hence his decision to turn away from politics to the more dedicated business of bhoodan.

Should Jayaprakash and Vinoba Bhave decide in the event of Nehru's departure from the political stage to return to active politics in conjunction with the Congress Socialist wing, the mass appeal of this group will be immeasurably strengthened and might conceivably assert itself successfully against the right. Believing in the Gandhian tenet that wherever evil exists it should be actively resisted, Jayaprakash played a dominant role in rousing public opinion on the Soviet brutalities in Hungary in 1956 and on Red China's aggression in Tibet, three years later. Though India's foreign policy under a Socialist government is unlikely to move away from nonalignment, its attitude to Communist expansionism will undoubtedly be more critical and more vigorously expressed.

What of the home front? Here the cry for compromise between urban and rural interests, between the need to accelerate industrialization and galvanize land reforms and peasant prosperity will be louder and more insistent. The grass-roots philosophy of Gandhi will have to be worked out in a modern, forward-looking context. The future of democracy in India will hinge largely on the success of this experiment, for while Nehru's sense of hustle has infused his country and countrymen with a realization that India has to catch up economically with the more advanced countries of the world, it has politically generated a confused state of public schizophrenia which makes it difficult for the average Indian to differentiate between the ethical and the expedient, between the values of democracy and Communism, between what is economically justifiable and politically right. This has tended to give the benefit of the doubt more often to the totalitarian world than to the democratic, and in the process has blunted individual and public consciousness and conscience within the country to the detriment of democratic policies and trends.

The mere advent of a Congress Socialist government spearheaded by Jayaprakash Narayan, J. B. Kripalani, and Asoka Mehta, with the moral support of Vinoba Bhave, would not automatically induce a change of outlook and method overnight. But it might persuade into being an outlook and method which while characteristically Indian would be politically Gandhian and economically more forward-looking and advanced. India, in other words, will have to move democratically but on economic lines different at least on the urban and industrial fronts from what Gandhi envisaged and advocated. Success will depend on whether personalities such as Jayaprakash and Kripalani, Vinoba and Asoka Mehta can work together to hammer out a political and economic program acceptable to all of them. Asoka Mehta's attitude to bhoodan is by no means as starry-eyed as Jayaprakash's, nor do Kripalani and Vinoba see eye to eye on all issues. But broadly the four men are agreed that Socialism in India can only survive and carry the country forward on democratic lines if its inspiration is Gandhian, not Marxist. The most single-minded of the four is Vinoba, the most clearheaded, Asoka. Jayaprakash lacks intellectual certitude, though his mass appeal as a political leader is still considerable. Kripalani is purposeful but inclined at times to be willful.

In recent months, the veteran C. Rajagopalachari, first Indian governor general, a former chief minister of Madras, and once a member of the Union Government, has formed a conservative or rightist party, in opposition to the Congress,* named the Swatantra (Freedom) party. "C. R.," as he is popularly known, is eighty, and though he is still mentally vigorous he is handicapped

* Swantra party.

physically by his advanced age. Some attribute his action to political pique, for despite his considerable experience he has been out of active politics for five years and is said to chafe at it. C. R., subtle and subterranean but clearheaded, is sometimes referred to maliciously as the Machiavelli of Madras or, after his home district, Salem, as the Savonarola of Salem. Supporting him in this project is M. R. Masani, a former Congress Socialist but now bitterly opposed to Nehru's foreign and domestic policies. Masani, who is fifty-four, is intellectually combative but has no political following. Educated in England, and highly sophisticated, he was returned to Parliament as the candidate of a tribal party, a fact which has occasionally provoked Nehru to derisive comment. If, with Nehru's withdrawal from political life, the Congress party continues as a compact monolithic organization there will be stronger popular demand for an opposition party, particularly from those sections which view with growing disquiet Communist attempts to build the Reds up as the only active opposition. Such a party could function most effectively as a Center party or perhaps a right-of-center group with the Congress Socialists and Communists to its left. But in the event of the Congress itself splitting into a left and right group, it would be difficult for the new opposition party to function effectively to the right of the right, while as a Center party it would be in danger of being crushed between the nutcracker of the right and the left. An opposition, right of the Congress right wing, would attract extreme religious support only from the more fanatical communal elements and be in many respects a retrograde group. In all likelihood the new opposition party to the right of the Congress right wing would end by being absorbed by the latter.

Therefore the chances of true democratic development in India really lie in the Congress splitting into two main groups, thereby fostering the growth of a stable party system in the country. The tendency in the states, as we have seen, is to develop on group rather than on party lines somewhat on the pattern of the French Fourth Republic. This tendency is likely to grow rather than to diminish.

Of the Congress personalities apart from Nehru, Krishna Menon excites the most lively and controversial interest abroad. Menon himself is controversial and can often be lively. In the United States and in some circles in Britain he is regarded as a baleful, sinister figure whose influence on Nehru and the country's foreign policy can do no one, except the Soviet bloc, any good. It must be confessed that Menon with his prickly personality and bristly tongue has done not a little to fortify this impression. He suffers neither fools nor wise men gladly. Menon has always been a lone wolf preferring to hunt in his own omniscient company rather than with the pack. He is sixty-two and has spent some thirty years of his life abroad. He is in fact a stranger in his own land, with no roots in the country and with no close affiliations, personal or political, with the Congress party. His strength, in so far as Indian politics goes, lies solely in his long, intimate association with Nehru, which is also his weakness, for it has drawn on him the active suspicion and hostility of others who would aspire to the throne. Menon's known leftist proclivities, economic and political, render him suspect, a feeling which his reported popularity with the armed forces has intensified, more particularly abroad. There is no danger of the armed forces ever rising en masse on Menon's behalf, and the picture and possibility of its happening are ludicrous in the extreme for those who know India intimately. Menon will vanish from the Indian stage with Nehru's departure.

Two other Congress personalities, now also much in the public eye, invite comment. They are Nehru's close relatives—his daughter Indira Gandhi, currently president of the Congress party; and his sister, the able Vijayalakshmi Pandit, who is now the Indian high commissioner in London. From many points of view the election of Indira Gandhi as Congress president while her father was India's prime minister was a tactical blunder which might have strategically unfortunate results, for the simultaneous association of father and daughter at the apex of the political pyramid could shake the pyramid more than somewhat. Mrs. Gandhi is a woman with a mind of her own, intelligent and, though sometimes glacial, not without charm. But it would be unusual and unnatural, considering the background of her career, that her opinions were completely uninfluenced by her father's. She also happens to be her father's only child, which ordinarily makes parental susceptibilities more sensitive. This could cramp the political style of both or either and in turn induce excessive caution or provoke precipitate action. The public mind, fastening on the two simultaneously, would find it difficult to disentangle the one from the other, whether in praise or censure, and the resultant double image would be a distortion of the real picture. There is no question of Nehru's attempting to create a dynasty of his own; it would be inconsistent with his character and career.

Mrs. Pandit, now fifty-nine, is some seventeen years older than her niece, and apart from being decorative she is a remarkably intelligent woman. It is well known that she does not share all her brother's views, particularly in the international field, but she has long political experience and has served with distinction as India's representative in Moscow, Washington, and London, as well as in the United Nations, where she was the first woman to be elected president of the Assembly. Had she remained in India rather than chosen to go abroad in the crucial decade after independence, there is little doubt that she would have been a minister at the Center and would have exercised more influence than she now possesses in the Indian political world. Absence may make the heart grow fonder, but it has a habit of making the mind grow less aware. With her brother at the country's helm and her niece directing the rudder of Congress, there is little place for her on any governmental or party boat except as a distinguished deckhand, which is a pity, for she has opinions of her own and occasionally the courage to express them.

There remain the Communists. Although the threat they pose to democracy in India and elsewhere in the free world is real, there is a tendency to overrate their sense of cohesion and unity and to underrate the inherent contradictions in their party and political thinking. The deviations in Communist policy since the Bolsheviks seized power in Russia are illustrative of the convolutions in their day-to-day tactics, for while their long-range objectives and strategy remain constant their short-term methods alter incessantly. Trotsky, who shared some of Lenin's light and glory in his lifetime, was degraded and deported to "a planet without a visa" not long after Lenin's death. In our day Stalin has suffered the same fate, and what awaits Khrushchev not even the stars can tell.

So it is with India's Reds, who, emulating the Bolsheviks, have been zigzagging to their target. To the man in the street, patriotism is a matter of basic loyalties. And nothing has more pitilessly exposed the Communists in India than their recent attempt to decry New Delhi's attitude over Peking's aggression in Tibet. Significantly, here again Moscow has been silent on the Indian attitude to Tibet. Can it be that the Russians do not really relish the early prospect of India turning Communist, fearful of being threatened on a vulnerable flank by the vast combined land mass and population of Asia's two largest countries with China abutting on some of the Soviet Asian republics? Mao Tse-tung has surely not forgotten the twists and turns of Soviet policy concerning China over the past thirty years or that Stalin disavowed the Chinese Communists at the Potsdam conference toward the end of the Second World War, and in May, 1945, assured the late Harry Hopkins that Chiang Kai-shek was the only leader fit to rule China. In August of the same year Moscow signed a treaty of friendship and alliance with Kuomintang China. Mao himself, whose dialectical loyalty is to Marx more than to Moscow, did not meet Stalin until five years later. Some twenty years before that, in a report compiled on the possibilities of a peasant rising in 1927 in his home province of Hunan, the Chinese leader had cold-shouldered even Marx by ignoring his precept that in colonial or semicolonial countries the proletariat or urban workers should spearhead the revolution. In doing so, he also ran counter to the precepts of Lenin and Stalin.

Mao's ruthless single-mindedness of purpose has found no reflection in the policy pursued by a single one of the Indian Communist leaders since the foundation of the Indian Communist party. These have looked in turn for direction from the British Communist party, from Moscow, and even from Peking, whose policies they once openly denounced, recanting their denunciation only at Moscow's behest. Their strategy, as we have seen, has been successively "right," "left," and "neo-Maoist." Today the Communist party of India broadly pursues the Chinese path, attempting to keep the anti-imperialist and anticapitalist forces in one camp, hoping to mobilize them, as Mao did, in a final assault on the so-called reactionary forces. But there is no sign of any Indian Mao among the Communist leaders of today.

None of the five general secretaries which the party has had since 1934—Dr. G. Adhikari, P. C. Joshi, B. T. Ranadive, Rajeshwar Rao, and Ajoy Ghosh—has been a man of outstanding distinction or individuality. None has left his impress on the party, the movement, or the country. One of the most forceful personalities on the top rungs is the old-time Communist S. A. Dange, who is rated higher as an agitator and orator than as a serious political student or thinker. But even he has made hardly a dent in the Congress armor, although he was returned to Parliament with the largest majority in the last general election. As Ellen Roy, widow of the late Manabendra Nath Roy has observed, the

Indian Communists "are no different from other Communists, except that they have to their credit probably more mistakes, more turn-abouts and somersaults than Communists elsewhere."

The reason for this is that, looking with one eye on Moscow and the other on Peking, they do not know where exactly they are going. If Mao today looks only to Moscow, it is because he has nowhere else to look. He may take pride, and does, that his was essentially a Chinese revolution, but just now he realizes that he has no foreign supporter whom he can exploit as a counter to Russia. Therefore for the moment Peking must perforce work with Moscow with the eyes of both on another country—India. Here is where China has the advantage of Russia by reason, first, of her territorial proximity to India and also because the two countries happen to be Asian—a fact of which both are acutely aware. If India were to go Communist, Peking's dependence on Moscow would decrease, and it might well be that, checkmated by China, Russia would attempt to expand farther eastward into Europe while China sought to seep southward into Asia. Beyond would lie other worlds which the Reds, if they succeed in Asia and Europe, might also try to conquer—the sprawling continents of Africa, the Americas, and the Antipodes. It is unlikely that this Wellsian nightmare will ever mature, but India's loss to the free world, while a grievous casualty to the cause of democracy, might precipitate the first faint beginnings of a head-on clash within the Communist camp itself. The Chinese and Russian revolutions have one thing in common: both wear a strong national veneer, and each is actuated primarily in its foreign policies by purely national considerations. The idea that countries committed to international Communism cannot be influenced by national interests is a myth which Russia and China have themselves exploded.

India, though wedded to democracy, has still to imbibe and implement fully the spirit and workings of democracy. As Manabendra Nath Roy warned many years ago, "In Asia the decisive moral resistance to Communism is bound to be weak because there is no democratic tradition to defend." The ifs of history are always speculative though interesting, but it is possible that India might have reached the goal of true democracy more quickly had she followed the Gandhian path rather than the way along which Nehru has led the country—courageously but often impulsively—over the past twelve years. For Gandhism, as we have noted, filled the Indian air with an Indian idea and impregnated Indian minds with the belief that through their own institutional forms a type of democracy suited to Indian conditions might be evolved. To the Mahatma democracy appeared as a pyramid broad-based on the villages and rising to its apex by way of towns, cities, and states to the pinnacle of the Center through a system of indirect elections in which every citizen had a voice.

In the past twelve years Nehru also has propelled the country on the path of progress, determined to make of India an advanced and a modern state. But in an odd way the India which is emerging, even if modern, seems inchoate and amorphous, neither Eastern nor Western, shedding ideals in the pursuit of ideas, most of them carried through by a growing bureaucracy of officials and functionaries whose caliber, both civic and administrative, declines daily. As the old core of administrators and civil servants shrinks, the new and monstrous regiment of officials, less well paid than they were and drawn from a strata which no longer represents the cream of the country's intelligentsia, swings into action much like the *kanpus* of Communist China, and always aware, like them, of the eyes of their taskmasters, political and administrative. Initiative has small scope in such surroundings, nor has intellectual integrity. Increasingly the country finds itself enmeshed in a gargantuan net of rules and regulations in which both bureaucracy and the politicians, even as they flounder in it, seem to delight. Over all reigns the new class of Congress rulers who in turn take their cue from a single, omnipotent individual.

Because of his predominating prestige and personality, Nehru's strangely split outlook is reflected in the country in matters both foreign and domestic. At home private enterprise beats a retreat before the growing battalions of the public sector, while the country is compartmentalized into linguistic factions, often influenced by caste and local ambitions; into warring trade-unions drawing their sustenance either from the Communists or from the Congress; into conflicting sectors of big business, now rapidly shrinking, and in the process demoralized enough to contribute indiscriminately to the coffers of the Congress or of the Communists. It is stateism in excelsis—the encroachment of the government into the life of every sector of society—the intellectual, the businessman, the artisan, peasant, and worker. Everything is grist to the government's mill—handicrafts, cooperative farms, Chinese rice planting, German, Russian, and British steel plants, Soviet technicians, the Colombo Plan, aid from America, private and public planning. The bewilderment generated by these confused and conflicting activities expresses itself in the average Indian alternatively through ire or irritation.

On the foreign front the picture as presented to the country's thoughtful citizens is equally confused. Gandhi would undoubtedly have approved of coexistence, which was in line with his own basic teachings, but he would never have compromised with evil in any form, whether Indian, Russian, or American. Until the Hungarian tragedy India's inclination, under Nehru's direction of foreign policy, to give the benefit of the doubt to the Soviet bloc seemed at times unconscionable, while even over Hungary the equivocations initially indulged in by the Indian representative at the Security Council caused more than a mild lifting of eyebrows. In many quarters they evoked bitter protest and anger. Since then the Indian Government has held the scales more evenly as between East and West, and China's aggression in Tibet vividly demonstrated that imperialism could be practiced by one Asian people against another. But the tedious and often tortuous tergiversations earlier displayed in the international field have left their trail in public doubts as to whether the country's foreign policy has always been influenced by strict adherence to the moral obligations of nonalignment.

Therein lies Nehru's weakness and India's danger; for while the inclination to dangle the carrot and wield the stick simultaneously is common to many governments, the sense of undue regimentation, of unnecessary governmental intrusion not only in the public spheres of commerce, industry, and professional life but also in the ordinary business of everyday life and living oppresses many in India, not all of whom belong to the so-called privileged or commercialized sections of the people. Indeed, not a few officials and others who though exercising office should constitutionally be beyond the reach of governmental influence or interference have been heard to complain of overzealous ministerial "advice." The excessive "bureaucratization" of a country ruled by a new class comparatively unused to authority and unfamiliar with the business of government creates the sensation of the state as a Great Leviathan to which the people are expected and encouraged to look for everything.

Yet, like Nehru, India's people have a resilience which might yet enable them to emerge through the vastly contrasting experiences of British rule, the Gandhian era, and the Nehru epoch to reach out to and achieve a synthesis of the three, blending the best in the Orient and the Occident—the robust resolution and imaginative but practical faith of Britain, the Indian roots of Gandhism, and the hustling modernism—with something also of the courage and impulsiveness—of Nehru. History and geography give India a vantage point from which to serve as a bridge between the varied civilizations of the world, for India herself represents a microcosm of human development from the primitive to the sophisticated, and might yet prove that while a country need not lose its consciousness of nationality it can safely keep its windows open to the winds of the world, provided the winds blow freely and are not channeled to knock down other people's chimneys and blow away their roofs. It is here that the need for "a decisive moral resistance to Communism" impinges on the conscience of the free world, including India. And it is here that Nehru has failed the free world. Both at home and abroad his so-called middle-of-the-road policies, not always middle, have left the Indian people wondering whether abroad democracy can be equated with Communism and whether at home the enforced retreat of private enterprise before the bludgeoning of the public sector, the growing forest of red tape, of rules and regulations, of intrusion into almost every domain of life, public and private, adds up to democracy or Communism, and asking themselves, "Where is India heading?"

The answer affects Asia as much as India. In a very real sense it also matters to Europe. Asia and Europe? Are the two really separate and distinct? In truth there are no such entities as Europe and Asia except that the characteristic mark which distinguishes European civilization from the Asian is the possession of the scientific spirit, where again Asia is catching up. But as science grows less exclusive and becomes the handmaid of the human race as a whole, even this distinction must disappear. To be obsessed with notions of being Asian or European is slightly out of date in the context of modern progress and thought, for in the culture and history of the East and the West different streams and currents have mingled their waters. Throughout history there has been a two-way traffic between the culture and thought of the East and the West. Within Asia itself exist three major civilizations—the Far Eastern, the Hindu, and the Islamic—with widely differing racial groups and languages. What affinity is there between the metaphysical outlook of the Indian and the severely practical mind of the Chinese, the former an introvert with his emphasis on the inner experience of man, the latter an extrovert more concerned with the study of man in relation to his fellow man? How closely again does the Celt approximate to the Teuton? No longer is the Westerner identified solely with the continent of Europe, for he has overflowed it. In that sense, the terms "Europe" and "Asia" are anachronistic.

By posing Asia as the antagonist of Europe, and vice versa, Asians and Europeans over the centuries have reared artificial images and mental barriers in their minds. Long before Alexander, the Greeks thought of Asia as the negative image and natural opponent of Europe. There is a division but it does not lie there. As an American observer, Professor John M. Steadman, remarks: "Europe and Asia are divided chiefly by time. Between them lie barriers more effective than oceans—the Industrial Revolution, the growth of modern science, and the evolution of modern parliamentary government. The antithesis of East and West refers ultimately to the consciousness of different stages of political and economic development; it distinguishes a world which has already experienced those metamorphoses from a world which, for the most part, has yet to undergo them."*

Primitive culture marks the first stage when man outgrew his animal nature, developed language and myths, employed animals to assist him, and learned the use of tools and fire. There followed the river-valley cultures of ancient Egypt, Mesopotamia, India, and China, characterized by the wheel, writing, laws, organized government, and a higher stage of cultural development. By 500 B.C. India had produced the Upanishads and the teachings of the Lord Buddha. China knew the philosophies of Confucius and Laotse, while Iran learned at the feet of Zarathustra, and in Palestine the biblical prophets preached. In this period Greece re-

* From the periodical *The American Scholar*, April, 1956.

veled in the glories of Homer and Heraclitus, of Plato and Parmenides, of Thucydides and Archimedes.

Civilization as we know it today is a synthesis of the Greek-Latin and West Asian cultures which, following the Renaissance, spread their influences throughout the world, and into this stream flowed the contributions of India, China, and even of primitive cultures. The world is thus mixed to a marked degree, and contains in its texture many varied, even conflicting, strands, but many also which unite and strengthen the entire fabric. According to modern science, our earth has lasted some 2,000 million years, whereas the human race has existed for around 600,000 years. Our knowledge of human history, however, covers some 6,000 years, and of this totality of written history the five-hundred-year history of conflict between the East and the West covers only a small span. The period of political freedom in Asia is even smaller. It is necessary to appreciate this if we are to approach and study the problem in its true perspective.

If our global life is to achieve and maintain intellectual, cultural, and scientific cooperation, emphasis must be placed on the things which unite men and not on those which divide them. Foremost among these, as we have seen, is science, once divisive but now potentially cohesive. As the late Maulana Abul Kalam Azad, former education minister in India, once pointed out, the Eastern conception of man's status is not only consistent with the progress of Western science but in fact offers an intelligible explanation of how scientific progress is possible. "If," said Maulana Azad, "man were merely a developed animal, there would be a limit to his advancement. If, however, he shares in God's infinity, there can be no limit to the progress he can achieve. Science can then march from triumph to triumph and solve many of the riddles which trouble man even to this day." Elaborating on the same theme, Maulana Azad explained: "If we think of man as only a progressive animal, there is nothing to prevent his using science for furthering interests based on the passions he shares in common with animals. If, however, we think of him as an emanation of God, he can use science only for furthering God's purposes, that is, the achievement of peace on earth and good will to all men."

The benefits of science, if they are to be shared universally, must be designed to foster the progress, peace, and unity of the world as a whole, composed as this is of various peoples at various levels of cultural, economic, political, and scientific advancement. The aim should be to build up integrated individuals in an integrated society, and both the East and the West with their differing concepts should contribute to this result. By blending the magnificent achievements of Western science with the Eastern spirit of man's affinity with God, a positive, purposeful synthesis would be achieved, employing science as an instrument not of devastation and destruction but of prosperity, peace, and progress. Here India can help—and help significantly, perhaps even decisively.

Index

Acharya, Sankara, 36
Adikhari, G., 119, 234
Ahmad, Mirza Ghulam, 59
Ali, Mir Laik, 154
All-India Congress Committee, 95–97, 113, 184
All-India Spinners Association, 89
All-India Trade Union Congress, 113, 129
All-India Village Industries Association, 89
Altamish, 37–38
Ambedkar, B. R., 87, 90, 162
Andhra, 103, 174; absorbs part of Hyderabad, 157; Communists in, 99; formed, 151–152; rice deal with Kerala, 128, 173; rulers of, 33; Socialists in, 113; terrorists in, 118
Arya Samaj, 58, 59, 60
Asian Conference, Colombo, 205
Asian Conference, New Delhi, 10
Asian Relations Conference, 1947, 191; 1954, 205
Asiatic Law Amendment bill, 69
Asoka, 31–32, 33, 56, 201
Assam, 196, 219
Aurangzeb, 41–42, 43, 44, 48, 55
Azad, Maulana Abul Kalam, 84–85, 241–242

Baghdad Pact, 207
Banaras, 37
Bandaranaike, S. W. R. D., 216
Bandung, Afro-Asian Conference, 205
Bannerjea, Surendranath, 78, 80
Basu, Bhupendranath, 64
Bengal, 82; refugees in, 143; partition of, 63. *See also* West Bengal
Bharatiya Jan Sangh, 93, 137
Bhave, Vinoba, 17, 89, 90, 173, 176–179, 227, 228, 229
Bhoodan yagna movement, 89, 173, 176–179, 227, 229
Bhutan, 166, 200
Bihar, 103, 219; politics in, 99, 138
Birth control, 185
Bombay, 71, 152; absorbs part of Hyderabad, 157; Communists in, 104; Pradesh Congress Executive, 173–174; reverence for cattle in, 8; State Assembly, 99
Brahmanism, 28, 29, 33–34, 36
Brahmo Samaj, 58, 59
British Commonwealth of Nations, 10, 162, 163, 187; Conference of Prime Ministers, 163. *See also* Great Britain

Calcutta, 71, 117; refugees in, 143
Calicut, 34, 46
Canal-waters dispute, 209
Caste, 6–7, 12, 27, 40, 41, 106. *See also* Harijans; Untouchables
Chambal power project, 181
Chandavarkar, Narayan, 64
Chang Kuo-ha, General, 195
Chavan, Y. B., 101, 173
Chelmsford, Lord, 79
Chen Yi, General, 195
Chiang Kai-shek, 196, 233
China, aggression in Tibet, 134–135, 228; Communist imperialism of, 50, 190–200, 202; expansionist tendencies of, 190–200, 202, 203, 204; and India, 190–200, 234, 235
Chou En-lai, 191, 194, 196, 204
Cochin, 47, 107
Colombo Plan, 237
Colombo Powers, 205
Communism, 13, 93, 94–95, 99, 102, 103–139, 166–167, 169, 173, 221, 233–236, 237, 239
Communist League, 113
Communist Party of India, 112, 113–139, 166, 234
Communists, in Kerala State, 99, 103–139, 166, 173

Congress new class, 96–104, 107–110, 168–169, 175–176, 218, 221, 238
Congress Parliamentary party, 98, 220, 225
Congress party, 14, 92, 94–95, 112, 121, 138, 139, 145, 146, 150–151, 163, 165, 166, 167, 204, 217, 218, 220, 224, 229, 230, 231; Avadi session, 15; Nasik session, 14; right wing, 22; weakening of, 16–17, 18, 19, 20
Congress Socialist party, 137

Dalai Lama (5th), 198; (13th), 194; (14th), 194, 198; crosses Indo-Tibetan border, 190, 195; at Tezpur, 204
Dange, S. A., 123, 134, 234
Dar Commission, 151
Dayananda, Swami, 58–59
Delhi, 143; Agreement of July, 1952, 161; Islamic achitecture in, 41; sacked, 42; Sultanate, 37, 38, 47
Democratic Socialist party, 107
Desai, Morarji, 14, 149, 223–224, 226
Deshmukh, C. D., 184
Dhebar, U. N., 97, 111, 204
Dixon, Sir Owen, 161
Doctrine of Lapse, 61
Dravida Munnetra Kazhagam, 138
Dutt, Rajni Palme, 114

East India Company, 44, 48, 58, 61, 78

Ganatantra Parishad, 99, 138, 148, 218
Gandhi, Mohandas Karamchand, 2, 17, 22, 23, 29, 32, 65, 102, 114, 148, 149, 150, 176, 201, 224, 227, 228, 237; asceticism of, 69–70; assassination of, 13, 88, 96, 137, 144; character of, 9–11; conservatism of, 8–9; during World War I, 84, 85–86; economic ideas of, 82–83; in England, 68, 70, 89, 90; era of, 66–88; heads Congress, 63; and Hinduism, 71–73; idea of *sarvodaya* society, 89; legacy of, 20–21, 22, 143, 176, 201, 220–221; and Nehru, 9–11, 16, 17, 19, 66, 73–75, 77, 90, 92, 218, 227; political and social contributions of, 69–75, 76–77, 79–80, 83–88, 89–90; on power, 96–97
Gandhi-Irwin Pact, 90
Gandhi, Mrs. Indira, 98; assessed, 231
George, K. C., 128
Ghose, Aurobindo, 67, 78
Ghosh, Ajoy, 119, 234
Gokhale, Gopal Krishna, 63, 64, 65, 78
Gopalan, A. K., 134
Gouri, K. R., 126
Graham, Frank, 160–161
Grant, Charles, 57
Granth Sahib, 41
Great Britain, in India, 45–65
Great Rebellion, of 1857, 51, 61

Halifax, Lord (Edward F. L. Wood), Lord Irwin, 89, 90
Harijans (Untouchables), 7, 27, 28
Hastings, Warren, 53–54
Hind Swaraj (Gandhi), 69, 70–71, 90
Hindu Mahasabha, 22, 137
Hinduism, 1–11, 12, 22–23, 55, 71–73
Hindustani Prachar Sabha, 89
Home Rule Movement, 80, 90
Hume, Alan Octavian, 62–63
Hutchinson, Lester, 114
Hyderabad, 145, 152–153; accedes to India, 154–157; as "B" state, 147; in first general elections, 156–157; terrorism in, 118

Ilbert bill, 62
Independent Labor party, 115
India: Aryan invasions of, 1, 24; British legal systems in, 28; British rule in, 46–65; and China, 190–200, 234–235; Civil Service in, 61–62; Communism in, 14, 21, 93, 94–95, 99, 102, 103, 104, 113–115, 139, 166, 169, 173, 221, 233–236, 237, 239; Congress new class in, 98–103, 110–111; contemporary personalities and politics in, 215–242; economic attainments and objectives, 166–189

(*see also* India, Government of: Five-Year plans); effect of Suez Canal on, 52; foreign policy of, 190–214; formation and integration of states of, 145–161; Great Britain in, 142–143; handicraft industries in, 34; Hellenic influence on, 30–31; Hinduism in, 1–11, 12, 22–23, 24–28, 32–33, 36, 38–40, 42–44; history of, 24–88; impact of West on, 92; independence, 1, 9, 13, 79, 84, 140, 142, 143; industrialization of, 56; irrigation and power projects in, 209–211; Islam in, 33, 34–35, 36, 37–44; literacy rate in, 7; new class in, 89–111; and Pakistan, 143–144, 153–161, 209; politics in, 12–23, 215–242; princes of, 60–62; problems of partition in, 143–144, 145; prospects for, 215–242; sends troops to Hyderabad, 156; sends troops to Srinagar, 158–159; Socialism in, 14–15, 19, 93, 96, 102, 113, 114–115, 138, 141, 166–167, 173, 227, 228, 230; and Tibet, 190–200

India, Government of: Act of 1919, 79, 80; Act of 1935, 82, 145, 216; Arms Act, 86; Central Directorate of Employment Exchanges, 105; Central Election Committee, 95; Congress Working Committee, 85, 95, 97, 98, 163; Constituent Assembly, 155, 162, 201; Constitution of, 2, 132, 133, 142, 161–164, 171–172, 216–217, 219–220; Council of Ministers, 219; Council of States, 145; Federal Assembly, 145; foreign-exchange requirements of, 186–187; Five-Year plans—*First:* 12, 103, 120, 124, 127, 141, 165, 166, 168, 169, 177, 179–180, 181, 183, 184, 185; land reform, 171–179; National Extension service, 170–171; reclamation, 171; rural development, 169–170; stresses agriculture, irrigation, and power, 169–170; *Second:* 8, 103, 120, 124, 126, 141, 166, 167, 168, 169, 177, 180; aims of, 181–186; effect of Suez Canal closure on, 186; irrigation projects, 180–181; *Third:* 187–189; general elections: first, 156; second, 165; Lok Sabha (House of the People), 100, 103, 119, 133, 134, 164, 173, 176, 219; National Congress: 66–68, 77, 79, 80–83, 90–91, 94–96, 98–103, 110–111, 114, 115, 133–136, 166–167, 171, 209, 220, 223, 227, 237; agrarian legislation of, 171–176; founded, 62–64; National Extension Service, 170–171; Parliament of, 95, 133 n., 135, 163, 193, 211, 220; Parliamentary Board, 95; Planning Commission of, 105, 131, 165, 171, 174, 177; reorganization of states of, 150–151, 154–161; Representation of the People Act of 1951, 164; States Department of, 146; States Reorganization Commission, 106, 148, 152; Supreme Court of, 162, 163; Thirty-Year Master Plan of, 127; United Provinces Provincial Committee of, 171; Welfare State of, 165; White Paper on Indian States, 147

Indian Councils Act, of 1861, 78; of 1892, 64; of 1909, 64

Indian National Trade Union Congress, 129

Industrial Revolution, 45, 240; effect of, on India, 48–51

Islam, in India, 33, 34–35, 36, 37–44

Ittehad-ul-Moslemean, 154

Iyer, Alladi Krishnaswami, 162

Iyer, Subramania, 64

Jammu and Kashmir State, accedes to India, 161; as state of Union of India, 211

Jan Sangh, 99, 102

Janata party, 99, 138

Jhansi, 61; Rhani of, 61

Jharkhand party, 99, 138, 219

Jinnah, Mohammed Ali, 76, 80, 81

John, A. J., 108

Jones, Sir William, 53, 56

Joshi, P. C., 118, 234

Junagadh, 145, 152–153; accession to India, 153–154

Kafur, Malik, 38
Kashmir, 145, 152–153, 199; accedes to India, 161; as "B" state, 147; dispatch of troops to, 86; dispute, 157–160, 208; National Conference, 161; status of, 157–160
Kautsky, John, 113 n., 116, 117
Kerala, 47, 103, 104; Communist party, 120; Education bill, 131–132, 133; formed, 106; population density of, 172; rice deal with Andhra, 173; rise and fall of Communists in, 99, 103–139, 166; Socialist party, 107, 108, 109, 138; State Assembly, 124, 132; State Public Service Commission, 132
Kesavan, C., 107
Khan, Liaquat Ali, 160
Khan, Syed Ahmed, 53, 54, 57, 58, 63, 64
Khilafat, 81
Khusru, Amir, 38
Kisan Mazdoor Praja (Peasants') party, 102, 137
Koraput, *gramdan* movement in, 179
Kripalani, Acharya J. B., 96, 97, 130, 137, 176, 229; assessed, 227
Krishnamachari, T. T., 162

Ladakh, 200, 212
Lenin, Nikolai, 114, 135, 233
Liberal party, 65
Liu Shao-chi, 197
Lohia, Rammanohar, 113, 137
Lok Sevak Sangh (social service body), 91
Lytton, Lord, 62

Macaulay, Thomas Babington, 53–54
MacMahon Line, 196
Madhya Bharat, 147
Madhya Pradesh, 93; ban on cow slaughter in, 8; power project for, 181
Madras, 106; elections in, 100
Maha Gurjarat Parishad, 138
Mal, Raj Todar, 41
Manipur, 219
Mao Tse-tung, 119, 135, 191, 194, 196–197, 233–234, 235
Maratha States, 61
Masani, M. R., 113, 115; assessed, 230
Mehta, Asoka, 113, 229; assessed, 227
Mehta, Phirozeshah, 64, 78
Menon, C. Sankara, 128
Menon, K. B., 134
Menon, Krishna, assessed, 231
Menon, Panampilly Govinda, 108, 109, 111
Moksha, 25, 27
Mongrol, 153
Montagu, Edwin, 79
Mookerjee, Shyama, 137
Morley-Minto reforms, 64
Moslem League, 64, 80, 81, 116, 133, 145, 146
Moslems, 27, 106, 144, 209, 212
Mountbatten, Louis, Lord, 145, 154, 157, 158, 159, 160
Muhammad, Bakshi Ghulam, 161
Munshi, K. M., 162
Mysore, 61, 152; as "B" state, 147; ban on cow slaughter in, 8

Nagpur, 6; resolution on land reform, 166, 168, 172, 173, 176, 179, 183
Naidu, Sarojini, 17
Naidu, Mrs. Sarojini, 84
Nair, M. N. Govendan, 110
Namboodiripad, E. M. S., 112–113, 115-116, 120, 122, 123, 132, 164, 166, 172
Naoroji, Dadabhai, 63 n., 64, 66, 70
Narayan, Jayaprakash, 90, 112–113, 114–115, 177, 229; assessed, 227–228
Nehru, Jawaharlal, addresses Congress of the U.S.A., 206; addresses U.N. General Assembly, Paris, 1948, 205; attitude on China, 190, 198; denounced by Communists, 117; economic objectives of, 166–189; foreign policy of, 190–191, 193, 194, 196, 197, 200–208, 211–212; and Gandhi, 9–11, 16, 17, 19, 66, 73–75, 76, 77, 90, 92, 227; on

Hungary, 136, 190, 198; influence of, on India, 215, 216–217, 219, 221, 222, 237, 238, 239; on Kashmir, 211–212; on Kerala Communists, 133–134; and reorganization of states, 150–151, 154–161; and Patel, 12–14, 23; plans for India, 11–12, 140–141; political attitudes of, 7, 9, 12–23, 50, 92–93, 97–98
Nehru, Motilal, 76
Nepal, 196, 200
North Bihar, 63

Orissa, 99, 103, 138, 148, 218; Hirakud project in, 180

PEPSU (Patala and East Punjab states) elections in, 100; formed, 147; politics in, 138–139
Pakistan, 76, 80, 83, 88, 158, 199; and India, 153–161, 209; paradox of, 212–213; problems of partition in, 143–144, 145; U.S.A. aid to, 207
Panchen Lama, 194, 198
Panchshila, 195–196, 204, 213, 214
Pandit, Viyayalakshmi, assessed, 231, 232–233
Pant, Govind Vallabh, 14, 133, 222; assessed, 224–225, 226
Passive Resistance Association, 69
Patel, Sardar Vallabhbhai, 12–14, 15–16, 17, 76, 97, 146, 147, 148, 150, 151, 157, 224
Patil, S. K., 14, 222, 223, 225, 226
Patwardhan, Achut, 113
Pillai, Pattom Thanu, 107, 108
Pillai, T. K. Narayan, 107
Polak, Mrs. H. S. L., 84
Poona Pact, 89–90
Poonch, 158
Prabhakara, 36
Pradesh Congress Committee, 113
Praja Socialist party, 96, 99, 100, 107, 108, 109, 120–122, 130, 133, 134, 137
Prasad, Rajendra, 14, 211, 220, 222, 223; assessed, 225, 226
Princely States, 82; integration of, 145–161
Prinsep, Henry T., 56

Punjab, 30, 54–55, 82, 93, 103, 152; ban on cow slaughter in, 8; power projects in, 180

Radhakrishnan, Dr., 225
Rai, Lala Lajpat, 65, 78
Raj, Prithvi, 37
Rajagopalachari, C., 225, 229-230
Rajasthan, 36, 93, 103; formed, 147; power projects in, 180, 181, 211
Rajjivbhar, Rajchandra, 69
Rajputana, Jainism in, 29
Rajputs, 35–36, 37
Ram Rajya Parishad group, 138
Ramamurthy, P., 126
Ramgarhias, 27
Ranadive, B. T., 118, 119, 123, 234
Ranga, N. G., 176
Rao, Rajeshwar, 119, 234
Rashtriya Swayamsevak Sangh, 138
Rau, B. N., 162
Revolutionary Socialist party, 108, 109, 121, 122
Rowlatt Act, 80
Roy, Ellen, 234
Roy, Manabendra Nath, 114, 234, 235–236
Roy, Ram Mohun, 53, 57–58
Russia, expansionist tendencies of, 200, 202, 203; Five-Year plans of, and India, 49

Samyukta Maharashtra Samiti, 99, 138
Sarvodaya (service), 179; society, 89
Satara, 61
Satyagraha (nonviolent noncooperation), 67–69, 75
Saurashtra, formed, 147
Savage, G. L., 180
Sen, Sukumar, 164
Shaftesbury, Earl of, 56
Shastri, Lal Bahadur, 226
Sikh Akali Dal, 138
Sikhs, 41, 43, 51; as refugees, 144
Sikkim, 196
Simla Convention, 196, 199, 200
Sind, 31, 34, 82; refugees from, 144
Singh, Gobind, 43

Singh, Hari, 151–158, 161
Singh, Ranjit, 43
Singh, Yuvraj Karan, 161
Sinha, Satya Narain, 226
Sino-Tibetan Agreement, May, 1951, 191, 192, 194, 199
Situramayya, Pattabhi, 151
Socialism, 50, 93, 96, 102, 107, 113, 114–115, 138, 141, 166–167, 173, 218, 227, 228, 230
Socialist party, 102, 114–115, 138
Southeast Asia Treaty Organization (SEATO), 207
Southeast Asian Youth Conference, in Calcutta, 117
Srinagar, India flies troops to, 158–159
Sriramulu, Potti, 151
Stalin, Josef, 122, 233, 234
Standstill Agreements, 146, 153, 154, 157–158
Steadman, John M., 239
Subramaniam, C., 101
Suez Canal, 52, 186, 202
Sun Yat-sen, 196–197
Sunderraya, P., 123–124
Swaraj (freedom), 65, 66, 78. See also *Hind Swaraj*
Swatantra party, 138, 229

Tagore, Rabindranath, 184
Talimi Sangh, 89
Tamil kingdoms, 38, 47
Tamil Nad, 126; Socialists in, 113
Tamils, 106
Tandon, Babu Purushottamdas, 14, 97
Taxila, 30; university of, 35
Telingana, 155; rebellion in, 171; terrorism in, 118, 119
Thomas, A. M., 128
Thomas, T. V., 129
Tibet, and China, 134–135, 136, 228; Foreign Affairs Bureau, 192; and India, 190–200
Tilak, Bal Gangadhar, 63–67, 78
Tito (Josip Broz), 119
Travancore, 47. *See also* Travancore-Cochin
Travancore-Cochin, 120, 125; Congress, 106–108; elections in, 100, 109–110; formed, 106; terrorism in, 118
Travancore Tamil Nad Congress, 107, 108, 109
Trivandrum Communist League, 113
Trotsky, Leon, 233

United Front of Anti-Communists, 133
United Front of Leftists, 108, 121
United Nations Security Council, 237; appeal to, on Hyderabad, 155; Kashmir dispute referred to, 159, 160–161; Tibet dispute referred to, 193
United States of America, Nehru addresses Congress of, 206; Point Four program of, 171; tariff barriers of, 49
Untouchables, 7, 9, 27, 28, 72, 87, 106, 163. *See also* Caste; Harijans
Upanishads, 25, 28, 57, 240
Uttar Pradesh, 93, 103; ban on cow slaughter in, 8; Communists in, 99; zamindari system in, 175

Valmiki, 25
Vimochana Samara Samiti, 133
Vindhya Pradesh, formed, 147
Vindhyas, 35
Vivekananda, 36

West Bengal, 103; Communists in, 99; population density of, 172; terrorism in, 118. *See also* Bengal
Wheare, Kenneth, 162–163
World Bank, 187, 209, 210
World War I, 49, 56, 80, 81, 84–86
World War II, 56, 79, 84, 114, 116, 145, 233

Young India (periodical), 86
Yunani, 39

Zamindari landlordism, 172, 175
Zhdanov line, 117, 118